K. C. PHILLIPPS

JANE AUSTEN'S ENGLISH

ANDRE DEUTSCH

FIRST PUBLISHED 1970 BY
ANDRE DEUTSCH LIMITED
105 GREAT RUSSELL STREET
LONDON WC1
COPYRIGHT © 1970 K. C. PHILLIPPS
ALL RIGHTS RESERVED
PRINTED IN GREAT BRITAIN BY
TONBRIDGE PRINTERS LTD
TONBRIDGE KENT
ISBN 0 233 96228 X

JANE AUSTEN'S
ENGLISH

THE LANGUAGE LIBRARY

EDITED BY ERIC PARTRIDGE AND SIMEON POTTER

ALREADY PUBLISHED

Adventuring Among Words	*Eric Partridge*
The Best English	*G. H. Vallins*
Better English	*G. H. Vallins*
Caxton and his World	*Norman Blake*
Chamber of Horrors	*'Vigilans'*
Changing English	*Simeon Potter*
Dictionaries: British and American	*J. R. Hulbert*
A Dictionary of Sailors' Slang	*Wilfred Granville*
A Dictionary of Theatrical Terms	*Wilfred Granville*
Early English	*John W. Clark*
English Dialects	*G. L. Brook*
Etymology	*A. S. C. Ross*
Good English: How to Write It	*G. H. Vallins*
A History of the English Language	*G. L. Brook*
Introduction to the Scandinavian Languages	
	M. O'C. Walshe
The Language of the Book of Common Prayer	
	Stella Brook
The Language of Dickens	*G. L. Brook*
The Language of Science	*T. H. Savory*
Modern Linguistics	*Simeon Potter*
The Pattern of English	*G. H. Vallins*
The Pitcairnese Language	*A. S. C. Ross*
Sense and Sense Development	*R. A. Waldron*
Spelling G. H. *Vallins* (*revised by* D. G. *Scragg*)	
Swift's Polite Conversation	
	Annotated by Eric Partridge
Tudor to Augustan English	*A. C. Partridge*
The Words We Use	*J. A. Sheard*

CONTENTS

	page
PREFACE	7
TABLE OF ABBREVIATIONS	8
PHONETIC SYMBOLS	9
INTRODUCTION	11
1 VOCABULARY	17
2 SENTENCE STRUCTURE	108
3 MODES OF ADDRESS	208
BIBLIOGRAPHY	217
SUBJECT INDEX	221
WORD INDEX	225

PREFACE

Some of the material in this book has also formed the basis of two articles published recently (1969); one in *English Studies* and one in *Neuphilologische Mitteilungen*; and this is reproduced by permission of the editors of these journals, Professor Zandvoort and Professor Mustanoja respectively.

I am particularly grateful to Professor Simeon Potter, joint editor of this series, who read the book in typescript, and whose suggestions have been of great value. I am also indebted to the Harold Cohen Library of Liverpool, for permission to read a very good BA dissertation of Miss Mary D'Arcy on the subject of Jane Austen's English; to the Library Staffs of Leicester University and of the British Museum; to my colleagues at Leicester, Miss M. M. B. Jones and Dr Richard Watson, who read and discussed with me various sections; to Miss Sylvia Gurney, for typing the manuscript; and last but not least, to my wife, for help with what Jane Austen, with characteristic *double entendre*, would have wished to call *typical errors*.

Leicester
December 1969   K. C. P.

TABLE OF ABBREVIATIONS

I have relied entirely on the edition of Jane Austen's novels by
Dr R. W. Chapman (OUP, 1923), and have used the following
abbreviations, with the number of the page where the quotation
occurs, in each case:

SS	*Sense and Sensibility* (first published 1811)
PP	*Pride and Prejudice* (first published 1813)
MP	*Mansfield Park* (first published 1814)
E	*Emma* (first published 1816)
NA	*Northanger Abbey* (first published 1818)
P	*Persuasion* (first published 1818)
MW	*Minor Works.* Collected and edited from the manuscripts by R. W. Chapman (OUP, 1954)

Other abbreviations:

EDD	*The English Dialect Dictionary*
EETS, OS	Early English Text Society, Original Series
ME	Middle English
MEG	*A Modern English Grammar* (Jespersen)
MEU	*A Dictionary of Modern English Usage* (Fowler)
NED	*The New English Dictionary*
OE	Old English
ON	Old Norse
SPE	Society for Pure English

PHONETIC SYMBOLS

The following letters are used as phonetic symbols with their usual English values: p, b, t, d, k, g, f, v, s, z, h, w, l, r, m, n. Other symbols are used with the values indicated by the italicized letters in the key-words which follow:

CONSONANTS

ʃ	*sh*ip	θ	*th*in
ʒ	plea*s*ure	ð	*th*en
tʃ	*ch*in	j	*y*es
dʒ	*judge*	ç	German i*ch*
ŋ	si*ng*		

VOWELS

i	s*i*t	*a*:	f*a*ther
i:	s*ee*	ɔ	h*o*t
e	g*e*t	ɔ:	s*aw*
a	f*a*t	u	p*u*t
ə	fath*er*	u:	s*oo*n
ə:	b*ir*d	ʌ	b*u*t

DIPHTHONGS

ei	d*ay*	ɔi	b*oy*
ou	g*o*	iə	h*ere*
ai	f*ly*	ɛə	th*ere*
au	n*ow*	uə	g*our*d

Square brackets are used to enclose phonetic symbols. A colon after a phonetic symbol indicates length.

INTRODUCTION

Anyone who embarks on a description of Jane Austen's English would do well to bear in mind the unfortunate example of Mr Collins conducting visitors around the garden of Hunsford Parsonage: 'Every view was pointed out with a minuteness which left beauty entirely behind' (*PP 156*). It is perhaps this awful warning, this fear of breaking the butterfly of art upon the wheel of pedantry, that has daunted students of English hitherto. There have been, it is true, a few articles in periodicals recently on Jane Austen's use of abstract terms, and one on her use of tenses, as well as a thoroughgoing German treatment of direct and indirect speech in the novels; but for a more general discussion of her language, we have had to rely on the thirty pages in the two appendices (one on vocabulary, one on grammar), which Dr R. W. Chapman added to his edition of *Sense and Sensibility*. To put it like this, however, is to give an unjust impression. In addition to his own unequalled knowledge of the novels, Dr Chapman had recourse to the advice, in philological matters, of Dr Henry Bradley. Only rarely have thirty pages contained so much information on language.

Part of the fascination of Jane Austen's English is the way in which it differs, in slight and sometimes barely definable, but nevertheless unmistakable ways from our own. Dr Chapman quotes a passage from *Persuasion* (*P 182*) to illustrate these slight differences. As he points out, in the last resort they cannot be pinned down: minor variations of construction blend with minute shifts in meaning to contribute to the distinctive narrative focus, as it were, of the novels. More of our pleasure in Jane Austen than we at first realize, perhaps, comes from the charm of the language.

The English of the dialogue is especially interesting. Differences of class, differences of age, differences of character all reveal themselves in slight variations of speech. The 'little

11

bit (two Inches wide) of Ivory' which Jane Austen claimed as
the range of her subject (*L* 134, p. 469), will stand minute
examination. The young and the elderly had something of a
'language barrier' between them then, as they have today. Mrs
Jennings, of *Sense and Sensibility* and Mrs Norris, in *Mansfield
Park*, are as different by nature as two elderly ladies could well
be; yet both have in common some of those syntactic peculiarities – the use of *sure* as a sentence adverb, for example – which
mark out, in Jane Austen's world, the not-so-young from the
young. There are sometimes two, or even three, distinct levels
of usage in regard to one expression (see *but however*, p. 197),
according to the social class of the speaker. And the minutest
details in speech may reveal some characteristic. How indicative
is Mrs Norris's familiar omission of an article in '*Coachman*
would attend us, out of his great love and kindness' (*MP* 189)!
If only she had been half so considerate to her niece! How well
Mr Elton's mingled officiousness and sycophancy is summed up
in his '*Exactly so*'! How typical of John Thorpe's inarticulate
attempts at wooing Catherine Morland is his use of *however*, in
the Austenian sense of 'at any rate', or the inclusion of the verb
to be in the wrong place here: 'But I say, Miss Morland, I shall
come and pay my respects at Fullerton before it is long, if not
disagreeable' (*NA* 123). Or there is Lady Bertram's phrase 'I
will tell you what' (*MP* 333, 339), by which she is very
occasionally roused from habitual lethargy to make some
original suggestion: 'And I will tell you what, Fanny . . . the
next time pug has a litter you shall have a puppy'.

Even similar characters are differentiated by their language.
On the face of it, Isabella Thorpe and Lucy Steele are somewhat
alike; opportunist vulgarians both. But their speeches show up
differences in the vulgarity of each: as becomes a great reader of
romances, Isabella's vulgarity is of a more flamboyant kind;
Lucy Steele is not prone, as she is, to uttering 'the grand idea'
(*NA* 119). Finally, there is Miss Bates, with an amorphous
syntax all her own; best summed up in her own definition of
her 'method' of speaking: 'I say one thing and then I say another,
and it passes off' (*E* 237). These various peculiarities of
dialogue it has been a pleasure to record.

Jane Austen's precise and confident use of abstract nouns has
recently attracted considerable critical attention; an attention

that indicates an increased awareness of her seriousness as a writer. The study of key words like *rational, elegance* and *mind* gives us insights whereby we deepen our appreciation of her world. Owing to the limited nature of her subject-matter, the same words tend to recur frequently; and they appear to be used, on the whole, with great consistency and sureness. As David Lodge has pointed out, in *The Language of Fiction* (p. 113):

> She puts every generation of readers to school, and in learning her own subtle and exact vocabulary of discrimination and evaluation, we submit to the authority of her vision.

It is true that a few abstract nouns, owing to the state of the language, do not appear so well discriminated as they are today: *grateful* and *gratifying*, for example, or *emergence* and *emergency* (p. 48); but, comparing her with her predecessors, we can see definite advances in this matter; for instance, neither Fielding nor Fanny Burney distinguishes, as she consistently does, between *complaisance* and *complacency* (pp. 27, 87).

As for grammar, Jane Austen set herself, on the whole, high standards, and when minor solecisms crept in, she often corrected these in later editions of those novels which were re-published in her lifetime, namely *Sense and Sensibility, Pride and Prejudice* and *Mansfield Park.* Indeed, quite apart from her very characteristic attention to detail and finish, it was imperative that she should seek to avoid 'errors' in the narrative, since in the dialogue she constantly used substandard usage as a means of exposing vulgarity. By her day, the grammarians had been hard at work prescribing, proscribing and pontificating about English usage for some fifty years. According to S. A. Leonard, who has chronicled the whole movement in his authoritative book *The Doctrine of Correctness in English Usage 1700–1800* (p. 12), there were two hundred titles on grammar, rhetoric, etc., published between 1750 and 1800, as compared with fewer than fifty in the first half of the century. Nothing illustrates the grammarians' influence better than to compare the status and acceptance of the later Verney and Wentworth ladies' correspondence at the beginning of the eighteenth century, with the letters of, say, Lucy Steele or Lydia Bennet. The solecisms of the earlier ladies are often identical with those of the later; but how differently they are received! The Verneys and Wentworths wrote a 'prelapsarian' English, as it were: their sentence-structure was not so much incorrect as non-existent. No-one then expected a lady, however nobly born, to write other than as she spoke, with, in Henry Tilney's words, 'a general deficiency of subject, a total inattention to stops, and a very frequent ignorance of grammar' (*NA* 27). But Lucy Steele's English, no worse and no better than her more high-ranking predecessors', is judged and found sadly wanting. When Edward Ferrars shows Elinor Dashwood one of his ex-fiancée's letters, his comment is: 'In a sister it is bad enough, but in a wife! – how I have blushed over the pages of her writing! . . . – this is the only letter I ever received from her, of which the substance made me any amends for the defect of the style' (*SS 365*). As for Elinor, aware, as all Jane Austen's heroines are, of 'the duty of woman by woman', she reads it and returns it 'without any comment'; but this, of course, is condemnation enough. Several other passages in the novels imply the same equation of good grammar and good breeding. Emma, anxious to prove that Robert Martin is not sufficiently 'genteel' to marry Harriet Smith, is disconcerted to find, on reading his letter proposing marriage, that there are no grammar mistakes; indeed, 'there were not merely no grammatical errors, but as a composition it would not have disgraced a gentleman' (*E 51*).

As this last quotation shows, the novelist's attitude to grammar and composition was not merely the negative and proscriptive one that the grammarians are often accused of inculcating. The composition of even a letter had its more positive side of content and arrangement. Apropos of a message written in a hurry and in embarrassment, Fanny Price reproaches herself: 'She had no doubt that her note must appear excessively ill-written, that the language would disgrace a child, for her distress had allowed no arrangement' (*MP 308*). And even 'arrangement' is not enough. Lady Bertram, 'addicted to letter writing, without having much to say', has formed for herself 'a very creditable, common-place, amplifying style, so that a very little matter was enough for her' (*MP 425*); but she finds that such a style is quite useless when she is for once brought face to face with real emotion and needs to express it. She begins her letter to Fanny about her son Tom's illness in the best eighteenth-century epistolary tradition:

> . . . This distressing intelligence, as you may suppose . . . has agitated us exceedingly, and we cannot prevent ourselves from being greatly alarmed, and apprehensive . . .

In the middle of her writing, her boy is brought home, and she continues her letter 'as she might have spoken' (but, unlike the Verney ladies, with benefit of grammar):

> He is just come, my dear Fanny, and is taken up stairs; and I am so shocked to see him that I do not know what to do . . . Poor Tom, I am quite grieved for him, and very much frightened, and so is Sir Thomas; and how glad I should be, if you were here to comfort me. But Sir Thomas hopes he will be better tomorrow, and says we must consider his journey. (*MP* 427)

One could say much, did space permit, about this broken-off letter, and its continuation. In some ways it represents in little the style of the narrator herself. She too relied on eighteenth-century abstractions, the assured manipulation of conventional terms like *liberality*, *propriety*, *delicacy*, on the one hand; and on the other, interpenetrating thoroughly with this style owing to her subtle and versatile use of *erlebte Rede*, there was the distillation of a more dramatic and realistic language from the best spoken English she heard about her. It was a language that could be polished, brilliant, profound or tender as the occasion warranted. With no other guide but genius, Jane Austen forged for herself a perfect vehicle for her purposes; a style that, like its creator, is still, perhaps, underrated.

I

VOCABULARY

That Jane Austen had a craftsmanlike interest in English words, we know from many of the incidental comments made in her letters, and from the remarks of some of the characters in the novels. She had a keen eye for the illogical expression; she hesitates, for example, over the phrases *yesterday morning* and *yesterday evening*:

> I called yesterday morning (ought it not in strict propriety to be termed yester-morning?). (*L* 39, p. 142)
> We all of us attended them both on Wednesday morning & last evening I suppose I must say. (*L* 39, p. 139)

And one has the impression that she agrees with Henry Tilney in his strictures, made in the best Johnsonian manner, on illogical expressions. He seizes on Catherine Morland's casual remark 'Isabella promised so faithfully':

> Promised so faithfully! – A faithful promise! – That puzzles me. – I have heard of a faithful performance. But a faithful promise – the fidelity of promising! (*NA* 196)

Again, when Catherine asks him if he thinks *Udolpho* 'the nicest book in the world', Tilney is ready with his special brand of quizzical pedantry:

> The *nicest* – by which I suppose you mean the neatest. That must depend upon the binding. (*NA* 107)

But here the moderating influence of his sister's ridicule is ready for him, too, in his turn:

> The word *nicest* as you used it (Eleanor explains to Catherine) did not suit him; and you had better change it as soon as you can, or we shall be overpowered with Johnson and Blair all the rest of the way. (*NA* 108)

17

Already, in Catherine's use of the word *nice* here, we see the tendency, noted by Fowler, for *nice* to become 'too great a favourite with the ladies'. Jane Austen's own use of the word is generally more precise; it usually means 'fastidious'. 'If we are so very *nice*,' says Maria Bertram as the amateur actors at Mansfield Park disagree over the choice of a play, 'we shall never act anything' (*MP* 141). So, too, in these passages:

A little beauty . . . and I am a lost man . . . He said it, she knew, to be contradicted. His bright, proud eye spoke the happy conviction that he was *nice*. (*P* 62)

My own *nicety*, and the *nicety* of my friends, have made me . . . an idle, helpless being. (*SS* 102)

It is rather surprising, perhaps, to find that other clergyman hero, Edmund Bertram, using the word a little more loosely:

And as well as I can judge by this light, you look very *nicely* indeed. (*MP* 222)

But Henry Tilney himself countenances a slightly wider meaning than 'fastidious':

Originally perhaps it (*nice*) was applied only to express neatness, propriety, delicacy, or refinement; – people were *nice* in their dress, in their sentiments, or their choice. But now every commendation on every subject is comprised in that one word. (*NA* 108)

In the letters (never intended, of course, for publication) expressions like 'Lady Bridges . . . is a *nice* woman' (*L* 56, p. 217) occur.

Another word that was losing its meaning in a way that she did not approve was *horrid*. Descriptive of the 'Gothic' romances, it retains a meaning nearer its etymology (Latin *horridus* 'prickly, rough, shaggy') of causing a bristling or shuddering with fear, and this meaning she endorses:

'. . . Midnight Bell, Orphan of the Rhine, and *Horrid* Mysteries. These will last us some time.'
'Yes . . . but are they all *horrid*, are you sure they are all *horrid?*' (*NA* 40)

But when Isabella Thorpe refers to *Sir Charles Grandison* (*NA* 41), and her brother to Fanny Burney's *Camilla* (*NA* 49) as *horrid*,

expressing thereby strong, though vague, disapproval, their
creator clearly does not approve of the extension of meaning:

> The finer performances of the London stage, which she knew on
> Isabella's authority, rendered every thing else of the kind 'quite
> *horrid*'. (*NA* 92)

Nowadays the use of this word as a mere expression of distaste
has gone so far that we have to use the noun *horror* attributively
to describe those films and 'comics' which owe their origin,
however remotely, to the novels of writers like Mrs Radcliffe.

Generally, slang is avoided in the letters. She introduces it, when
she does use it, apologetically, quoting someone else's usage:

> So, Lady Bridges – in the delicate language of Coulson Wallop, is
> *in for* it. (*L* 29, p. 102)
> Tho' I like praise . . . I like what Edward calls *Pewter* too. (*L* 106,
> p. 420)

In the novels, too, certain words, however much they may be in
vogue, are clearly not to be used by the more refined of her
characters. Such a word is *beau*. In the mouths of the Steeles the
word epitomizes the vulgarity and blatant husband-hunting
which she pillories: 'Lord! Anne,' cries Lucy Steele, 'you can
talk of nothing but *beaux*; – you will make Miss Dashwood
believe you think of nothing else' (*SS* 124). Even worse is Mrs
Elton's inappropriate flirtatiousness with poor Mr Woodhouse:
'Here comes this dear old *beau* of mine, I protest' (*E* 302).

A special type of 'slang' which Jane Austen particularly
disliked was what she called *novel-slang*; she meant by this what
we now understand as the clichés of the romantic novelist. In a
letter to Anna Austen, criticizing her niece's attempts at a novel,
she writes:

> Devereux Forester's being ruined by his Vanity is extremely good;
> but I wish you would not let him plunge into a 'vortex of Dissipation'. I
> do not object to the Thing, but I cannot bear the expression; – it is
> such thorough *novel-slang* – and so old, that I dare say Adam met with it
> in the first novel he opened. (*L* 101, p. 404)

Sir Edward Denham, in the unfinished *Sanditon*, who has read
'more sentimental novels than agreed with him', speaks such
novel-slang frequently:

The Novels which I approve are such as display Human Nature with Grandeur – such as show her in the Sublimities of intense Feeling . . . where we see the strong spark of Woman's Captivations elicit such Fire in the Soul of Man as leads him . . . to hazard all, dare all, atcheive [*sic*] all, to obtain her . . . They hold forth the most splendid Portraitures of high Conceptions, Unbounded Veiws, illimitable Ardour, indomptible Decision. (*MW* 403)

It is not a common device of Jane Austen's to illustrate eccentricity with special vocabulary, as she does here. More often, as I hope to show, it is with loose syntax and vulgar turns of phrase that the less admirable characters reveal themselves in speech. Occasionally, however, a vocabulary that is too slangy, or too technical, is the object of her ridicule. She wisely avoids being too nautical in the descriptions of Portsmouth in the last volume of *Mansfield Park*; John Thorpe, however, has his special vocabulary, referring to horses as *cattle* (*NA* 85), and speaking of a horse 'taking the *rest*' (*NA* 62), i.e. a means of checking or 'arresting' a horse (NED *rest* n. 3). As for vulgarity, Mrs Norris in particular has several inelegancies: her recommendation for Fanny's upbringing ('*breed* her up with the Bertrams' *MP* 7) suggests the pheasants' eggs to put under a spare hen in a borrowed coop, which she had acquired, or, to use Maria Bertram's down-to-earth word, *spunged* (*MP* 106), from the housekeeper at Sotherton. Likewise Mrs Norris's phrase *on the catch*, apropos of Maria's engagement to Mr Rushworth – ('there were girls enough *on the catch* for him if we had been idle. But I left no stone unturned' *MP* 189), indicates her calculating and opportunist attitude to matchmaking. Similar faults are apparent in Tom Bertram's over-colloquial summing-up of the prospects regarding the Mansfield living: 'Dr Grant . . . was a short-neck'd, apoplectic sort of fellow, and, plied well with good things, would soon *pop off*' (*MP* 24). Anne Steele's expression *to make any bones of* is also probably substandard: 'She never *made any bones of* hiding in a closet . . . to hear what we said' (*SS* 274).[1]

Here, too, one might mention, though they are more a matter of idiom than vocabulary, stale and awkward circumlocutions like

[1] The phrase nevertheless has a long ancestry, being first quoted in the NED from the Paston letters, though then it was usual to speak of *finding bones in*, the finding of bones in fish, etc., causing hesitation in eating.

Mrs Allen's 'I did *not above half* like coming away' (*NA* 238), and Lucy Steele's 'You think the little Middletons rather too much indulged; perhaps they may be *the outside of enough*' (*SS* 122).

It is true that certain colloquialisms do occur, spoken by some of the best people, and some of them have a modern ring. A disagreeable task was a *fag* (*NA* 29); to be tired was to be *fagged* (*MP* 178) or *dog-tired* (*L* 91, p. 371); a sore eye was 'a sad *bore*' (*L* 17, p. 50); to be eager about a matter was to be *wild* (*PP* 280) to do it or *mad for* it (*MP* 416); a dance, according to Sir John Middleton, was *a little hop*. This last, however, occurs in a conversation in which Sir John uses some increasingly inelegant expressions. First Mrs Dashwood demurs at his suggestion that her daughters will be eager to *catch* the newcomer Willoughby; and the scene culminates in Marianne 'warmly' objecting to Sir John's expression, 'You will be setting your cap at him':

> That is an expression, Sir John . . . which I particularly dislike. I abhor every common-place phrase by which wit is intended; and 'setting one's cap at a man' or 'making a conquest' are the most odious of all. Their tendency is gross and illiberal. (*SS* 45)

Though, according to Austen-Leigh's *Memoir* (p. 88), 'she read French easily, and knew something of Italian', Jane Austen seems to have felt that foreign phrases in conversation were generally pedantic or affected. Emma has no opinion of Mrs Elton, 'with her Mr E., and her *caro sposo*' (*E* 279), and it is in this same novel, which has a tendency to be almost chauvinistic at times, that she points a difference between English and French 'amiability':

> Your amiable young man can be amiable only in French, not in English. He may be very *aimable*, have very good manners, and be very agreeable; but he can have no English delicacy towards the feelings of other people. (*E* 149)

Yet James Benwick, in *Persuasion*, is described as *too piano* (*P* 172); an *alfresco* party is held at Donwell (*E* 357); she prefers the rare French spelling *invalides* for *invalids* to describe the hypochondriacal Parker family (*MW* 410); and talks – there is indeed no English equivalent – of a *cottage ornèe* (sic) being built at Sanditon (*MW* 377). When her brother William, and

Henry Crawford, leave Mansfield, Fanny cries 'con amore, . . .
but it was con amore fraternal and no other' (MP 282); and the
Crawfords, in their town-bred sophistication, are prone to
phrases like menus plaisirs (MP 226) and tout ensemble (MP
230). One senses from the following passage in her letters,
however, that Jane Austen felt that foreign phrases in conversation were an affectation:

> She has an idea of your being remarkably lively; therefore get ready the
> proper selection of adverbs, & due scraps of Italian and French. (L 38,
> p. 135)

The forcefulness and weight of a word, its lightness or seriousness in its context, is something that changes considerably
with the centuries. Certain words could obviously be used with
less serious import than today. Such a word is evil. In one of the
letters she describes the house being painted, and 'we find no
evil from the smell' (L 85, p. 341). Robert Martin's situation
as a yeoman farmer, not a gentleman farmer, is seen as an evil
(E 472), and Mrs Norris, when dining at the parsonage where
there was a large table, always managed 'to experience some
evil from the passing of the servants behind her chair' (MP 239).
When we use the word, we now mean something more
positively malignant than the suggestion of mere inconvenience
or drawback conveyed by these passages. Again, when Jane
Fairfax is said to be 'disgustingly . . . suspiciously reserved'
(E 169), Jane Austen intends only the comparatively mild
etymological force of 'distastefully', not the stronger modern
connotation of 'nauseatingly'. So in the letters, where she
describes a newly-wed husband as not quite so foolishly doting
as she had feared: 'He seems more engrossed by his feelings
towards our family, than towards her, which you know cannot
give any one disgust' (L 25, p. 85).[1] A milder force is also

---

[1] There are contexts, however, in which both the words disgust and
evil are beginning to acquire more force. When Lydia returned to
Longbourn after her escapade, with no sense of remorse, 'Elizabeth was
disgusted and even Miss Bennet was shocked' (PP 315); and, for evil,
we have Emma's dismissal of the suggestion that Mr Knightley should
marry Jane Fairfax: 'If it would be good to her, I am sure it would be evil
to himself; a very shameful and degrading connection'. (E 225).

apparent in her use of the word *repulsive*; it generally means 'tending to repel by coldness of manner' rather than 'offensive' or 'loathsome':

Mary was not so *repulsive* and unsisterly as Elizabeth. (*P* 43)
Having seen him so seldom, his reserve may be a little *repulsive*. (*MP* 199)

Less force than in present contexts is presumably also to be conveyed by the use of the word *oppress* here:

My mother desires her very best compliments . . . and a thousand thanks, and says you really quite *oppress* her. (*E* 173)
She was *oppressed*, she was overcome by her own felicity. (*SS* 363)

A comparable hyperbole today would be *overwhelm*; *oppress* has too many sinister suggestions.

The phrase *to a degree* (also *in a degree*) is also milder and less extreme in the six novels than it is today. It now normally means 'to a high degree'; in the novels the meaning is 'to some extent':

I never saw quite so wretched an example of what a seafaring life can do; but *to a degree*, I know it is the same with them all. (*P* 20)
One is familiar with Shakespeare *in a degree* . . . from one's earliest years. (*MP* 338)

A word that seems rather strong and pretentious to use of a country ramble is Mrs Elton's verb *explore*:

We had a delightful *exploring* party from Maple Grove to Kings Weston. (*E* 354)

Mr Knightley's reply, however, suggests that he regards this word as somewhat inappropriate:

You had better *explore* to Donwell . . . That may be done without horses. (*E* 354)

While the words *expose* and *exposure* occur, as they do today, in weighty contexts with the sense of unmasking an evil, as when Wickham claims to be held back by respect for the elder Mr

Darcy's memory from *exposing* his son (*PP* 207), they also occur with more trivial import. The verb used reflexively indicates something less offensive than it does today: 'to make an exhibition of oneself' is clearly the meaning here:

> You will have my sketches . . . or my poem. I shall do something to *expose myself*. (*E* 365)
> Lydia will never be easy till she has *exposed herself* in some public place or other. (*PP* 230)

But where Mr Elton uses the word in reference to the inclusion of a riddle in a private collection of riddles, it suggests a pretentiousness on a par with his wife's use of the verb *explore*:

> Being my friend's, I have no right to *expose* it . . . to the public eye. (*E* 71)

It is now archaic or dialectal to use the verb *suffer* in the milder sense of 'to allow':

> Fearful of wearying her with too much wisdom at once, Henry *suffered* the subject to decline. (*NA* 111)
> Fanny said she was rested, and would have moved too, but this was not *suffered*. (*MP* 96)

The word *genius* in the novels generally describes an altogether milder quality than the outstanding capacity for imaginative thought and creative ability that it suggests in present English. The modern meaning of *a genius*, applied to an individual, was developing, and seems to occur once, if only by negative implication: Sir Thomas Bertram was aware that he must not 'expect a *genius*' (*MP* 186) in his son-in-law, Mr Rushworth. In a few instances, too, something nearer the modern meaning of the abstract noun may be implied:

> I have no wish to be distinguished . . . Thank Heaven! I cannot be forced into *genius* and eloquence. (*SS* 91)
> To drive about the grounds, and see his *genius* take fire. (*MP* 244)

Otherwise, what is described by this word is a quality of mind in no way exceptional or outstanding: inherent ability, aptitude, and inclination for study and for developing the mind:

'(Fanny Price) says that she does not want to learn either music or drawing.'
'To be sure . . . that is very stupid indeed, and shows a great want of *genius*'. (*MP* 19)
Mrs Allen . . . had neither beauty, *genius*, accomplishment, nor manner. (*NA* 20)

On the other hand, in contrast to all these words in which the meaning has become more extreme, the verb *to tease* now has more playful implications than when used in the novels; the meaning in these next sentences corresponds to the NED definition (*tease*, v. 2): 'to worry or irritate by persistent action which vexes and annoys'; now less common than the lighter senses of the word:

Her cousins might attack, but could hardly *tease* her. (*MP* 157)
Could she not see that we wanted her gone! – how *teazing* [*sic*] to Edward! (*SS* 244)

The word *regard* in the sense of 'affection' shows the same tendency: it was a much stronger and less casual word than it now is:

Having never even fancied herself in love before, her *regard* had all the warmth of first attachment. (*PP* 227)

Another word which has since Jane Austen's day acquired a less intense, more casual import, and one now mixed with suggestions of condescension, is *amiable*. Mary Crawford intends a high compliment when she bids Fanny Price farewell with 'Good bye, my dear, my *amiable*, my excellent Fanny' (*MP* 364). And we have already noted the high standards which Mr Knightley understood by English, as opposed to French, *amiability* (*E* 149).
In addition to differing thus, over the centuries, in their forcefulness, many words undergo what J. Copley (*Shift of Meaning*, p. 5) has called a 'moral deterioration'. Of words used by Jane Austen that have undergone this process, we might mention, for instance, *chat* and *chatty*, which now tend to have disparaging overtones. Mr Woodhouse, however, means nothing detrimental when he says that Miss Bates is 'very

chatty and good-humoured' (*E* 171). Good-natured flow of conversation or letter-writing is clearly meant:

> In their daily intercourse, in business, or in *chat*. (*MP* 465)
> The first page is in her usual . . . jealous, inconsistent style, but the remainder is *chatty* and harmless. (*L* 48, p. 171)

The word *genteel* also occurs without the sarcastic implications now so often present:

> Lucy was certainly not elegant, and her sister not even *genteel*. (*SS* 231)
> Like other ladies she is considerably *genteeler* than her parents. Mrs Armstrong sat darning a pair of stockings. (*L* 39, p. 142)

Respectable, also, had hardly yet acquired its present overtones of smugness and conformity; normally the word means 'worthy of respect' with no sarcastic reservations. 'You,' Elizabeth Bennet accuses her sister Jane, 'wish to think all the world *respectable*' (*PP* 135). One must always be on the look-out for irony in the novels, but I think there is none intended when she writes, in *Sanditon*, of 'A Gentleman's Carriage . . . & by the quantity of Luggage taking off, bringing . . . some *respectable* family determined on a long residence' (*MW* 406). G. B. Stern considers, in *Talking of Jane Austen* (p. 171), that there is only one context in the novels where the suggestion of mockery is added: 'To work in his garden was one of his (Mr Collins's) most *respectable* pleasures' (*PP* 156). Even this, I would say, is 'not proven'; this may be a rare word of praise for Mr Collins, gardening being the only sphere in which he can show what she would call any 'solid' achievement.

The words *candid* and *candour* often carry suggestions today of being frank to the extent of being outspoken, of telling truths that are home truths. This is an implication rarely found in the eighteenth century. A character like Mrs Candour in *The School for Scandal* is, in practice, outspoken, but this is not the point of her name; Mrs Candour retails scandal under the guise of being *candid*, or charitable. Dr Johnson's first definition of *candid* is 'free from malice; not desiring to find fault', a meaning now obsolete, according to the NED. This is Jane Austen's normal usage also, as seen in the description of the most candid character in the novels, Jane Bennet, by her sister Elizabeth:

Affectation of *candour* is common enough; – one meets it everywhere.
But to be *candid* without ostentation or design – to take the good of
every body's character and make it still better, and say nothing of the
bad – belongs to you alone. (*PP* 14)

Dr Chapman is wrong, however (*mirabile dictu*) in saying that
the modern meaning of telling the truth without regard to the
consequences never occurs:

You know I *candidly* told you I should form my own opinion; . . . You
may believe me. I never compliment. (*E* 321)

The suggestion of self-satisfaction, sometimes unwarranted,
which the noun *complacency* now frequently carries, is generally
not the usage of the novels, though the compound *self-
complacency* (*SS* 298) is used in a more pejorative way:

The word 'home' made his father look on him with fresh *complacency*.
(*E* 191)
Amid the cares and the *complacency* which his own children suggested.
(*MP* 21)

Discontent tends now to be used with some disapproval, and
also to indicate a state of mind of some duration. In the novels
it is often used of a more temporary emotion arising from a
particular situation, and has something of the more neutral
meaning of our own *dissatisfaction*. The expression 'patient
discontent' in the second quotation here, would hardly be
possible now except as a paradox:

Fanny was confused, but it was the confusion of *discontent*. (*MP* 277)
Now she should not know what was picturesque when she saw it. Such
were her thoughts, but she kept them to herself, and put on her bonnet
in patient *discontent*. (*NA* 177)

The words *irritation*, *irritability* etc., like *discontent*, are often
used by Jane Austen with pity rather than disapproval; and the
last quotation here shows that irritation can be caused by
pleasurable as well as unpleasant emotions:

Sir Thomas knew not how to bring down his conversation or his voice
to the level of *irritation* and feebleness. (*MP* 429)
Marianne entreated her, with all the eagerness of the most nervous
irritability, not to speak to her. (*SS* 180)

> She was now in an *irritation* as violent from delight, as she had ever been fidgetty from alarm and vexation. (*PP* 306)

Indulge and *indulgence* now generally have disparaging overtones. The following contexts, however, show them used to mean enjoyment and pleasure free from any suggestion of unrestrained self-gratification:

> Elizabeth . . . resolved soon after breakfast to *indulge* herself in air and exercise. (*PP* 195)
> I was glad you made her play so much, for having an instrument at her grandmother's, it must have been a real *indulgence*. (*E* 170)

But elsewhere we see the modern derogatory sense of humouring or gratifying at the expense of a certain relaxation of standards. Marianne Dashwood's excessive grief at Willoughby's leaving her is described as an *indulgence* (*SS* 83).

The word *scheme*, meaning a plan, now tends to be coloured with suggestions of self-seeking and deviousness. It sometimes has this meaning in the novels also (*SS* 78), but it is also used in the sense of a project for pleasure and enjoyment, a jaunt or a pleasure trip. This meaning now survives only in dialect:

> The *schemes* of amusement . . . which Sir John had been previously forming. (*SS* 53)
> I did not once put my foot out of doors . . . Not one party, or *scheme* or anything. (*PP* 319)
> That will be a good time for our *scheme* to Beaulieu. (*L* 54, p. 205)

The word *sly* has undergone a more continuous process of deterioration in meaning through the centuries. Both the favourable sense 'skilful' and the less flattering one 'crafty' have been present from the beginning, but the former survives dialectally, and also in the corresponding noun *sleight*, as in *sleight of hand*. The sense of artifice, and then of insidiousness, gradually developed and increased until now it so predominates that *sly* hardly seems a word to use of a hero, as Mrs Gardiner uses it in a letter chiefly in praise of Mr Darcy here:

> I thought him very *sly*; – he hardly ever mentioned your name. But *slyness* seems the fashion. (*PP* 325)

Similarly Mrs Palmer, teasing Marianne Dashwood, is not perhaps so blunt as she now appears to be:

Oh! don't be so *sly* before us . . . for we know all about it. (*SS* 111)

It is curious how words which are etymologically quite neutral can acquire, as the language develops, pejorative overtones. In Shakespeare's day, when the word was first used, an *inmate* signified the mate or associate of another in the same dwelling or one who lived with another as lodger or subtenant in the same house. Only since the early nineteenth century has the word come to be connected with a prison, an asylum, or some kind of institution for the mentally sick; no such meaning occurs in the novels:

His mind . . . was at leisure to find the Grants and their young *inmates* really worth visiting. (*MP* 238)
Her brother saw her only as the supposed *inmate* of Mansfield Parsonage. (*MP* 295)

The NED informs us that, if used with reference to physical stature or size, the adjective *great* expresses some feeling such as surprise, contempt or admiration. We should now substitute the neutral adjectives *large* or *big* in contexts like the following:

Mr Elton being the adoration of all the teachers and *great* girls in the school. (*E* 143)
How does Lord Macartney go on? – (opening a volume on the table and then taking up some others.) And here are Crabbe's Tales, and the Idler, . . . if you tire of your *great* book. (*MP* 156)

To marry greatly, in the following, means to marry into a high rank in society; a rare use of the adverb, according to the NED, which quotes this example:

If you encourage her to expect to marry *greatly*. (*E* 64)[1]

Female is a word that seems impersonal to the point of rudeness today. According to the NED (*female* B 2b), the word

---

[1] Cf. 'Maria is *nobly* married' (Sir Thomas Bertram) *MP* 319. Mr Rushworth is not strictly of the nobility, but he is one of the wealthiest men in the novels, comparable with Mr Darcy, and no doubt, like him, in Mrs Bennet's phrase, 'as good as a lord'.

is 'now commonly avoided by good writers, except with contemptuous implication'. This was not so in the novels:

> As he and the *females* of the family were sitting together. (*PP* 351)
> The affectation and coquetry of an elegant *female*. (*PP* 109)

Also too impersonal for modern taste is the word *object* applied to persons, sometimes in deeply felt contexts, meaning the person for whom, or to whom, one's aims and ambitions are directed. Thus Edmund Bertram describes Mary Crawford and Fanny Price as 'the two dearest *objects* I have on earth' (*MP* 264). Similarly in the following: .

> Emma divined what every body present must be thinking. She was his *object* and every body must perceive it. (*E* 220)

The noun *closet* in the novels has the general meaning, implicit in its etymology, of a small enclosed room; often an antechamber or dressing-room. As Copley points out (*op. cit.* p. 39), the Victorian use of the *water-closet* has spoilt the word for other use, though the participial adjective from the verb, *closeted*, seems to have escaped contamination:

> Do you think the minds . . . which are indulged in wanderings in a chapel, would be more collected in a *closet*? (*MP* 87)
> My mother's room is . . . large and cheerful-looking, and the dressing *closets* so well disposed. (*NA* 196)

Peculiarity cannot now be divorced from derogatory suggestions of eccentricity. It clearly does not always have such connotations.

> (Mary Crawford) began, . . . with all that openness of heart, and sweet *peculiarity* of manner . . . which are so much a part of herself. (*MP* 352)

The word *peculiar* is used rather as we now use *particular*, in antithesis to *general*:

> That was too general a sensation for any thing of *peculiar* anxiety to be observable. (*E* 218)

On the other hand, the word *particular*, as sometimes used, is a good instance of the process contrary to all those we have been discussing; that of a word losing its undesirable overtones since Jane Austen's day. As used by her, *particular* means 'singular', 'conspicuous' or 'odd':

> 'I would have given the world to sit still.'
> 'Then why did not you?'
> 'Oh! my dear! it would have looked so *particular*.' (*NA* 134)

Similarly, Tom Bertram apologizes to Mr Yates for his father's *particularity* (*MP* 191) in objecting to *Lovers' Vows*.

Certain other words, as used in the early nineteenth century, show the same tendency of retaining pejorative connotations since lost. *Expensive*, for example, can be applied to people as well as things, and it then means 'extravagant, improvident, wasteful':

> His character is now before you; *expensive*, dissipated, and worse than both. (*SS* 210)
> Those false ideas of the necessity of riches, which I was naturally inclined to feel, and *expensive* society had increased. (*SS* 323)
> His *expensiveness* is acknowledged even by himself . . . self-denial is a word hardly understood by him. (*SS* 350)

A word which rarely has unfavourable overtones today is *assiduous*, which normally means 'perseveringly hardworking, diligent'. The less favourable suggestion of 'obsequiously attentive' which *assiduous* and *assiduity* have in the novels is now, according to the NED, archaic. The most *assiduous* characters (in this sense) in Jane Austen are the Steeles, and Mrs Clay in *Persuasion*:

> Mrs Clay . . . possessed . . . *assiduous* pleasing manners, infinitely more dangerous attractions than any merely personal might have been. (*P* 34)
> The thorough want of delicacy . . . which her attentions, her *assiduities*, her flatteries at the Park betrayed. (*SS* 127)

The word *compliment*, similarly, could carry a less favourable implication of conventional praise. 'It was no *compliment*' in the next quotation means, not 'It was an insult' but 'It was not mere flattery':

'These are the finest looking home-baked apples I ever saw in my life . . .' And I am sure, by his manner, it was no *compliment*. (*E* 238)

So also with the verb:

Must not *compliment*, I know . . . that would be rude. (*E* 323)

But *compliment* also occurs in the more favourable modern sense (*PP* 189).

To admire now conjures up ideas of approving, respectful wonder, not always present in Jane Austen's use of the word:

Anne . . . *admired* again the sort of necessity which the family-habits seemed to produce, of every thing . . . being to be done together, however undesired and inconvenient. (*P* 83)

Eclat means today signal success or applause for success, a meaning which occasionally occurs in the novels (*MP* 183); more commonly, the word is used less favourably, to mean a public display of one's feelings, an outburst or a row:

It was a great object with her to escape all enquiry or *eclat*; but it was her intention to be . . . cool. (*P* 214)
The difficulties of . . . subduing feelings, concealing resentment, and avoiding *eclat*. (*E* 137)

From the meaning of exciting pity for its littleness and meanness, the word *pitiful* acquires a still more unfavourable meaning, becoming virtually a synonym for 'mean', 'scrimping'. It is perhaps a slightly vulgar extension of meaning, however, not resorted to by the best characters:

Nobody loved plenty and hospitality more than herself – nobody more hated *pitiful* doings (Mrs Norris). (*MP* 31)
When one has the means of doing a kind thing . . . I hate to be *pitiful* (John Thorpe). (*NA* 47)
Very little white satin, very few lace veils; a most *pitiful* business! (Mrs Elton). (*E* 484)

The word *rate*, now commonly neutral in meaning, acquires a pejorative suggestion of mediocrity in contexts like this:

The children . . . were talked to and admired amid the usual *rate* of conversation. (*E* 219)

Her brother's disposition to look down on the common *rate* of social intercourse. (*E* 97)

Quite often, Jane Austen's use of a word is nearer to the etymological sense than our own. Her use of *secure*, from Latin *securus* with the more original meaning of 'free from care, untroubled', illustrates this. The normal modern meaning, of course, is 'safe'.[1] *Secure* is used by Jane Austen in contexts of courtship, meaning 'confident of the affection of another', as well as in the more general sense of 'free from care':

Though feeling almost *secure* . . . for Charlotte had been tolerably encouraging, he was comparatively diffident. (*PP* 121)
He spoke of apprehension and anxiety, but his countenance expressed real *security*. (*PP* 189)
Her apprehensions once raised, paid by their excess for all her former *security*. (*SS* 312)

The word is used, followed by the preposition *of*, in contexts where we should now prefer the earlier derivative of the Latin *securus*, viz., *sure*:

(Mrs Dashwood) hastened to shew both letters to her daughters that she might be *secure* of their approbation. (*SS* 24)
Now that she . . . had carried her point and was *secure* of her walk. (*NA* 103)

Secure also occurs, however, with its more modern meaning (*MP* 473).

Our current meaning of the word *ascertain*, as Copley points out (*op. cit.* p. 21), stresses discovery rather than certainty. But the first definition in Johnson's Dictionary is 'to make certain, fix'. According to Dr Chapman, *ascertain* never means merely 'to find out' in the novels, though in the third quotation here we see how the transition of meaning came about:

[1] This quotation from Ben Jonson nicely differentiates the earlier use: 'Man may *securely* sin, but *safely* never' *Epode; Not to Know Vice at All.*

B

How could it ever be *ascertained* that his mind was truly cleansed? (*P* 161)

She seized, with an unsteady hand, the precious manuscript, for half a glance sufficed to *ascertain* written characters. (*NA* 169)

For one morning I think you have done pretty well. You have already *ascertained* Mr Willoughby's opinion in almost every matter of importance. (*SS* 47)

To prevent in the sense of the original Latin *præventus*, from *prævenire*, 'to come before, to anticipate', familiar to Anglicans from its occurrence in the Liturgy, can be illustrated from the novels. When Edmund Bertram comes to fetch Fanny Price from her mother's family at Portsmouth, he enters just in time 'to *prevent* their sitting down to the breakfast table' (*MP* 445); this does not mean that the Prices had no breakfast. So also in the following:

'Fanny, you do not want to go, do you?'
'If you put such a question to her,' cried Edmund, *preventing* his cousin's speaking, 'Fanny will immediately say, no.' (*MP* 217)

The verb *to canvass* is connected with the noun meaning 'coarse cloth'. The NED attributes the connexion to the idea of sifting or shaking up papers in a canvas bag, hence to examine a question thoroughly. Jane Austen's normal use of the word, meaning 'to discuss a subject', is thus seen to be nearer the etymology than the more specialized, and now commoner meaning of soliciting support for a political candidate. This political use does occur in the novels (*SS* 113); but the meaning of 'to discuss' is more common:

We think so very differently on this point, Mr Knightley, that there can be no use in *canvassing* it. (*E* 65)

The whole of what Elizabeth had already heard . . . was now openly acknowledged and publicly *canvassed*. (*PP* 138)

Besides its normal significance of a happening (*NA* 232), the word *event* commonly has a more etymological meaning of 'outcome'; a happening seen as a result of what has gone before. The older meaning survives today in a phrase like *in the event*:

It was, perhaps, one of those cases in which advice is good or bad only as *the event* decides. (*P* 246)
Dearest you will always be, whatever the *event* of this hour's conversation. (*E* 430)

The etymology of *fact*, from Latin *factum*, a thing done, is more apparent in instances like these than in most modern contexts :

Wall torn down – apples stolen – caught in the *fact*. (*P* 23)
Enscombe however was gracious, gracious in *fact*, if not in word. (*E* 257)
Remiss, perhaps, more in thought than *fact*. (*E* 377)

The word *essay* tends now to be confined more and more to the meaning of a written composition, a meaning that dates and derives, according to the NED, from Montaigne. The earlier and more etymological meaning of 'a trial or attempt' is evident here :

It will not do – very sorry to check you in your first *essay* – but indeed it will not do. (*E* 350)
Miss Crawford made her first *essay* (at horse-riding) with great credit. (*MP* 66)

It is now obsolete to use *act* in the etymological sense of *do* with an object : (He could sometimes *act* an ungracious, or say a severe thing; *E* 93). But in the sense of taking the part of a character in a play, or performing an insincere or simulated action, the verb *act* is still found with the object *part*. The phrase occurs in this sense in the novels (*E* 145); but *to act a part* also means 'to participate in an action or affair in a direct way'. Curiously, we can still use *play a part*, but not *act a part*, in this straightforward way :

He must by this time be ashamed of the part he had *acted*. (*NA* 222)
The part which I *acted*, is now to be explained. (*PP* 198)

To discover is used by Jane Austen in several senses which have now been largely ousted by the predominant modern one of obtaining knowledge of a thing for the first time. The original meaning was concrete : 'to uncover or lay bare'; in senses more immediately derived from this the word is used of the finding of

people – Lydia and Wickham, for instance, after their elope-
ment:

> That generous compassion which induced you to take so much trouble
> . . . for the sake of *discovering* them. (*PP* 366)

And of the disclosure or manifestation of feelings or talents:

> His sisters' uneasiness had been equally excited with my own; our
> coincidence of feeling was soon *discovered*. (*PP* 198)
> As Marianne was *discovered* to be musical. (*SS* 35)

We must likewise forget the modern scientifically-coloured
meaning of the word *experimental*. In this quotation from
Northanger Abbey it retains the earlier meaning: 'by experience'
rather than 'by experiment':

> (General Tilney's) departure gave Catherine the first *experimental*
> conviction that a loss may be sometimes a gain. (*NA* 220)

So Boswell describes one of Johnson's observations as '*experi-
mentally* just' (*Life*, III, 199).

Another word which, since Jane Austen's day, has become
increasingly adapted to a world governed by change, is *idea*.
This word occurs in the novels with the meaning of a notion or
an impression, however unoriginal. *Idea* today suggests at once
something vaguer and more in flux:

> There is something of dignity in his countenance, that would not give
> one an unfavourable *idea* of his heart. (*PP* 258)
> Till called on by the General for her opinion of it, she had very little
> *idea* of the room in which she was sitting. (*NA* 213)
> His visit hitherto had given her friend only good *ideas* of him. (*E* 205)

Similarly in the following, where *ideas* means topics of conversation. One could run short of *ideas* today for a lecture or
dissertation, where originality is called for, but hardly for a
conversation:

> She wanted to talk . . . Yet time and her aunt moved slowly – and her
> patience and her *ideas* were nearly worn out before the tete-a-tete was
> over. (*PP* 257)

The word *idea* is now more often seen in regard to future
projects and developments, and could hardly now mean 'the
mental image or picture of something previously seen or known,
and recalled by the memory' (NED *idea* 8a. *Obsolete*):

> She had merely intended to discompose Elizabeth, by bringing forward
> the *idea* of a man to whom she believed her partial. (*PP* 269)

A more precise word than *idea* would also occur in the two
following sentences: *fears* in the first, and a *protestation* or
avowal in the second:

> His collar-bone was found to be dislocated, and such injury received in
> the back, as roused the most alarming *ideas*. (*P* 53)
> 'Had I the command of millions . . . your brother would be my only
> choice.' Catherine . . . thought her friend never looked more lovely
> than in uttering the grand *idea*. (*NA* 119)

We no longer use the phrase *in idea* meaning 'in imagination' or
'in the mind's eye':

> She saw her *in idea* settled in that very house in all the felicity which a
> marriage of true affection could bestow. (*PP* 98)

The last two quotations here also have overtones of the further
meaning, now often conveyed by the word *ideal*, of a standard of
perfection. It is some such combination of meanings that
Thompson intends in his famous lines:

> Delightful task! to rear the tender thought,
> To teach the young *idea* how to shoot. (*The Seasons* 1152)

Two words whose derivatives are not always easy to disentangle
from each other are *sense* and *sensibility*. The two stand in
antithesis, of course, in the title of the first published novel.
While it has often been pointed out that Elinor and Marianne
Dashwood are not merely exemplars of these two qualities
respectively, Lord David Cecil's distinction (*Poets and Story-
tellers*, p. 121) points an essential difference in what these two

words connote: 'The issues between Elinor and Marianne are the issues between Rousseau and Dr Johnson'.

Sense occurs, as today, with the meaning of 'common sense, sensibleness': 'Do not speak ill of your *Sense*, merely for the Gratification of your Fancy' is Jane Austen's advice to her niece Fanny Knight (*L* 140, p. 481). The word also occurs, as again it still does, with the meaning of awareness: 'Jane Fairfax's *sense* of right' (*E* 446). In at least one context, *sense* may also retain the meaning of 'feeling', and be nearer in import to *sensibility*:

> Such apparent devotion to Miss W., as it would have been impossible for any woman of *sense* to endure. (*E* 441)

As for the word *sensibility*, this was defined by Dr Johnson as 'quickness of sensation or perception'. It denotes a more than ordinary responsiveness, whether to nature, or to the arts, or to human feelings. This could be an admirable quality, though in excess it was reprehensible. In one of her letters, Jane Austen clearly approves:

> Fanny's calling gave great pleasure & her *Sensibility* still greater, for she was very much affected at the sight of the Children. (*L* 117, p. 436)

She seemed to feel that this sensitivity to human relationships was the worthiest kind of sensibility, as when she makes Emma say:

> I could not excuse a man's having more music than love – more ear than eye – a more acute *sensibility* to fine sounds than to my feelings. (*E* 202)

With the negative there was the further complication that *insensibility*, besides meaning 'insensitivity' (*PP* 204), could mean, as today, actual unconsciousness. After Louisa Musgrove's accident, her sister Henrietta faints away, is revived, and is 'kept, by the agitation of hope and fear, from a return of her own *insensibility*' (*P* 112).

It was possible to pay a high price for sensibility. It is suggested, for instance, that the qualities of sensibility and *complacency* (in the non-pejorative sense of 'serenity') are not often found together: Mr Darcy was deceived into thinking that Jane Bennet was indifferent to Bingley because 'there was a

constant complacency in her air and manner, not often united
with great *sensibility'* (*PP* 208); Fanny Price, on first going to
Mansfield, has to be persuaded by Edmund out of too great
'sensibility of her situation' (*MP* 17); and finally, Marianne
Dashwood is perhaps the classic example in English literature of
sensibility carried to extreme. Elinor, we are told, saw with
concern 'the excess of her sister's sensibility' (*SS* 7).

So far the words *sense* and *sensibility* are fairly clearly
distinguished. Problems arise, however, with the adjective
sensible, which relates to both nouns, and by the latter half of the
eighteenth century could have at least four distinct meanings:
two from *sense* in its meanings of 'gumption' and 'awareness';
and two from *sensibility* signifying 'sensitivity 'and 'consciousness' (in the medical sense). There is no doubt that, as C. S.
Lewis points out,[1] the word was overburdened with meaning.
The first of these four meanings of *sensible*, now the commonest
one, of 'having good sense', was the last to develop. Dr Johnson
only barely recognized it in his Dictionary: 'In low conversation
it (*sensible*) has sometimes the sense of reasonable, judicious,
wise'. But this meaning was common and correct enough by
Jane Austen's day: Mr Collins, she tells us, was 'not a *sensible*
man' (*PP* 70).

The most frequent meaning of *sensible* in the novels, however,
is 'aware' or 'conscious', though perhaps with greater depth of
feeling than is conveyed now by either of these two words. Like
these two words, *sensible* is constructed either with a clause
following or with *of*:

> The little girl who was spoken of . . . as seeming so desirably *sensible*
> of her peculiar good fortune. (*MP* 15)
> They soon became *sensible* that the authority of a servant who had
> known him since he was four years old . . . was not to be hastily
> rejected. (*PP* 264)

In the later eighteenth century, the third meaning of 'sensitive'
had been fairly common:

> One (poem) was on the parting of two lovers; very *sensible*; and so
> tender. (Richardson, *Sir Charles Grandison*, I 23)

[1] *Studies in Words*, p. 163. See also S. I. Tucker, *Protean Shape*,
pp. 249–251.

It is a measure of the way this overburdened word was shedding some of its earlier connotations that this meaning rarely, if ever, occurs in the novels. But the adverb *sensibly* in the following may well bear a meaning corresponding to *sensibility* rather than *sense*:

> He expressed himself . . . as *sensibly* and as warmly as a man violently in love can be supposed to do. (*PP* 366)

Professor Empson draws attention to the following passage, describing Lady Bertram's feelings on her husband's return from Antigua, in which again the adverb derives from *sensibility* rather than *sense*; with the further suggestion, besides 'in her sensibilities or feelings' of 'perceptibly to the feelings of others':[1]

> She had been almost fluttered for a few minutes, and still remained so *sensibly* animated as to put away her work . . . and give all her attention . . . to her husband. (*MP* 179)

The negative *insensible* certainly connotes sensibility and not sense; indeed, *insensible* hardly ever seems to have meant, in the late Modern English period, 'having no sense, irrational'. By far the commonest meaning of *insensible* in the novels is 'insensitive':

> Any young man . . . must have been *insensible* indeed, not to become an immediate convert to the excellence of such works. (*SS* 47)

The fourth meaning of *sensible* is 'conscious' in the medical sense; we must bear in mind that *conscious* and *unconscious* regularly mean 'embarrassed' and 'unembarrassed' respectively:

> We hastily . . . implored him not to die . . . I was overjoyed to find him yet *sensible*. (*MW* 99)
> Charles . . . could only turn his eyes from one sister, to see the other in a state as *insensible*. (*P* 110)

Most of the words we are discussing present few difficulties to the intelligent modern reader. They stand out as having, to our

[1] *The Structure of Complex Words* p. 306. Cf. also Fielding: These words had a *sensible* effect on the coachman. *Joseph Andrews*, I 44

minds, an unusual meaning, which is generally ascertainable from the context. Words more likely to mislead are those for which a modern reading is possible; but probably not the one intended. Consider the word *development* here:

> To these recollections was added the *development* of Wickham's character. (*PP* 213)

This would mean in present English the way Wickham's character was evolving and changing. But in fact Wickham's character remains the same throughout the novel; Jane Austen means here the gradual unfolding or disclosing of what had hitherto been unknown about his character. Similarly, Emma's discovery that she has been in love with Mr Knightley all along is described as 'a *development* of self' (*E* 409), i.e. self-revelation. This meaning relates more closely to the oldest, and now obsolete, use of the verb *develop*, which is concrete: 'to unfold or unfurl anything rolled up'. The NED quotations show that the earliest metaphorical uses of this verb applied to people. Most of those which have a non-personal subject occur after Jane Austen's day; and the word was later in the nineteenth century much coloured by ideas of evolution. She uses the verb with only a personal subject, and it tends to mean either (a) 'to find out, ascertain', or (b) 'to uncover oneself, be brought into fuller view':

> (a) On *developing* from amidst all her perplexity of words in reply, the meaning, which one short syllable would have given. (*NA* 242)
> (b) The experience of three and twenty years had been insufficient to make his wife understand his character. *Her* mind was less difficult to *develope*. (*PP* 5)

With the abstract noun *development* the first NED definition applies, more or less: 'a gradual unfolding . . . a fuller disclosure or working out of the details of anything'. The idea of further revelation or disclosure is rarely absent:

> She was nearly fainting: all her former habitual dread of her uncle was returning, and with it compassion for him . . . on the *development* before him (the disclosure of the play rehearsals going on in his absence). (*MP* 176)

Never, since reading Jane's second letter, had she entertained a hope
of Wickham's meaning to marry her . . . Surprise was the least of her
feelings on this *developement*. (*PP* 279)

Another word which does not always mean what we understand by it today is *character*. It tends often to mean the
character as viewed by public opinion; in other words reputation
or good repute; or perhaps, occasionally, something approaching
that favourite modern word *image*. There is in the novels a
fairly frequent phrase, now obsolete, *by character*, meaning 'by
repute'. The last NED quotation for this phrase (*character* n.
13c), is from *Persuasion*:

I have been acquainted with you *by character* many years. (*P* 187)
A family . . . whom Emma well knew *by character*. (*E* 23)

In this sense a *character*, or reputation, is built up, or to use her
word, *established*:

He is now perhaps sorry for what he has done, and anxious to re-
establish a *character*. (*PP* 227)

The following passages can hardly be understood without
taking into account this public aspect of *character*:

Sir Thomas . . . remained . . . in town, in the hope of . . . snatching her
from farther vice, though all was lost on the side of *character*. (*MP* 451)
You chose to tell me that you liked me against your will, against your
reason, and even against your *character*. (*PP* 190)
(Wickham) promises fairly, and I hope among different people, where
they may each have a *character* to preserve, they will both be more
prudent. (*PP* 313)
The parsonage . . . had never borne a bad *character* in her time. (*MP*
31)

A small word which can sometimes mislead is the adverb
quite. In its earliest meaning, which Jane Austen always adheres
to, *quite* is purely an intensive, signifying 'completely, to the
fullest extent'. We can compare our present use of *quite right* or
quite alone. More recently, *quite* has increasingly become what
C. Stoffel, in his *Intensives and Down-toners* (pp. 38–67) calls a
'down-toner', since to protest about the extreme degree of an
attribute may perhaps argue a certain hesitation. So *quite good*

has become equivalent, more or less, to *fairly good*. In the novels, however, *quite* is always intensive:

> Every body said how well she looked; and Mr Bingley thought her *quite beautiful* and danced with her twice. (*PP* 12)
> They . . . entered a room splendidly lit up, *quite full* of company and insufferably hot. (*SS* 175)

With the verb *to lounge* the sense that now predominates is that of reclining or lolling on an easy chair; from this sense, indeed, the noun *lounge* has developed as a widely used, if somewhat non-U equivalent of a drawing-room. Neither verb nor noun has this meaning in the novels, where both derive from an earlier meaning, 'to stroll, to saunter':

> While three or four Officers were *lounging* together, passing in & out from the adjoining card-room. (*MW* 327)
> The comparatively quiet state of the house, from Tom and Charles being gone to school . . . and her father on his usual *lounges*. (*MP* 388)

The commonest meaning of *apparent* today is 'that which appears', often in contrast to what is.[1] Jane Austen's use of this word may mislead, therefore, since she still uses it with the more etymological sense (Latin *apparēre* 'to come forth, show oneself') of 'open, evident, not hidden':

> He saw Mrs Rushworth, was received by her with a coldness which ought to have been repulsive, and have established *apparent* indifference between them for ever. (*MP* 467)

The following are rather doubtful; but I take them to have the older meaning of 'evident(ly)' or 'manifest(ly)' rather than the modern one of 'to all appearances':

> Such shameful, insolent neglect of her, and such *apparent* devotion to Miss W., as it would have been impossible for any woman of sense to endure. (*E* 441)
> When she considered how little useful, how little self-denying his (Tom Bertram's) life had (*apparently*) been. (*MP* 428)

[1] Perhaps we should not press this too far. In a loyal leader on Prince Charles, the editor of *The Guardian* can still write of the Prince of Wales's 'agreeable nature, his charm and *apparent* dedication' (June 27, 1969). In such a context, however, the word has special overtones.

It is sometimes difficult to pin down why a word is used differently from present English. If asked, we should probably say that the words *undoubtedly* and *certainly* were more or less interchangeable synonyms. But when Emma replies to Frank Churchill's observation that she has known Miss Fairfax from a child: 'I have known her from a child, *undoubtedly*' (*E* 203), we realize that *certainly* would be far more likely in such a context today, since Frank Churchill's statement has already removed any doubt. Still more so in the following:

'Fetch them both. Invite them both . . . I shall think you a great blockhead, Frank, if you bring the aunt without the niece.'
'*Undoubtedly* if you wish it, I will endeavour to persuade them both.' (*E* 255)

Similarly, we might consider *altogether* and *on the whole* as interchangeable; but when, after giving Mrs Clay freckles, a projecting tooth, and a clumsy wrist, the novelist describes her as '*altogether* well-looking' (*P* 34), we realize that *on the whole* is the phrase we should prefer here today.

There was a general tendency for abstract words to be less restricted in meaning than they are today. Thus the verb *to comprehend*, besides meaning 'to understand' (*MP* 6), frequently occurs in the sense of 'to include, comprise' from which the current meaning of the adjective *comprehensive* derives:[1]

The party . . . *comprehended* a great many people who had real taste. (*SS* 250)
Far from *comprehending* him or his sister in their father's misconduct. (*NA* 242)
Till they were forward enough in their rehearsal to *comprehend* all his scenes. (*MP* 166)

Like *comprehend* in having a wider signification than today is the noun *view*. Apart from phrases like *with a view to*, we tend now

[1] 'With a courteous, *comprehensive* smile to all' (*P* 226). Semantically, the two meanings of 'understand' and 'comprise' are not as distant from each other as at first appears; both can be rendered colloquially by the phrasal verb *to take* (a thing) *in*.

to prefer the word *prospect* when the meaning is that of outlook and aims for the future:[1]

> Their different situations and *views* – that John was at Oxford, Edward at Merchant-Taylors', and William at sea. (*NA* 32)
> So natural . . . as to confirm all the daughter's *views* of happiness in being with her. (*MP* 371)

When the emphasis is on motivation rather than prospects, a word like *motive* or *intention* is now more usual. The use of *view* in such contexts she will have found in her eighteenth-century predecessors; it is something of a cliché in Richardson's novels that gentlemen who go courting should have *honourable views*:

> It was plain that he could have no serious *views*, no true attachment. (*MP* 228)
> I would not have been induced by any selfish *views* to go on. (*E* 438)

As with *view*, so also with *situation*; some of its meanings in the novels are now taken over by synonyms. It is used of betrothals (*MP* 125); of pregnancy, where *condition* tends now to be preferred (*SS* 107); as well as in the modern meaning of a place of employment. It also means place or rank in society, where *position* is now more usual:

> From *situation* Mrs Clay was . . . a very unequal, and in her character . . . a very dangerous companion. (*P* 16)

So also with the verb:

> *Situated* as we are with Lady Dalrymple, cousins, we ought to be very careful not to embarrass her. (*P* 166)

Another fairly common meaning of *situation* is 'a place of residence': Lydia and Wickham, on marrying, were always moving from place to place 'in quest of a cheap *situation*' (*PP* 387). A final quotation will illustrate how general the application of this word was:

> Here is a young man . . . with every thing to recommend him; not merely *situation* in life, fortune, and character. (*MP* 316)

[1] Contrariwise, as we shall see, *prospect* occurs meaning 'visual outlook' where *view* is now more normal.

If *situation* occurs where we now use *position*, the latter word is found with the meaning of 'proposition'. We can compare the verb *to posit*:

> Your first *position* is false. (*PP* 136)
> Catherine's feelings contradicted almost every *position* her mother advanced. (*NA* 239)

Both the noun and the verb *value*, with the adjective *valuable*, had a wider currency than they now have. In the now obsolete sense of 'estimate and appreciation of, or liking for, a person or a thing', the noun *value* is common in the novels; it is followed by either *of* or *for*. For all General Tilney's faults, his son Henry assures Catherine that he had had a true appreciation of his dead wife: 'His *value of* her was sincere' (*NA* 197). Similarly:

> In every thing but a *value for* Edmund, Miss Crawford was very unlike her. (*MP* 81)
> His two other children were of very inferior *value* . . . Anne . . . was nobody, with either father or sister. (*P* 5)

So with the verb, meaning 'to appreciate' or reflexively, 'to pride oneself':

> He would enjoy her liveliness – and she has talents to *value* his powers. (*MP* 199)
> I, who have *valued myself* on my abilities. (*PP* 208)

We should now prefer a word like *estimable* or *admirable* instead of *valuable* in contexts like the following:

> In good hands she will turn out a *valuable* woman. (*E* 58)
> (The custom of family prayers) was a *valuable* part of former times. (*MP* 86)

Variety occurs where we now prefer *variation*, or even *variegation*:

> Poor Fanny's mind was thrown into the most distressing of all its *varieties*. (*MP* 364)
> How wonderful the evergreen! . . . how astonishing a *variety* of nature. (*MP* 209)
> The *varieties* in the fitting-up of the rooms . . . the common necessaries . . . were contrasted with some few articles of a rare species of wood. (*P* 98)

Comfortable now tends to mean either (of things) 'affording contentment' or (of people) 'in a state of content and tranquil enjoyment'. As used in both the letters and the novels, however, it is a word of wider application, being often equivalent to 'comforting, cheering':

> Every symptom was then so favourable . . . as the day advanced, all these *comfortable* appearances gradually changed. (*L* 40, p. 144)
> Her mother, perceiving her *comfortable* suggestion to have had no good effect. (*NA* 236)

Jane Austen's use of this word recalls at times the meaning of 'consolatory, fortifying' which we associate with the King James Bible; except that it often occurs in mild and trivial contexts:

> They had not met him. *Comfortable* hopes, however, were given that he would find Mr Crawford at home. (*MP* 75)
> Mrs Welby takes her out airing in her barouche, which gives her a headache – a *comfortable* proof, I suppose, of the uselessness of the new carriage. (*L* 72, p. 280)

The noun *comfort* is used in the plural more widely than in the modern stereotyped phrases, *home comforts*, or *creature comforts*. While Mrs Norris protested at the Grants' extravagant eating, she maintained that 'Nobody loved plenty and hospitality more than herself . . . the parsonage she believed had never been wanting in *comforts* of any sort' (*MP* 31). Or again, considering Maria Bertram's prospects of marriage to the foolish but wealthy Mr Rushworth, Sir Thomas pondered: 'Her feelings probably were not acute . . . but her *comforts* might not be less on that account' (*MP* 201).

The adjective *strong* has a wider application than is usual today. It quite often occurs as an intensive, where *great* is now usual:

> There must have been some *strong* indiscretion. (*MP* 438)
> Father and mother were in much too *strong* and recent alarm to bear the thought. (*P* 55)
> A source of as lively pain as her mind could well be sensible of, under circumstances of otherwise *strong* felicity. (*P* 251)

In the sense of 'courses of action' the word *measures* is much
restricted in use today; occurring chiefly in phrases like 'to take
(stern) *measures*' etc. In the novels the plural noun on its own
has a wider currency in this sense:

> Mr Elton must now be left to himself. It was no longer in Emma's
> power to superintend his happiness or quicken his *measures*. (*E* 91)
> I condescended to adopt the *measures* of art so far as to conceal from him
> your sister's being in town. (*PP* 199)

There has been a general tendency, since the early nineteenth
century, to limit the overlapping and confusability of similar-
sounding and near-synonymous words. *Elocution* is now clearly
distinguished from *eloquence*, *emergence* from *emergency*, *grateful*
from *gratifying*, *character* from *characteristic*, *qualification* from
quality, *purport* from *purpose*, and, generally speaking, *receipt*
from *recipe*:

> A well-judging steady young man, with better notions than his
> *elocution* would do justice to. (*MP* 186)
> It was absolutely necessary . . . to think of something, and in this
> *emergence* . . . she observed . . . (*PP* 177)
> The prospect of their relationship was highly *grateful* to her. (*PP* 125)
> A lucky contraction of the brow had rescued her countenance from the
> disgrace of insipidity, by giving it the strong *characters* of pride and
> ill nature. (*SS* 232)
> Every *qualification* is raised at times . . . to more than its real value; . . .
> she was sometimes (inclined) . . . to rate good-breeding as more
> indispensable . . . than good-nature. (*SS* 215)
> Coming as he did from such a *purport* fulfilled as had taken him away
> (*MP* 334)
> The housekeeper . . . had . . . given her the *receipt* for a famous cream
> cheese. (*MP* 104)

It is not merely that many words have a wider variety of
meaning in the novels than they now have; several verbs also
show a greater versatility of construction than is now possible.
A favourite construction, for instance, is the verb *determine* with
an impersonal subject and a personal object. This is now rare:

> (A headache) grew so much worse . . . that . . . it *determined* her not
> to attend her cousins to Rosings. (*PP* 187)
> The very great uncertainty . . . *determined* him on sending home his
> son. (*MP* 38)

Continue can have a personal object also:

> Should her disposition be really bad . . . we must not . . . *continue* her
> in the family. (*MP* 10)

So also the verb *recover*, which cannot now have a personal
object:

> It required a long application of solitude and reflection to *recover* her.
> (*P* 81)

Consequently it cannot now be used in the passive with a
personal subject, as in 'A young lady who faints, must be
recovered' (*E* 333); a young lady cannot now be recovered,
although, in a different and less personal sense, her dead body
can.

Induce and *acquit* present a converse situation: they now
normally have only a personal object, whereas in the novels an
impersonal object occurs:

> Maria's guilt had *induced* Julia's folly. (*MP* 467)
> Tom's extreme impatience to be removed to Mansfield . . . had
> probably *induced* his being conveyed thither too early. (*MP* 427)
> She could not *acquit* his unsteadiness. (*MP* 159)

Apply, meaning 'to concentrate', as in practising a musical
instrument, occurs in the novels intransitively; it is now used in
this sense only as a reflexive verb. We now associate the simple
intransitive verb *apply* almost entirely with that characteristic
twentieth-century phenomenon, the application form:

> I should have been a great proficient. And so would Anne, if her health
> had allowed her to *apply*. (*PP* 173)
> Catherine said no more, and, with an endeavour to do right, *applied* to
> her work. (*NA* 241)

But the phrase *to work out*, when the subject is impersonal, can
now occur intransitively only; whereas in the novels, an
impersonal subject, and a transitive verb are found:

> Every thing would *work out* a happy conclusion. (*MP* 335)

We are now approaching the subject of transitivity and intransitivity, the grammar of which we shall discuss in more detail later (p. 152). The question of transitivity is not merely a syntactic question, however, but also a semantic one. Notice here the unusual intransitive sense of the verb *wring*, and the equally unfamiliar transitive usage whereby *to participate* becomes equivalent to the verb *to share*:

> Elinor's heart *wrung* for the feelings of Edward. (*SS* 268)
> Indulging in very dreadful fears, and trying to make Edmund *participate* them. (*MP* 34)

Parallel with such a construction, we find *participation of* (*MP* 300, 367), not *participation in*.

It would be wrong, however, to say that because so many words had a wider range of meaning and less limited constructions than they now have, Jane Austen's use of language was imprecise. On the contrary, she clearly enjoyed using language with precision, underlining a word's meaning by indicating its etymology, for example:

> You have an understanding, which will prevent you from receiving things only *in part*, and judging *partially* by the event. (*MP* 313)

And she sometimes restores or refurbishes the meaning of a word or phrase by bringing it back to its more original sense, as in the case of *trials*, *business*, *hopeless* and *common sense* in the following:

> After many pauses and many *trials* of other subjects, Elizabeth could not help reverting once more to the first. (*PP* 82)
> Their presence was a restraint both on her and on Lucy. It checked the idleness of one, and the *business* of the other. (*SS* 247)
> The surgeon was with them . . . They were sick with horror while he examined; but he was not *hopeless*. (*P* 112)
> Though in a legal sense she may be called Nobody, it will not hold in *common sense*. (*E* 62)

With words like *aggravate* and *transpire* she shows an awareness of the true meaning of words whose significance is now apt to be obscured. *Aggravate* does not mean 'annoy' in the novels, *disinterested* does not mean 'uninterested', and *it transpired* is not the equivalent of *it happened*:

> To have it so clandestinely formed . . . severely *aggravated* the folly of her choice. (*MP* 452)
> The only two *disinterested* letters; all the rest had been mere applications for money. (*P* 51)
> Fanny learnt from her, all the particulars which had yet *transpired*. (*MP* 449)

The one usage to which the purist might object is *infer* in the sense of 'imply', though in fact the NED (*infer* 4) has several instances of this:

> An alacrity and cheerfulness which seemed to *infer* that she could taste no greater delight. (*SS* 144)

In short, though Jane Austen sometimes seems to have had a freer hand with abstract nouns than we have, it was a freedom that rarely led to imprecision. To a great extent this was due to her inheritance from the eighteenth century. As Mary Lascelles, in *Jane Austen and her Art* (p. 107), puts it:

> To us Jane Austen appears like one who inherits a prosperous and well-ordered estate – the heritage of a prose style in which neither generalisation nor abstraction need signify vagueness, because there was close enough agreement as to the scope and significance of such terms.

Indeed, since her vocabulary is somewhat circumscribed by the limitations of her subject-matter, and the same words tend to recur, we can work out with some precision just what she means by certain key terms. She is quite clear, also, as to the distinctions to be preserved in differentiating qualities of personality like, for instance, shyness and reserve (*SS* 94), or vanity and pride (*MW* 347); or as to the difference between sense and meaning (*P* 186).

Let us take, however, as an example, her use of a key word like *elegance*. Etymologically, the word is connected with the Latin *eligere* 'to choose', and the original meaning is sometimes resorted to. Thus Emma has doubts whether Frank Churchill, who has inherited his father's affability, may not show an indifference to rank in society that amounts to *inelegance of mind* (*E* 198). In like vein, Mrs Piozzi, alias Mrs Thrale (*British Synonymy* I 37) had referred to the etymology of this word when distinguishing its special meaning:

> The word *elegant* can scarcely be used with more propriety than on such occasions, when people *elect* as pleasing what produces a train of ideas most congenial to our own particular fancy. Pearls are, on this principle, accounted by many people to be more elegant than diamonds; which we all allow to be finer, handsomer, and infinitely more beautiful.

We gain further evidence of what Jane Austen means by *elegance* when we consider those who have it and those who do not. Neither of the Steele sisters attains it, for instance; the elder sister has not even the minimum prerequisite of gentility:

> Lucy was certainly not *elegant* and her sister not even genteel. (*SS* 231)

Lucy had 'a smartness of air, which though it did not give actual *elegance* or grace, gave distinction to her person' (*SS* 120). Mrs Elton tried very hard, but Emma suspected 'that there was no *elegance*; – ease but not elegance' (*E* 270). Good looks counted for little in the matter. If Mrs Elton's 'not unpretty' face does not ensure her elegance, Miss Campbell's plainness, on the other hand, is no bar:

> Miss Campbell always was absolutely plain – but extremely *elegant* and amiable. (*E* 161)

But when elegance occurred with beauty, it was a great enhancer of it. Jane Fairfax is the model of this type of beauty in the novels, Emma's 'bloom of full health' suggesting handsomeness rather than elegance. Jane Fairfax had 'a style of beauty, of which *elegance* was the reigning character, ... elegance which, whether of person or mind, (Emma) saw so little in Highbury. There, not to be vulgar, was distinction, and merit' (*E* 167). Note the precision of this: elegance of person is a distinction; elegance of mind is merited. Qualities of *mind*, as we shall see, are both innate and acquired: *elegance* in this sense must be worked for.

Elegance was ascribed more freely than now to people; the

transference of the sense of refined and choice adornment from things to people occurring readily:

A young woman, pretty, lively, with a harp as *elegant* as herself. (*MP* 65)

But we should hesitate to attribute elegance to a man, as both Marianne Dashwood and her creator apply it to Willoughby (*SS* 45, 42). And again, the Eltons do not qualify: for all Mr Elton's smoothness, elegance is expressly denied him (*E* 135).

The allied quality of *delicacy* is also one in which Jane Fairfax excels. Frank Churchill dwells on the delicacy both of her mind (*E* 439) and her complexion (*E* 478). This is the quality that both Crawfords so sadly lack. Henry had 'an active sanguine spirit, of more warmth than *delicacy*' (*MP* 326); while Mary, Edmund finally recognized, had 'faults of principle, . . . of blunted *delicacy* and a corrupted, vitiated mind' (*MP* 456). Colonel Brandon, quite apart from his flannel waistcoat, is *delicate* in this sense also. The meaning here is clearly 'scrupulous'; perhaps in his case, 'overscrupulous':

Colonel Brandon is so *delicate* a man, that he rather wished any one to announce his intentions to Mr Ferrars than himself. (*SS* 287)

In the letters, the word is found in antithesis to *coarse*:

Lady Hales, with her two youngest daughters, have been to see us. Caroline is not grown at all *coarser* than she was, nor Harriet at all more *delicate*. (*L* 4, p. 10)

Another word of frequent occurrence is *liberal*. A basic meaning of this word is 'generous, free from miserliness, kind to those less fortunate', as when the apothecary Mr Perry is said to be so *liberal* that he is prepared to attend Jane Fairfax without charge (*E* 162); or when Admiral Croft, having, like most gentlemen of the Navy, '*liberal* notions', does not haggle over the terms of his tenancy of Kellynch Hall (*P* 17, 32). The word has, since Jane Austen's day, been much influenced by political developments, and these overtones we have to forget. Usually it is still more or less closely related to attitudes to money and possessions, this quotation from *Emma* suggesting the sense development:

> A very narrow income has a tendency to contract the mind, and sour the temper. Those who can barely live . . . may well be *illiberal* and cross. (*E* 85)

That magnanimity which ought to be, but is not always, the consequence of wealth, is often the meaning. Matchmakers like John Dashwood, who think of marriage chiefly in terms of gain and aggrandizement, are stigmatized as *illiberal*:

> Her wish of bringing Marianne and Colonel Brandon together was hardly less earnest, though rather more *liberal* than what John had expressed. (*SS* 378)

Other characters who lack this kind of *liberality*, though perhaps they have more excuse, are Lucy Steele (*SS* 367), and Mrs Bennet (*PP* 236). And we have seen that expressions which reduce human relationships to what is merely mercenary or predatory, are condemned by Marianne Dashwood on the grounds that 'their tendency is gross and *illiberal*' (*SS* 45). Comparable with such financially coloured meanings of the word *illiberal* is Jane Austen's use of *narrow-minded*, meaning, in effect, 'mercenary'. Henry Tilney apologizes to the Morlands for his father's *narrow-minded* counsel which led him to expel Catherine from Northanger because she was not rich enough to be his daughter-in-law (*NA* 247). Similarly, Dr Johnson had described an acquaintance as '*narrow*, not so much from avarice, as from impotence to spend his money' (Boswell's *Life* III, 40). For the sense of 'Puritanical', not often needed in the novels, we find the word *precise*, which continues to have its Tudor and seventeenth-century meaning in certain contexts:

> We must not be over *precise*, Edmund. As Mr Rushworth is to act too, there can be no harm. (*MP* 141)
> Miss Crawford found a sister without *preciseness* or rusticity. (*MP* 41)

To return, however, to *liberality* in its wider implications, we note that this word describes a basic positive quality of a gentleman, as *delicacy* and *propriety* are its negative counterparts. Robert Martin's letter proposing marriage to Harriet, so unexpectedly gentleman-like, had expressed 'good sense, warm attachment, *liberality, propriety*, even *delicacy* of feeling' (*E* 51) ; and Henry Crawford, in approaching Sir Thomas about Fanny's hand, had evinced a similar combination of qualities : 'He had done it all so well, so openly, so *liberally*, so *properly*' (*MP* 314).

If we ask, 'What then, does Henry Crawford, even a Henry Crawford refined and improved by his love for Fanny, lack?' we touch on the dimension which makes *Mansfield Park* the most profound of the six novels. We are reminded of Newman's famous definition of a gentleman, and of the limitations of a gentleman, in the eighth discourse of *The Idea of a University*. Jane Austen's diagnosis of the defect in the Bertram family applies to Henry Crawford also : '*Principle*, active principle, had been wanting'. David Lodge (*op. cit.* p. 102) rightly sees *principle* as a key word in *Mansfield Park*. What activates principle is religion; practical Christianity, in fact. The Bertrams 'had been instructed theoretically in their religion, but never required to bring it into daily practice' (*MP* 463). *Principle*, in Jane Austen's vocabulary, is a word with religious implications. She wonders, in one of her last letters, at the combination of a lively imagination and good judgement in her favourite niece, Fanny Knight; and comes to the conclusion: 'Religious *Principle* I fancy must explain it' (*L* 141, p. 486). The word occurs in the plural also. Miss Taylor had given Emma *principles* (*E* 462), and no doubt it was remembering these, as well as Mr Knightley's rebuke, that led her to weep tears of remorse all the way home in the carriage after being rude to Miss Bates.

Two favourite normative adjectives are *tolerable* and *rational*. It is interesting to follow the fortunes of the latter word in the novels. In *Pride and Prejudice*, the book which its author criticized for being 'rather too light, and bright, and sparkling', and which has some of the hardness, as well as some of the sparkle, of a jewel, *rational* qualities are well to the fore. It is a word we hear, for instance, from Mr Bennet. By standards of *rationality* deficiencies, and extravagances, are constantly being measured. Charlotte Collins (née Lucas) writes her friend Elizabeth an account of her new home which is 'Mr Collins's picture of Hunsford and Rosings *rationally* softened' (*PP* 147).

Lydia Wickham's fortune is likely to fall below the norm: 'neither *rational* happiness nor worldly prosperity, could be justly expected' (*PP* 307). In various contexts in the later novels, however, depths of feeling can justify conduct which, judged by merely rational standards, seems questionable; and in such circumstances it is rationality, and not feeling, that is demoted or downgraded. Fanny's determination to reject Henry Crawford at all costs is a case in point: 'Never, Fanny,' expostulates Edmund, 'so very determined and positive! This is not like yourself, your *rational* self' (*MP* 347). In *Persuasion*, above all, mere rationality often seems quite dethroned:

> Mr Elliot was *rational*, discreet, polished – but he was not open. There was never any burst of feeling, any warmth of indignation or delight. (*P* 161)
> Subjects . . . such as were wont to be always interesting . . . insinuations highly *rational* against Mrs Clay. But just now she could think only of Captain Wentworth. (*P* 178)

Lady Russell 'had a cultivated mind, and was, generally speaking, *rational* and consistent' (*P* 11), but her advice caused the heroine much pain. At the end of the novel, Lady Russell's values are in a new priority:

> She was a very good woman, and if her second object was to be sensible and well-judging, her first was to see Anne happy. (*P* 249)

It is perhaps not far-fetched to connect this down-grading of *rational* with a corresponding promotion of the word *enthusiasm*. Dr Johnson's numerous definitions of *enthusiasm* in his Dictionary are predominantly unfavourable: 'a vain belief of private revelation, a vain confidence of divine favour, heat of imagination, violence of passion'. All these, of course, recall the etymology: Greek *enthousiázein*, 'to be inspired, sent into ecstasy, possessed by a god'. The kindest of Johnson's definitions are 'elevation of fancy, exaltation of ideas'. When Willoughby is encouraged by Marianne Dashwood to appreciate Cowper and Scott 'as he ought', and to admire Pope 'no more than is proper', the process is summed up in the sentence: 'He acquiesced in all her decisions, caught all her *enthusiasms*' (*SS* 47). The reader is to take *enthusiasms* with a due sense of criticism, though clearly the word was more acceptable to Jane Austen than it had been to the great lexicographer. We can discern a further stage in the word's advancement when James Stanier Clarke, the worthy but rather obtuse librarian of the Prince Regent, urges her, in 1815, to 'delineate . . . the Habits of Life and Character and *enthusiasm* of a Clergyman' (*L* 113a, p. 430). She replies, perhaps still with some irony, though not enough for him to notice: 'The comic part of the character I might be equal to, but not the good, the *enthusiastic*' (*L* 120, p. 443). When, however, Anne Elliot is said to prize 'the frank, the open-hearted, the eager character beyond all others. Warmth and *enthusiasm* did captivate her still' (*P* 161), the word has shed all the pejorative connotations of the previous century. Perhaps we should see this change in the light of two conflicting statements in the letters. In 1809 she had written 'I do not like the Evangelicals' (*L* 65, p. 256); in 1814, 'I am by no means convinced that we ought not all to be Evangelicals, & am at least persuaded that they who are so from Reason and Feeling, must be happiest & safest' (*L* 103, p. 410). The commitment is only partial, and the priority of reason over feeling is significant; moreover as late as 1816 a clergyman annoyed her with a sermon that stressed conversion and regeneration (*L* 133, p. 467). Nevertheless, such passages as that quoted from *Persuasion* are straws in the wind. On the same page, much graver sins of Mr Elliot's than lack of enthusiasm are deplored:

> She saw that there had been bad habits; that Sunday-travelling had been a common thing; that there had been a period of his life . . . when he had been, at least, careless on all *serious* matters . . . How could it ever be ascertained that his mind was truly cleansed? (*P* 161)

No passage better illustrates the difference between the early and the late novels. There are echoes of Mr Collins in the narrative here; with the vital difference, however, that irony is completely absent. We have crossed the threshold into the nineteenth century. Especially notable is the use of *serious*, meaning in effect 'religious'. The first NED quotation (*serious* a. 2) for this meaning is 1796. Elsewhere in *Persuasion*, the adverb also occurs in this sense:

'There is so little real friendship in the world! – and unfortunately' (speaking low and tremulously) 'there are so many who forget to think *seriously* till it is almost too late.' (*P* 156)

Another word which often carries theological implications is *appointment*, where we should now prefer something like *dispensation*; in a phrase like 'the merciful *appointment* of Providence' for example (*MP* 455). This is a word that suggests not so much Evangelicalism as the more rational piety of the earlier eighteenth century:

Without presuming to look forward to a juster *appointment* hereafter. (*MP* 468)
(Elasticity of mind) which, by a merciful *appointment* ... seems designed to counter-balance almost every other want. (*P* 154)
But I am getting too near complaint. It has been the *appointment* of God, however secondary causes may have operated. (*L* 147, p. 498)

Tolerable, like rational, is a common normalizing word. Only a minimal standard is implied, but Jane Austen is anxious not to dwell on scenes which, in human terms, are less than *tolerable*:

Let other pens dwell on guilt and misery. I quit such odious subjects as soon as I can, impatient to restore every body, not greatly in fault themselves, to *tolerable* comfort. (*MP* 461)

Sure enough, on the next page to this, when an attempt is made to rescue what can be saved from the Bertrams' catastrophe, the adverb occurs twice: Mr Yates, though not very 'solid', gave a hope of being '*tolerably* domestic and quiet'; and Edmund talked over his disappointment with Fanny till he became 'very *tolerably* cheerful again'. When Isabella, Mrs John Knightley, and her father, Mr Woodhouse, meet, the word is much bandied about; for both father and daughter have the limited aspirations of hypochondriacs:

'And do you see her, sir, *tolerably* often?' asked Isabella in the plaintive tone which just suited her father. (*E* 94)
I do not know but that the place agrees with her *tolerably*. (*E* 94; also *E* 105)

Certain words do seem particularly characteristic of certain of the novels. If *rational* is an adjective that typifies *Pride and*

Prejudice, a key word in *Sense and Sensibility* is the verb *to support*, with the sense of 'to endure' or 'to bear up'. It occurs at least a dozen times; chiefly apropos of Elinor Dashwood, who in her role as exemplar of fortitude, self-control and good sense, is called upon to *support* everything from her mother's exhausted body (*SS* 334) to a conversation in embarrassing circumstances:

> Elinor took no notice of this, and directing her attention to their visitor, endeavoured to *support* something like discourse with him. (*SS* 89)

See also *SS* 141, 146, 185 etc.

A key word in *Emma* is *superior*. It occurs at least thirty times. Among other things, this points to the comparative absence of evil characters in this novel; no insidious Wickham, unscrupulous Crawford, or odious Mrs Norris. We blush for the Eltons, but, apart from their treatment of Harriet Smith at the ball, they give us no reason to hate them. The word is constantly needed, however, to contrast the 'superior' characters with the 'tolerable' ones; Jane Fairfax and Miss Campbell, Mr Knightley and Frank Churchill, Harriet Smith and Robert Martin (or *vice versa*, depending on who is speaking), and so on. *Superior* sometimes occurs with ellipsis of the thing compared; usage which now recalls tradesmen's jargon. Here we have a characteristic of Jane Austen's English which we shall have occasion to mention again, more than once; or rather, of the development of English since her day. Certain words used straightforwardly by her have since acquired ironic overtones, because they are now so much associated with strenuously unsuccessful attempts at gentility. The recent history of words like *genteel* and *respectable*, which we have already discussed, shows the same trend as the word *superior*:

> She is not the *superior* young woman which Emma's friend ought to be. (*E 36*)
> I am fond of *superior* society. (*PP 26*)

This last is Sir William Lucas; clearly the irony is already beginning. And indeed, if there is any potential for irony in a word, we can be sure that Jane Austen will exploit it.

One of the most interesting words in her vocabulary is *mind*.

The word has been a principal subject of an article by Gilbert
Ryle, entitled *Jane Austen and the Moralists*. Tracing her use of
this word back to English moralists like Shaftesbury, Ryle
observes:

> *Mind* often used without the definite or indefinite article, (stands) not
> just for intellect or intelligence, but for the whole complex unity of a
> conscious, thinking, feeling and acting person.[1]

Mind, as we shall see, does not in fact always mean quite the
same thing in every context; and perhaps it is unreasonable to
expect that it should. Jane Austen is a novelist, not a terminolo-
gist. But the remarkable thing is how consistently such a word,
on the whole, is used. We can form a fairly clear idea of what
she means by *mind* if we consider passages where the word
appears distinguished from others. The *mind/person* distinction,
so common in Richardson, is well to the fore:

> You would rather talk of her person than her *mind*. (*E* 39)

But we also regularly find *mind* distinguished from *understanding*. Mrs Bennet, for instance, was a woman of 'weak
understanding and illiberal *mind*' (*PP* 236). This and several
other passages suggest that the merely cognitive faculty is
usually separated out;[2] and certainly she does not locate the
mind entirely in the head:

> The pain of her *mind* had been much beyond that in her head. (*MP* 74)

[1] p. 121. Ryle is not quite correct in assuming that there are no
eighteenth-century novelists who use the word *mind* in this basic and
comprehensive way. Such a meaning is surely implicit in instances like
the following from Richardson; though admittedly I have found no earlier
novelist writing *mind* with no article as in the quotations from *Persuasion*
on p. 62:
> Miss Barnevelt, a Lady of masculine features, and whose *mind* belied
> not those features; for she has the character of being loud, bold, free,
> even fierce when opposed. (*Sir Charles Grandison*, I 57)

[2] Usually, but not always: thus Jane Fairfax is Miss Campbell's
superior 'both in beauty and acquirements'; Nature had given her the
advantage 'in feature' and in 'higher powers of *mind*' (*E* 165). Here *mind*
seems to come nearer to intellectual ability.

Or consider this passage, describing Mrs Smith in *Persuasion*:

> A submissive spirit might be patient, a strong understanding would
> supply resolution, but here was something more; here was that
> elasticity of *mind* . . . which was from Nature alone. (*P* 154)

The mind, obviously, has innate qualities. In some respects, for
instance, Mary Crawford is better endowed with mind than
Fanny; she has more 'energy of character' and this is why she
can manage a horse better. 'I cannot but think that good
horsemanship has a great deal to do with the *mind*,' says Maria
Bertram, praising her (*MP* 69). But the mind is also something
that can be *formed*; and in Miss Crawford's case a defective
education has corrupted it:

> They have injured the finest *mind*! – for sometimes, Fanny, I own to
> you, it does appear more than manner; it appears as if the mind itself
> was tainted. (*MP* 269)

Fanny's mind, on the other hand, had been formed by Edmund
himself: 'Having formed her *mind* and gained her affections, he
had a good chance of her thinking like him' (*MP* 64). Whereas
elegance and accomplishments are embellishments connected
with manners[1] and understanding, qualities of *mind* relate to
morals, and are related here, for instance, though the
equivalence is only partial, to disposition:

> To be distinguished for elegance and accomplishments . . . could have
> had . . . no moral effect on the *mind* . . . His cares had been directed to
> the understanding and manners, not the disposition. (*MP* 463)

Mind, in fact, as used by Jane Austen, represents the basic and
essential foundation of the whole personality. Contemplating the
ill-assorted match of James Benwick and Louisa Musgrove,
Captain Wentworth ponders:

[1] This, however, is to beg the important question of what is meant by
manners. As David Lodge points out (*op. cit.* p. 100), by *manners* Edmund
Bertram at least can mean 'morals'. As a clergyman he looks forward to
influencing public *manners*: 'The *manners* I speak of, might rather be
called *conduct*, perhaps, the result of good principles' (*MP* 93). Lord
Chesterfield had already suggested that the word *mœurs* should be
imported from French to cover ambiguities in such contexts. See Logan
Pearsall Smith, *Needed Words* SPE tract XXXI.

I confess that I do think there is a disparity . . . and in a point no less essential than *mind*. (*P* 182)

No doubt there is something rough and ready about much of this. Perhaps it is contexts like these that have prompted C. S. Lewis's observation, in *A Note on Jane Austen* (Essays in Criticism IV, 363): 'All is hard, clear, definable; by some modern standards, even naively so'. But it often serves astonishingly well. Consider the passage (it is too long to quote in full) in which she traces the origins of Maria Bertram's delinquency (*MP* 463), contrasting the flattery of Aunt Norris with the coldness and severity of Sir Thomas, and so on. This 'case history' is summed up with the awareness and confidence of a modern writer, sophisticated in psychology; yet the terminology is not psychological jargon, but plain abstract words, made to do just what she wants them to do.

Mary Lascelles (*op. cit.*) and Howard B. Babb in his *Jane Austen's Novels, The Fabric of Dialogue* have rightly stressed the paramount importance of these conceptual and abstract terms in the six novels. As Jane Austen herself put it in one of her letters, in a jocular reference that is nevertheless capable of a wider application: 'Like my dear Dr Johnson . . . I have dealt more in Notions than Facts' (*L* 49, p. 181). But a second important strand, in her narrative as well as in her dialogue, is the colloquial. The overspill from dialogue to narrative is, of course, all the greater because her varied and versatile use of *erlebte Rede*, which we shall discuss later (pp. 204–207), means that the distinction between dialogue and narrative is often not sharp. I also hope to show that by her frequent use of such conversational syntax as the preposition at the end, the retained accusative, free grammatical conversion, and the elided preposition which makes an intransitive verb virtually transitive, Jane Austen indicates her debt to the best and most idiomatic conversation that she heard around her. Further evidence of this debt is her occasional choice of everyday words, and words still retaining physical and concrete suggestions, used meta-phorically, rather than more abstract expressions. A typical instance is the verb *to sink*. It is used meaning (a) a fall in prices, (b) transitively, intransitively and reflexively of the decline of a person's position in society or in the estimation of others, and (c) more generally, of any sort of decline or deterioration:

(a) Bread has *sunk* & is likely to *sink* more, which we hope may make Meat *sink* too. (*L* 85, p. 336)
(b) The dignity of Miss Woodhouse, of Hartfield, was *sunk* indeed. (*E* 276)
I wish I may not *sink* into 'poor Emma' with him at once. (*E* 464)
If she were not taken care of, she might be required to *sink* herself for ever (by an unequal marriage). (*E* 28)
(c) The intimacy between her and Emma must *sink*; their friendship must change into a calmer sort of goodwill. (*E* 482)
I do not see that the language (of an attempt at a novel) *sinks*. Pray go on. (*L* 98, p. 396)

In the following transitive instance, the word means 'obliterating, abolishing (in imagination)'. John Thorpe had misled General Tilney into thinking Catherine Morland a rich heiress: 'By doubling what he chose to think the amount of Mr Morland's preferment ... bestowing a rich aunt, and *sinking* half the children' (*NA* 245).

Comparable with the verb *sink* in sometimes appearing slightly incongruous today in abstract contexts are the nouns *burst* and *push*:[1]

This was the spontaneous *burst* of Emma's feelings. (*E* 411)
One of those extraordinary *bursts* of mind which do sometimes occur. (*P* 51)
Here is a fine *burst* of country; I wish you had my seat. (*MP* 81)
She made a sure *push* at Fanny's feelings here. (*MP* 364)
Her quick eye soon discerned in his the consciousness of having made a *push* – of having thrown a die. (*E* 81)

[1] With *burst* we are uncomfortably reminded of Shaw's *Pygmalion*, and poor Eliza Doolittle's attempts at polite speech:
(Drink) never did him no harm what I could see. But then he did not keep it up regular; on the *burst* as you might say, from time to time. (*Pygmalion* Act III)
But cf. Fanny Burney: With all her gentleness and resignation, *bursts* of sorrow break from her still. (*Diary* II, 301)

A physical and concrete word like *stretch* is sometimes used effectively in abstract contexts:

> He had given a reason for his interference, which asked no extraordinary *stretch* of belief. (*PP* 326)
> The horror and distress you were involved in – the *stretch* of mind, the wear of spirits. (*P* 183)

Similarly the reverberations of pain in Fanny Price's wounded feelings are vividly realized in the word *stab*:

> It was a *stab* . . . He would marry Miss Crawford. It was a *stab*, in spite of every long-standing expectation. (*MP* 264)

Another everyday word that bears an abstract meaning in the novels which it no longer has is *speak*. *To speak* often means 'to manifest' or 'to indicate'. It is constructed with either a single complement or with a pronoun and complement. The first construction is last illustrated from the NED (*speak* v. 29) from Jane Austen, the second from Sir Walter Scott:

> There was . . . a want of spirits . . . which if it did not denote indifference *spoke* a something almost as unpromising. (*SS* 22)
> The ploughs at work, and the fresh-made path *spoke* the farmer. (*P* 85)
> She had heard nothing lately of Lady Catherine that *spoke her awful* from any extraordinary talents. (*PP* 161)
> She had never . . . seen . . . any thing that *spoke him* of irreligious or immoral habits. (*PP* 207)

In a now obsolete usage for which the last NED quotation (*place* v. 6) is from *Mansfield Park*, the verb *to place* occurs in the abstract sense of 'to attribute' or 'ascribe', followed by *to*, *on* or *in*:

> She . . . *places* her disappointment . . . *to* her being . . . less affluent. (*MP* 421)
> I *place* my hope of better things *on* a claim to the protection of Heaven. (*L* 99.1, p. 508)
> *Placing* his whole happiness *in* being on intimate terms in Camden-place. (*P* 140)

The verb *to cross* can be used abstractly, much as we say *to cross one's mind*:

> Such an imagination has *crossed* me, I own (*E 112*.)

Another favourite figurative usage is from taxation: comparison with a tax is made in respect of its burdensomeness and its obligation; and there is often the suggestion also, of the price to be paid for a benefit:

> In the course of the sleepless night, which was the *tax* for such an evening. (*E* 434)
> She gloried in being a sailor's wife, but she must pay the *tax* of quick alarm for belonging to that profession. (*P* 252)
> One of the sweet *taxes* of Youth to chuse in a hurry & make bad bargains. (*L* 84, p. 330)

Among similar financial metaphors, we might mention the noun *amount*, used figuratively to mean 'the total effect, what something amounts to':

> This was the *amount* of the whole story. (*E* 334)
> In the general *amount* of the day there was deficiency. (*E* 367)

There is also *arrear*, used figuratively of an amount still being owed:

> The forbearance of her outward submission left a heavy *arrear* due of secret severity. (*E* 353)
> Miss Bingley . . . paid off every *arrear* of civility to Elizabeth. (*PP* 387)
> I am sure you must have been under great *arrears* of rest. (*L* 117, p. 437)

And finally, *account* is quite often used metaphorically:

> Every thing he had done for William, was to be placed to the *account* of his . . . attachment to her. (*MP* 301)
> Mr Weston . . . added a virtue to the *account*. (*E* 206)

Financial metaphors of this sort are made much of in an article by Mark Schorer on *Fiction and the Matrix of Analogy* (Kenyon Review XI, 539–60). He argues that the last novel, *Persuasion*, has a 'stylistic base derived from commerce and property, the counting house and the inherited estate'. It has been objected by Howard Babb (*op. cit.* p. 239) that Schorer sees metaphors from finance, banking etc., where they do not necessarily exist. Nevertheless, financial metaphors are fairly frequent in all the novels; not merely in *Persuasion*. The question which Schorer dismisses as irrelevant to the purpose of his article is still worth asking in a general way here: viz., how far 'a persistent reliance on commerce and property for concepts of value is the habit of Jane Austen's mind, the very grain of her imagination'.

We must avoid giving the impression, however, amid this discussion of figurative usage, that she relied heavily on metaphor; she did not. On the whole, she preferred unadorned language, and there are several instances in the novels of extravagant figurative language being ridiculed. Mr Collins and Mary Bennet are both prone to metaphors that are extravagant and stale. Habits of irony led her to be suspicious of metaphorical language:

> I shall be able to send this to the post to-day, which exalts me to the utmost pinnacle of human felicity, and makes me bask in the sunshine of prosperity, or gives me any other sensation of pleasure in studied language which you may prefer. (*L* 17, p. 53).

In general, she preferred her metaphors dead. A favourite recurring word is *light*, where we should probably now have a still more dead figure like *aspect*:

> Those that best pleased her, as placing his conduct in the noblest *light*, seemed most improbable. (*PP* 320)
> In what a disgraceful *light* might it not strike so vain a man! (*PP* 252)

Occasionally, what appears to us as the converse of this process of metaphorization occurs, when an abstract noun has a more concrete meaning than is now usual. While Elinor Dashwood writes a letter, her sister Marianne sits watching the *advancement* of her pen (*SS* 203); and *regard*, in the same novel, as well as being used, as we have seen, in the sense of 'esteem', also occurs more literally, meaning 'to look at'.

> He turned round again, and *regarded* them both. (*SS* 176)

Similarly *course* occurs with the concrete meaning of a path taken on a walk: '(General Tilney) would meet them by another *course*' (*NA* 179); and *succeed* and *succession* occur in the less abstract senses of literally following in, or occupying, a position vacated by another:

Sinking into the chair which he had occupied, *succeeding* to the very spot where he had leaned and written. (*P* 237)
The counter which seemed to promise the quickest *succession*. (*SS* 220)

The contrary process, however, is more common. Thus *revolve*, which is now a verb of concrete meaning only, signifying 'to rotate', has an abstract sense of 'to think over, to consider'. Copley (*op. cit.* p. 136) quotes precedents for this meaning from Shakespeare, Dryden and Pope:

> In *revolving* lady Catherine's expressions, however, she could not help feeling some uneasiness. (*PP* 360)

Similarly the verb *to penetrate* can be used in an abstract way not now usual, meaning 'to pierce or touch the feelings of a person':

> Sir Thomas . . . came forward with a kindness which astonished and *penetrated* her. (*MP* 178)

The word *stout* hardly ever occurs in its usual concrete modern sense, describing physical size; it tends to have more abstract meanings: either 'in good health', especially of recovery from illness, or 'resolute, firm in mind':

> A neighbour of ours . . . was here for his health last winter, and came away quite *stout*. (*NA* 54)
> I think I can be *stout* against any thing written by Mrs West. (*L* 101, p. 405)
> I am delighted to hear you speak so *stoutly* on the subject. (*E* 405)

In the abstract sense of 'proud, haughty', the adjective *high* now tends to be restricted to phrases like *high and mighty* and the Biblical *high-minded*. It occurs more often in this sense in the novels, but in colloquial usage; it is not a word used by the best speakers:

> It was all pride . . . She had long suspected the family to be very *high* (Isabella Thorpe). (*NA* 129)
> He is a most disagreeable, horrid man . . . So *high* and so conceited (Mrs Bennet). (*PP* 13)

The word *branch* freely occurs metaphorically, where we should now tend to write *aspect* or *part*:

As Emma saw his spirits affected . . . she immediately led to such a
branch of the subject as must raise them. (*E* 80)
In chapel they were obliged to divide, but Mr Crawford took care not
to be divided from the female *branch*. (*MP* 408)

Receive is commoner in the novels in abstract senses than it is
today. We receive things, or news; Jane Austen's characters
receive ideas, emotions, and so on, in a way that suggests less
passivity on the part of the recipient. A phrase like 'received
opinion' is a survival from this wider use:

Anne did not *receive* the perfect conviction which the Admiral meant to
convey. (*P* 173)
The horror of a mind like Fanny's, as it *received* the conviction of such
guilt. (*MP* 440)
Because Mr Elliot's manners had . . . pleased her . . . she had been too
quick in *receiving* them as the certain result of the most correct opinions.
(*P* 249)

Allow is also commoner in abstract contexts in the novels than it
would be today. A misleading example occurs when, in her
prejudice, Elizabeth listened to Wickham's slanderous account
of the Darcy family and '*allowed* that he had given a very
rational account of it' (*PP* 84). This would mean today
that she said as much; whereas the meaning is probably
'considered and admitted in her mind'. *Admit*, also, often
means in the novels a mental, rather than a spoken acknow-
ledgement; notably in the uneventful, yet exciting, climax of
Emma:

She touched – she *admitted* – she acknowledged the whole truth . . . It
darted through her, with the speed of an arrow, that Mr Knightley
must marry no one but herself! (*E* 408)

But we may be sure that Emma did not say a word about this!
   Other instances where *allow* and *admit* occur with wider
meaning than today are the following:

She had been *allowing* his attentions some time. (*MP* 466)
I thought too ill of him, to invite him to Pemberley, or *admit* his
society in town. (*PP* 201)
Dearest Miss Morland, what ideas have you been *admitting* ? (*NA* 198)

The eighteenth-century reflexive use of *allow*, *to allow oneself in*, now quite obsolete, occurs once in the novels:

> Mr Crawford *allowed himself in* gallantries which did mean nothing. (*MP* 363)

We may compare Richardson:

> Persons . . . that yet *allow themselves in* liberties which no good man can take. (*Sir Charles Grandison* I, 279)

Two notable words used in abstract senses which they no longer have are *to collect*, meaning 'to infer', much as we can still use the verb *to gather*; and the noun *addition*, used in social contexts of persons who are assets or acquisitions:

> You mean to return a favourable answer, I *collect*. (*E* 52)
> I was very much pleased with what I *collected* to have been your behaviour on the occasion. (*MP* 315)

I cannot find this figurative use of *addition* covered by the NED quotations:

> His ease and cheerfulness rendered him a most agreeable *addition* to their evening party. (*PP* 345)
> In my opinion, these Crawfords are no *addition* at all. (*MP* 102)
> Mr Tilney drank tea with us, and I always thought him a great *addition*. (*NA* 238)

The word *article* tends now to be used, either of a literary composition, or as an item of material things which come under the head of a classification: *an article of clothing*, for example. Jane Austen uses the word in more abstract contexts, where we now prefer *item*:

> Such an *article* of Mansfield news. (*MP* 424)
> The superior degree of confidence towards Harriet, which this one *article* marked, gave her severe pain. (*E* 410)

Occasionally a differentiation is discernible between a word used in more concrete and in abstract senses. Thus in its usual more concrete modern sense of a provision of a room or rooms, the word *accommodation* seems to occur in the plural only:

> Used only to a large house himself . . . and without ever thinking how many advantages and *accommodations* were attached to its size. (*E* 204)
> Better *accommodations* (for holding a ball) he can promise them. (*E* 250)

In the singular the word occurs with a more abstract group of meanings, all derived from the idea of adjustment to the arrangements of others:

> A letter . . . the offer of a small house . . . written in the true spirit of friendly *accommodation*. (*SS* 23)
> The man who fetches our letters every morning . . . shall inquire for your's [*sic*] too . . . you can have no scruple to accept such an *accommodation*. (*E* 295)
> It is the custom at Winchester . . . to come away a fortnight before the Holidays . . . Really it is a piece of dishonourable *accomodation* [*sic*] to the Master. (*L* 81, p. 315)

One can insist too much, however, that words in the novels have a merely concrete or a merely abstract significance. This is to forget that Jane Austen is a mistress of *double entendre*. Thus Elizabeth Bennet, visiting Pemberley, sees Darcy's portrait:

> As she stood before the canvas, on which he was represented, and fixed his eyes upon herself, she thought of his *regard*. (*PP* 251)

The card game of *Speculation*, 'the easiest game on the cards', played at Mansfield, is a *tour de force* of sustained double meaning. In the course of it, Mary Crawford, who symbolically 'stakes her last' and loses to Fanny, learns that Edmund Bertram intends to take up residence as incumbent of the parsonage at Thornton Lacey:

> All the agreeable of her *speculation* was over for that hour. It was time to have done with cards if sermons prevailed. (*MP* 248)

During the game, Henry Crawford, Mary's brother, now thoroughly in love with Fanny, refers 'with something of *consciousness*' (i.e. with both embarrassment and a guilty conscience) to his bad behaviour on the occasion when he went to Sotherton to advise Mr Rushworth on 'improving' his estate, and whispers to Fanny:

> I should be sorry to have my powers of *planning* judged of by the day at Sotherton. (*MP* 245)

Planning is here used in the technical, Reptonian sense of 'improving' a house and garden; but also with the deeper meaning of organizing his life. Compare the 'rationality of *plan*' which Emma mistakenly attributes to Frank Churchill (*E* 205).

It is in line with her preference for the everyday colloquial word, such as *sink* or *push*, that Jane Austen also often chooses that most idiomatic of English turns of phrase, the phrasal verb. The different phrasal verbs have varied greatly in meaning and currency in the three hundred years or so that they have been extensively used; and it is in her choice of these that some of the more marked divergences from our own usage occur. Notice the difference here, for instance, between *to turn off*, meaning 'to deteriorate' (of weather), *to turn away*, meaning 'to dismiss or sack an employee', and *to turn up*, where we now use *turn out*:

> At that season of the year a fine morning so often *turned off*. (*MP* 401)
> My uncle Philips talks of *turning away* Richard, and if he does, Colonel Forster will hire him. (*PP* 68)
> With all the chances against her of house, hall, place, park, court, and cottage, Northanger *turned up* an abbey. (*NA* 141)
> He was come to see how it might *turn up*. (*E* 81)

Or again, we may consider the difference between *to lay out*, still a colloquial expression for 'to spend' and *to lay out for*, meaning 'to make tentative suggestions for, to drop hints to obtain':

> *Lay-out* half-a-guinea at Ford's. (*E* 200)
> By *laying out* a few kisses in the purchase of a frank. (*L* 30, p. 104)
> After *laying out for* some compliments of being deeply regretted in their old neighbourhood, which Anne could not pay. (*P* 137)[1]

[1] Cf. Richardson: He had *laid out for* several opportunities to get into my company. (*Sir Charles Grandison* I, 441.)

And as a final trio, we may note *come into*, meaning 'to fall in with (a person's tastes, inclinations etc.)'; *come to*, meaning 'to come round, be appeased'; and *come across*, meaning 'to cross one's mind, occur to one':

> Miss Marianne would not object to such a scheme, if her elder sister would *come into it. (SS* 154)[1]
> I never saw Lucy in such a rage . . . but now she is quite *come to* (Anne Steele). (*SS* 272)
> The many laughs we have had together would infallibly *come across* me. (*MP* 133)

We now *put away*, rather than *put up* a letter (though *put away* also occurs in the novels – *PP* 205), and *break off*, rather than *break through*, an engagement:

> Has Emma read it all? *Put it up, put it up.* (*E* 304)
> Her three notes . . . I was forced to *put them up*, and could not even kiss them. (*SS* 329)
> He was quite mistaken in supposing she had the smallest desire of *breaking through* her engagement. (*MP* 200)

To *bring in* a candidate for Parliament meant 'to cause him to be elected':

> Alethea in her letter hopes for my interest, which I conclude means Edward's – & I take this opportunity . . . of requesting that he will *bring in* Mr Heathcote. (*L* 60, p. 233)

To *put to* a horse was a regular expression for harnessing it to a carriage. This is rare, if not obsolete now, though the NED quotations show that the phrase was transferred from the harnessing of horses to the coupling of wagons to a railway engine:

> James will not like *to put* the horses *to* for such a little way. (*E* 8)
> You know how impossible my father would deem it that James should *put-to* [*sic*] for such a purpose. (*E* 228)

[1] Cf. Richardson: Whether we are so much in the right to *come into* their taste, is another thing. (*Ibid.* I, 8)

One is similarly reminded of the continuity of language, despite technological change, in her use of *to ring up*:

> As soon as she had *rung up* the maid to take her place by her sister. (*SS* 311)

To open on, or *upon*, with a personal object, means to begin a conversation etc., with the person or persons concerned:

> Mr John Knightley now came into the room . . . and *opened on* them all with the information of the ground being covered with snow. (*E* 125)
> The walk in the rain had reached Mrs Elton, and her remonstrances now *opened upon* Jane. (*E* 295)

To stand up or *to stand up with* (a person) often has a meaning equivalent to *to dance*:

> Five couples are not enough to make it worth while *to stand up*. (*E* 248)
> When Mr Elton would not *stand up with* me. (*E* 406)

The converse is *sitting down* (*L* 1, p. 2) where we now say *sitting out*. *To speak for* is a phrase equivalent to *to order*:

> Suppose you *speak for* tea. (*MP* 180)
> The bell was rung, and the carriages *spoken for*. (*E* 128)

Finally, I append some miscellaneous examples of phrasal verbs at variance with our own usage:

> But, my dear, we must *touch up* the Colonel to do something (Mrs Jennings). (*SS* 292) .
> Always *putting forward* to prevent Harriet's being obliged to say a word. (*E* 156)
> I could not help *putting forward* to invite them again. (*L* 44, p. 159)
> Now, poor girl, her peace is *cut up* for some time. (*E* 137)
> Scarcely had she begun . . . than she found her subject *cut up* – her hand seized. (*E* 129; also MP 434)
> We are just the kind of people . . . to be *treated about* among our relations. (*L* 43, p. 152)
> Of Mrs Ferrars's resolution that both her sons should marry well, and

of the danger attending any young woman who attempted to *draw him in*.[1] (*SS* 23)

Your arts . . . may . . . have made him forget what he owes to himself and to all his family. You may have *drawn him in*. (*PP* 354)

Your eyes steadily fixed on him . . . or only *looking off* just to note down any sentence pre-eminently beautiful. (*MP* 227)

We have seen that Jane Austen, through Marianne Dashwood, conveys her disapproval of the 'gross and illiberal' expressions of matchmakers; nevertheless, the business of matchmaking is of paramount importance in the novels, and the more acceptable vocabulary she uses has its interest. An important and frequent verb is *to attach*, usually, but not always (see *E* 141), used of affections between the sexes. The verb can be used in a variety of ways: (a) reflexively, followed by the indirect object for the person of the opposite sex; (b) transitively; a usage which seems to be her own development – it is first illustrated in the NED from her writing; (c) as a participial adjective, both present and past: *attaching*, meaning 'pleasing, engaging', and *attached*, meaning something approaching to 'engaged' or 'affianced':

(a) To *attach myself* to your sister, therefore, was not a thing to be thought of. (*SS* 320)

(b) He never wished to *attach* me. (*E* 427)
    The man who could seriously *attach* my sister. (*SS* 17)

(c) His manners . . . are of a kind I well know to be more solidly *attaching* to Marianne. (*SS* 338)
    Whenever he were *attached* he would willingly give up much of wealth to be allowed an early establishment. (*E* 204)

This last development of *attaching* and *attached* invites comparison with *engaging* and *engaged*; and the parallel extends to the use of *engage*, with the sense of 'betroth', as a transitive verb, in a way not possible today:

Being . . . in daily expectation of Morland's *engaging* Isabella. (*NA* 244)

---

[1] Cf. Richardson: He said, her Nephew might be taken with me, and I might *draw him in*, or be drawn in by him. (*Pamela* I, 15)

There was a difference of degree, however, as this quotation makes clear:

> He came to . . . announce an *attachment* . . . More than an attachment indeed . . . *an engagement* – a positive engagement . . . Frank Churchill and Miss Fairfax are engaged. (*E* 395)

Clearly something definitive is implied by the latter word in such contexts; but this is by no means the only use of the verb *to engage*; it is regularly used, in *Northanger Abbey* and elsewhere, to mean engaged or 'booked' for a dance:[1]

> He must have thought it very odd to hear me say I was *engaged* the other evening, when he saw me sitting down. But I really had been *engaged* the whole day to Mr Thorpe. (*NA* 72)

Frank Churchill intends a play, not apparent on a first reading of *Emma*, on the two meanings of *engaged* in this passage (one of several which suggest that, in Mr Woodhouse's phrase 'that young man is not quite the thing'):

> Frank turned instantly to Emma, to claim her former promise; and boasted himself an *engaged* man. (*E* 325)

The verb *engage* illustrates very well the tendency we have already noted, in the novels, for words to be more elastic in meaning, and more versatile in construction, than they are today. *Engage* runs through a whole gamut of meanings, of varying intensity according to context, all basically having the idea of a pledge or previous involvement, whether this be of a promise or an accepted invitation, or some mental pre-occupation. The verb can be followed by various constructions: an infinitive, the preposition *for*, a personal object, and so on:

> It is so uncertain, when I may have it in my power to return, that I dare not *engage* for it at all. (*SS* 65)
> Wear the necklace, as you are *engaged* to do. (*MP* 263)

[1] Henry Tilney's analogy between dancing and matrimony (*NA* 77) is borne out also by another usage: *to apply for*, or *to aspire to* a lady's *hand* (*PP* 90, *NA* 134), merely meant to ask her for a dance.

If she might judge from his complexion, his mind was not very differently *engaged*. (*PP* 256)
Miss Lucas . . . goodnaturedly *engaged* Mr Collins's conversation to herself. (*PP* 102)
As soon as I could *engage* her alone. (*SS* 321)

Detach and *disengagement* are words used correspondingly of the end of a love-affair:

Regardless of the sentiments of either, I had *detached* Mr Bingley from your sister. (*PP* 196)
Lest she might wound Marianne still deeper by treating their *disengagement* . . . as an escape. (*SS* 184)

A third verb used along with *attach* and *engage* in such contexts, and one which has acquired some of the 'gross and illiberal' tendencies she deplored, is *to fix*:

Some of those little attentions and encouragements which ladies can so easily give, will *fix* him, in spite of himself. (*SS* 223)
If a woman conceals her affection . . . from the object of it, she may lose the opportunity of *fixing* him. (*PP* 21)

The two speakers here, however, are John Dashwood and Charlotte Lucas respectively, and their creator endorses the pragmatist matrimonial views of neither. The word *fix* seems already to be too blunt for the more acceptable characters to use in such contexts. However, it is used, in the letters, of less important arrangements:

I have also been . . . trying to *fix* Mary for a walk this afternoon. (*L* 43, p. 151)

And it also occurs intransitively, meaning 'to settle' (in a place):

I had once some thoughts of *fixing* in town myself. (*PP* 26)

The prospect for an unmarried girl of no fortune was bleak; for Jane Fairfax there waited the dreadful prospect of being a governess, 'the *governess-trade*', as she bitterly calls it, comparing it with the slave-trade (*E* 300). Infinitely preferable was marriage and an *establishment*; the security and status of a household of her own:

> Suppose you were to have one of the Miss Owens settled at Thornton Lacey . . . I dare say they are trying for it . . . for it would be a very pretty *establishment* for them. (*MP* 289)
> Catherine will be amply provided for, & not like my Frederica endebted [*sic*] to a fortunate *Establishment* for the comforts of Life. (*MW* 277)

But only the wealthy could afford an *establishment* for a fallen woman, as Sir Thomas Bertram did for his daughter Maria (*MP* 465).

By marriage family connections are made, and the words *connect* and *connection* are frequent in matrimonial contexts. Mary Crawford, in Sir Thomas Bertram's eyes, would have been 'so eligible a *connection*' for Edmund (*MP* 452); Lucy Steele is described as 'inferior in *connections*, and probably . . . in fortune' to Elinor Dashwood (*SS* 140). 'Upon my word,' says Emma of Robert Martin's proposal to Harriet, 'he will *connect himself* well if he can' (*E* 50). Similarly the verb *to ally* and the noun *alliance*, now used, if at all in matrimonial contexts, of the dynastic marriages of important people, occur, in the novels, of lowlier matches, though with a suggestion of aggrandizement in certain instances:

> A young woman of inferior birth, of no importance . . . and wholly *unallied* to the family! (*PP* 355)
> His daughters he felt . . . in quitting it (the name of Bertram) . . . would extend its respectable *alliances*. (*MP* 20)
> I need not so totally despair of an equal *alliance* as to be addressing myself to Miss Smith! (*E* 132)[1]

This last sentence, spoken by Mr Elton, also illustrates the frequent verb *to address*, used of courtship and proposals of marriage. Sir Thomas Bertram warns Fanny, when she refuses Crawford: 'You may live eighteen years longer in the world, without being *addressed* by a man of half Mr. Crawford's estate,

---

[1] This dynastic approach to marriage was still sufficiently alive at the end of the nineteenth century, in the highest circles, for Lady Bracknell's contemptuous remark, in *The Importance of being Earnest* (Act I): 'to marry into a cloakroom and form an *alliance* with a parcel!'

or a tenth of his merits' (*MP* 319). The noun is even more common, and is less obsolete with this meaning today than the verb is. In the sense of 'proposal of marriage' it seems always to occur in the plural:

> He considered her rather as one . . . still overpowered by the suddenness of *addresses* so wholly unexpected. (*MP 326*)

But this is by no means the only use of this frequent noun. It occurs (a) rarely, in the sense of 'speech', and (b) more frequently, with the meaning 'skill, adroitness, contrivance':

> (a) He was at liberty to hear Margaret's soft *address*, as she spoke her fears. (*MP 356*)
> (b) If you can persuade Henry to marry, you must have the *address* of a French-woman. (*MP 42*)
> By a little of that *address*, which Marianne could never condescend to practise. (*SS* 145)

Still more common is the meaning of 'bearing, deportment':

> His manners are certainly not the happiest in nature. – But we are not all born . . . with the same powers – the same *address*. (*SS* 299)

The commonest modern meaning of this word only rarely occurs (*SS* 209). Jane Austen's regular word for this is *direction*; the verb *to direct*, meaning 'to address a letter' also occurs:

> It was then folded up, sealed and *directed* with eager rapidity. Elinor thought she could distinguish a large W in the *direction*. (*SS* 161)

The word *air*, meaning 'bearing or presence', is clearly a synonym of *address* in the sense of 'bearing'. We now use *air* in a more neutral way, with a specifying adjective phrase usually: *an air of triumph, of disgust* etc. The word used on its own in the novels tends to be complimentary:

> She could see him instantly before her, in every charm of *air* and address. (*PP* 206)
> Henry, though not handsome, had *air* and countenance. (*MP 42*)

The last word here, *countenance*, frequently crops up when characters are being summed up as to their eligibility. Only rarely does this word mean 'face':

He . . . stationed himself so as to command a full view of the fair performer's *countenance*. (*PP* 174)

More often, it means the habitual expression, animated or otherwise, on the face. In some contexts, it is explicitly differentiated from facial features:

He is not so handsome as Wickham; or rather he has not Wickham's *countenance*, for his features are perfectly good. (*PP* 257)
There might be resemblance in *Countenance*; & the complexion, & even the features be very unlike. (*MW* 324)

A quality much admired in a member of the opposite sex was *openness*. It is the quality that Bingley has ('Bingley was endeared to Darcy by the easiness, *openness*, ductility of his temper', *PP* 16), and Jane Fairfax and Mr Elliot (*P* 161) so markedly lack. *Openness* could be overdone, however. Eleanor Tilney keeps the golden mean here, her manner being 'neither shy nor (the contrast is with Isabella Thorpe) affectedly *open*' (*NA* 56). *Ease* and *easy* are also ambivalent words to apply to people. As we have noted, apropos of Mrs Elton, *ease* is no substitute for *elegance* (*E* 270). Ease in such contexts means 'lack of restraint'; but it borders on familiarity, of the kind summed up in the devastating antithesis applied to John Thorpe: '*Easy* where he ought to be civil, and impudent where he might be allowed to be *easy*' (*NA* 45).

These are what we should call personal qualities, by which we mean qualities of personality or of the individual as a person. But by the words *personal* and *person*, Jane Austen tends to mean 'of the body, physical':

She . . . possessed, in an acute mind and assiduous pleasing manners, infinitely more dangerous attractions than any merely *personal*. (*P* 34)
His influence . . . was heightened . . . by that *person* of uncommon attraction . . . which it was no merit to possess. (*SS* 333)

So also with the adverb, *personally*:

I do not think her *personally* vain. Considering how very handsome she is, she appears to be little occupied with it. (*E* 39)

It is the word *personable*, in present English, that alone retains this connexion with physical beauty.

As to the words used to describe these *personal* qualities, there are differentiations. *Handsome* is the word one instantly associates with Emma Woodhouse; it is in fact the third word in the novel:

Emma Woodhouse, *handsome*, clever, and rich. (*E 5*)

Harriet Smith, on the other hand, can claim to be merely 'a very *pretty* girl' (*E* 23), whereas *pretty* is an adjective that Mrs Weston rejects to describe Emma:

Pretty ! say beautiful rather. Can you imagine any thing nearer perfect beauty than Emma altogether ? (*E* 39)

At a lower level than this poor Mary Musgrove had 'even in her bloom, only reached the dignity of being "a *fine* girl" ' (*P* 37).

Bloom is a word that often occurs in descriptions of heroines. It means a state of great beauty, and especially of fine complexion, associated with young womanhood. Emma, at twenty-one, had 'a *bloom* of full health' (*E* 39); Anne Elliot, at twenty-seven, had 'every beauty excepting *bloom*' (*P* 153); 'her *bloom* had vanished early' (*P* 6). A final enhancer of beauty could be a temporary excitement, producing – it is one of her favourite words – *a glow*. We recall the Victorian dictum: 'Horses sweat, gentlemen perspire, and ladies *glow*'. A *glow* was not always a sign of happiness, however; in the second instance here Emma's *glow* is due to rage at Mr Elton's treatment of Harriet:

She thought there was an air of greater happiness than usual – a *glow* both of complexion and spirits. (*E* 298)
Her heart was in a *glow*, and she feared her face might be as hot. (*E* 328)

It is curious that all these words, *pretty*, *beauty*, *bloom* and *glow* can be applied to men as well as women. Mr Woodhouse

describes Mr Elton as 'a very *pretty* young man' (*E* 14);[1]
Wickham had 'all the best part of *beauty*' (*PP* 72); General
Tilney was 'past the *bloom*, but not past the vigour of life' (*NA*
80); and Henry Crawford is described as 'in the first *glow* of
another scheme' (*MP* 246).

The word *pretty*, in fact, is widely used, and seems to mean
little more than the vaguest approval. It occurs a good deal in
the letters, but in the novels the exemplary characters do not
use it, unless they literally mean 'attractive to look at':

What a bloom of full health, and such a *pretty* height and size. (*E* 39)
Mrs Allen thought them very *pretty* kind of young people. (*NA* 236)
And to say the truth it was not very *pretty* of him not to give you the
meeting (Mrs Jennings). (*SS* 171)
We have called upon Miss Dusautoy and Miss Papillon, and been very
pretty. (*L* 97, p. 391)
There were people enough . . . to have made five or six very *pretty*
Basingstoke assemblies. (*L* 36, p. 127)

She perhaps considered that this was one of those words, like
nice, which was used too indiscriminately.

The words *distinguish* and *distinction*, in the sense of 'singling
out with special attention', frequently occur in matrimonial
contexts:

Sir Thomas . . . could not avoid perceiving . . . that Mr Crawford was
somewhat *distinguishing* his niece. (*MP* 238)
To Marianne it had all the *distinguishing* tenderness which a lover's
heart could give. (*SS* 71)
He never *distinguished* her by any particular attention, and . . . others
. . . who treated her with more *distinction* again became her favourites.
(*PP* 285)

Dr Chapman thinks that when Jane Austen writes of Miss Bates
that her youth had passed without *distinction* (*E* 21), she
probably means, 'without any offer of marriage'. This is usage
which can be found in Richardson. Harriet Byron agrees to give
her friends an account of all attentions paid to her: 'of every

[1] *Pretty fellow* is a regular eighteenth-century collocation, with no
pejorative overtones. Tom Jones, it will be remembered, 'began . . . to
have the name of a *pretty fellow* among all the women in the neighbourhood' (*Tom Jones* I, 154). The phrase must refer to good looks; Mr
Elton and Tom Jones have nothing else in common! See further S. I.
Tucker, *Protean Shape* p. 223.

address, and even of every silent and respectful *distinction*' (*Sir Charles Grandison* I, 18).

The words *conscious* and *consciousness*, describing both sexes in contexts of courtship, are generally used in a way that reminds us more of the eighteenth century than of the twentieth. The meaning is often akin to, but not identical with, 'self-consciousness'. Etymologically, the word implies a sharing of knowledge, and a frequent meaning in the novels is that of 'awareness, self-consciousness or embarrassment' caused by some extra or hidden knowledge that the *conscious* person has:

> You look *conscious*. Young ladies have great penetration in such matters. (*PP* 362)
> He was very sure there must be a lady in the case . . . and Mr. Elton . . . looked very *conscious* and smiling. (*E* 68)

Sometimes the noun seems to mean 'having a guilty conscience':

> Every look and action had shown how deeply she (Jane Fairfax) was suffering from *consciousness*. (*E* 418)
> Harriet expressed herself . . . without reproaches . . . and yet Emma fancied there was a something of resentment . . . It might be only her own *consciousness*. (*E* 451)

The negative *unconscious*, meaning 'unembarrassed', occurs:

> Emma could look perfectly *unconscious* and innocent. (*E* 189)

The question of illegitimacy, and its effect on a person's eligibility in the marriage market, occurs occasionally in the novels. Jane Austen's much praised sense of justice is evident in her terminology here. In the narrative she herself uses the neutral term *natural daughter*, free alike from condemnation or sentimental condoning. Harriet Smith, she tells us, was 'the *natural daughter* of somebody' (*E* 22). It is plain that if Lady Middleton's 'delicacy' was shocked by the mention of 'a *natural daughter*' (*SS* 66, and Chapman's note), her creator's was not. Mr Knightley, in his annoyance at Emma's foolish patronage of Harriet, is provoked to a stronger term:

> A degradation to *illegitimacy* and ignorance, to be married to a respectable, intelligent gentleman-farmer! (*E* 62)

On the other hand, Mrs Jennings's expression 'the little *love-child*' (*SS* 196) sentimentalizes a social evil; this is one of the many instances where Mrs Jennings is not a model.

Social intercourse is a topic second in importance only to courtship in the six novels; and here too we notice that some of the commonest words have slightly different implication from their present use. The word *conversation*, which is in any case not frequent,[1] occasionally has the meaning of 'a topic of conversation', much as we say '*the talk* of the town':

> It has been attended by circumstances which, for the sake of every one concerned in it, make it unfit to become the public *conversation*. (*SS* 196)

The word *conversible* (now *conversable*, and beginning to be accented on the first syllable), is fairly common. It means 'given over to conversation' as well as, of persons, 'easy to talk to':

> The evening was quiet and *conversible*. (*E* 100)
> If I find him *conversible* I shall be glad of his acquaintance. (*E* 150)
> She is very *converseable* in a common way. (*L* 39, p. 142)[2]

A frequent word with the meaning of 'conversation' is *discourse*. Its usual modern meaning, 'a lecture, sermon or treatise', occurs only once (*MW* 343):

> And then to turn the *discourse* she began admiring the house. (*SS* 124)
> There was no want of *discourse*. The bride and her mother could neither of them talk fast enough. (*PP* 316)

The stir and hubbub of conversation is described as a *buz(z)*:

> As soon as a general *buz* gave him shelter, he added . . . (*MP* 245)
> The almost ceaseless slam of the door, and ceaseless *buzz* of persons walking through. (*P* 183)

---

[1] Note, however, the precision of: All the rest of his *conversation* or rather talk, began and ended with himself. (*NA* 66)

[2] Cf. for the omission of the preposition, *live-able*: Work for five summers at least before the place is *live-able*. (*MP* 241)

A frequent verb, used of conversation, is *to start*. Some original meanings of this word are 'to leap, to caper, to move with a bound from a position of rest'. The suggestion of suddenness is more often present than it would be today. Ideas are *started* in conversation rather like hares, and the general impression is that talking was both more exciting, and more keenly appreciated, than nowadays:

> As for the navy . . . I was too old when the subject was first *started* to enter it. (*SS* 103)
> She took the first opportunity . . . of Eleanor's being in the middle of a speech about something very different, to *start* forth her obligation of going away very soon. (*NA* 221)
> She *started* no difficulties that were not talked down in five minutes. (*MP* 129)

Thoughts and emotions also *start* to the mind:

> She was within half a minute of *starting* the idea, that Sir Thomas was . . . unkind. (*MP* 424)
> The highly probable circumstance of an attachment to Mr Dixon, which she had so naturally *started* to herself. (*E* 168)

The noun *start* also occurs with this meaning, intermediate between 'a beginning' and 'a surprise':

> To Mr John Knightley was she indebted for her first idea on the subject, for the first *start* of its possibility. (*E* 135)

The verb *to notice* meant not merely 'to observe with the eye', but also 'to pass remarks about a thing in conversation':

> You must have heard him *notice* Mrs Clay's freckles. (*P* 35)
> Edward was the first to speak, and it was to *notice* Marianne's altered looks. (*SS* 242)

Conversely, a *remark* can be something noticed but not spoken:

> She scrupled to point out her own *remarks* to him, lest it should appear like ill-nature. (*MP* 66)

Notice also occurs in the sense of 'treating with favour and attention' and 'recognizing or acknowledging':

A girl who wanted only a little more knowledge and elegance to be quite perfect. She would *notice* her; she would improve her. (*E* 23)
The mortification of Mrs Elton's *notice*. (*E* 285)
But Jane and Elizabeth . . . agreed in wishing . . . that she should be *noticed* on her marriage by her parents. (*PP* 314)

As to the manner of speaking in conversation, the word *accent* is used to describe, not so much the idiosyncrasies of a speaker, as the variability in quality of voice appropriate for an occasion. We should now prefer the word *tone*:[1]

Some one was talking there in a very loud *accent*. (*MP* 182)
'They will be brought up,' said he, in a serious *accent*, 'to be as unlike myself as is possible.' (*SS* 103)

A trio of derogatory epithets which occur in social contexts are *rattle*, *quiz* and *puppy*. John Thorpe springs to mind as exemplifying precisely the empty-headed garrulity associated with the first of these words:

Catherine . . . knew not how to reconcile two such very different accounts of the same thing; for she had not been brought up to understand the propensities of a *rattle* nor to know to how many idle assertions and impudent falsehoods the excess of vanity will lead. (*NA* 65)

The word *quiz* originally meant a person who is odd or eccentric in appearance or character.[2] By a rare extension of the meaning from persons to things, Jane Austen has John Thorpe apply the word to his mother's hat. This is the only *NED* quotation in this extended usage:

Where did you get that *quiz* of a hat, it makes you look like an old witch? (*NA* 49)

Hence the verb *to quiz*, meaning 'to note eccentricities, and poke fun at them' (*MP* 49). Finally, there was a new development of the noun, as one who laughs at or quizzes others. Jane Austen does not appear to have this last usage, however; and

---

[1] Cf. Gray, *Ode on the Spring*:
        Methinks I hear, in *accents* low
        The sportive kind reply.
This use in the plural is barely obsolete; it flourished in Victorian ballads.
[2] Cf. Fanny Burney: Now really, Princess Royal, . . . I cannot suffer you to make such a *quiz* of yourself. (*Diary*, V, 357)

even with the agent-noun *quizzers*, erroneous, as Dr Chapman thinks, for *quizzes*, she seems to mean, in the context, an object of quizzing rather than one who quizzes:

> I will shew you the four greatest *quizzers* in the room . . . I have been laughing at them this half-hour. (*NA* 59)

A *puppy* meant, and still means in old-fashioned English, an impudent and empty-headed young man. An abstract noun *puppyism* occurs:

> So truly the gentleman, without the least conceit or *puppyism* . . . I have a vast dislike to *puppies*. (*E* 321)

An important ingredient of all conversation was *intelligence*, that is 'information' or 'news'. This is the commonest meaning of *intelligence* in the novels, its usual modern meaning being generally conveyed by some such word as *genius*, though the adjective *intelligent* does occur in its modern meaning:

> It was yet in his power to give her fresher *intelligence* of her former friends. (*PP* 143)
> His arrival was soon known at the Parsonage, for Mr Collins . . . hurried home with the great *intelligence*. (*PP* 170)

In one context the plural[1] seems to refer to the various faculties of the mind:

> There seems something more speakingly incomprehensible in . . . memory, than in any other of our *intelligences*. (*MP* 209)

And in yet other instances, the meaning seems to be 'understanding' in the sense of communication, as when Mr Knightley observes that there are 'symptoms of *intelligence*' between Frank Churchill and Jane Fairfax (*E* 343). The *NED* considers this usage rare if not obsolete today. See also *SS* 298.

In the quite frequent occurrence of *intelligence* for *news*, we have the contrary of the preference for simple words like *burst* and

[1] The early Modern English use of plural nouns like *powers* (*SS* 127) and *parts* (*SS* 127) still occurs in such contexts.

start, which we discussed above. Other Latinate words which remind us of Augustan prose rather than our own when they occur so frequently are *felicity*, *solicitude* and *complaisance*, where we should now prefer *happiness*, *care* (or *anxiety*) and *willingness to please*:

> In chatting with Miss Tilney . . . a new source of *felicity* arose to her. (*NA* 80)
> His own previous opinion as to the universal *felicity* and advantage of firmness of character. (*P* 116)
> The civil enquiries which then poured in . . . amongst which she had the pleasure of distinguishing the much superior *solicitude* of Mr Bingley's. (*PP* 35)
> Elinor . . . saw that *solicitude* in his disturbed and melancholy look. (*SS* 204)
> We must not suffer her good nature to be imposed on . . . She must not be left to her own *complaisance*. (*MP* 135)
> She had never received from her more than outward attention, nothing beyond the observances of *complaisance*. (*P* 16)

Another Latinate word that would tend now to be replaced by a native one is *sensation*, where we should now have *feeling*. The reason for this change is obvious: *sensation* has been increasingly confined to the third *NED* group of meanings: 'an excited or violent feeling', or 'an event which caused a "sensation" in this sense':

> Of the lady's *sensations* they remained a little in doubt. (*PP* 262)
> The balmy air, the sparkling sea, and your sweet looks . . . afforded *sensations* which are to raise ecstacy [*sic*] even in retrospect. (*MP* 415)

All the same, her astringency of mind leads Jane Austen to be more sparing of this word than Samuel Richardson. The following sort of sentence, so typical of Richardson, is not to be equalled in the six novels; parallels occur only in the unfinished *Sanditon*, in the mouth of Sir Edward Denham, whose fancy 'had been early caught by all the impassioned, & most exceptionable parts of Richardsons'. (*MW* 404). This is the kind of passage, no doubt, that she would consider 'exceptionable':

His heart must be proof against those tender *sensations*, which grow into ardour, and glow, in the bosom of a man pursuing his first and only Love. (*Sir Charles Grandison* I, 321)

The narrow horizons of the early nineteenth century, compared to today, can be seen in various aspects of vocabulary: in the word *country*, for example, meaning 'county' or 'a country district'. While the word *county* occurs (*MP* 40), the ideas of exclusiveness, and so on, which a phrase like *a county family* now suggests, are assigned to the word *country*:

The party was rather large, as it included one other family, a proper unobjectionable *country* family. (*E* 214)

In passages like these in the letters, the meaning is clearly Hampshire:

There were but 50 people in the room; very few families indeed from our side of the *Country*. (*L* 27, p. 91; also *L* 75, p. 294)

This use of *country* can sometimes mislead. Robert Martin's having been bid more for his wool 'than any body in the *country*' (*E* 28), merely means in the area, or perhaps in the county; and when Wickham wonders whether Darcy will remain 'in this *country* much longer' (*PP* 78), he merely means in Hertfordshire. Darcy does not contemplate going abroad. The use of this last word, incidentally, shows a similar narrowness of outlook. *Abroad* in the novels means 'out of the house'. Like the lovers in Henry Carey's *Sally in our Alley*, Mrs Price goes '*abroad*' only on Sundays (*MP* 408); Mr John Knightley does not like 'going *abroad*' on snowy evenings. (*E* 113)

In antithesis to the country is *town*, by which London is often meant:

It is an excellent thing to have Frank among us again, so near as *town*. (*E* 304)
Entirely against his judgment, a scene painter arrived from *town* (not Northampton; see *MP* 190). (*MP* 164)

Instead of going to *Town* to put myself into the hands of some Physician
. . . I am going to Winchester. (*L* 145, p. 494)[1]

The noun *race* is also used in a narrower sense than now, of a
family: the Morlands were not 'an irritable *race*' (*NA 233*),
though General Tilney came to regard them as a 'forward,
bragging, scheming *race*' (*NA 246*). The word *famous*, too,
reflects in its use a similar limited outlook to the word *country*.
The mass media of the twentieth century transmit fame throughout the country and beyond; *famous* in Jane Austen's time
often meant merely 'well known in that locality':

He is gone into Cornwall to order a Vessel built for himself by a *famous*
Man in that Country. (*L 55*, p. 213)
My mother says the orchard was always *famous* in her younger days.
(*E* 238)
The housekeeper . . . had . . . given her the receipt for a *famous* cream
cheese. (*MP* 104)

Famous thus becomes a general term of approval in colloquial
use: 'excellent, first-rate'. In the novels, however, it is not a
meaning given to the word by the best people. Those rather
similar characters, Tom Musgrave in *The Watsons* and John
Thorpe in *Northanger Abbey* have it:

A *famous* ball last night, was it not? (*NA* 61)
I shall order a Barrel of Oysters, & be *famously* snug. (*MW 335*)

A word which had a similar development to *famous*, though
without its suggestion of slang, was *capital*. Referring to
Fanny Burney, she writes of 'the *capital* pen of a sister author'.
(*NA* 111) The word is still used today by elderly speakers with
the suggestion of 'first-rate':

Her performance was pleasing, though by no means *capital*. (*PP* 25),
At Winchester, where there is a Hospital, & *capital* Surgeons. (*L* 145
p. 494)

[1] It comes as a surprise to find Jane Austen referring, in 1814 (*L* 104,
p. 413), to the capital with the opprobrious epithet later made famous by
Cobbett, *the Wen*. But the NED has this use as early as 1783.

In at least one context, however, the word has a meaning nearer the etymology: 'of the first importance':

Such a *capital* piece of Mansfield news, as the certainty of the Grants going to Bath. (*MP* 425)

Hence, too, Miss Bingley's weak joke at the expense of the Bennets:

'I think I have heard you say, that their uncle is an attorney in Meryton.'
'Yes; and they have another, who lives somewhere near Cheapside.'
'That is *capital*,' added her sister, and they both laughed heartily. (*PP* 37)

An interest of Jane Austen's that is sometimes reflected in her vocabulary is *the picturesque*. According to the Biographical Notice, written by her brother Henry, and published with the posthumous first edition of *Northanger Abbey* and *Persuasion* in 1818, 'at a very early age she was enamoured of Gilpin on the Picturesque' (*NA* 7). William Gilpin, in the first of his *Essays on Picturesque Beauty*, defined the word *picturesque* precisely, distinguishing it, at the outset, from *beautiful*:

A distinction . . . between such objects as are beautiful, and such as are picturesque – between those, which please the eye in their natural state, and those which please from some quality, capable of being illustrated in painting.[1]

Jane Austen had trained her eye in the *picturesque*, in this true sense of the word:

The prospect from the drawing-room window, at which I now write, is rather *picturesque* as it commands a perspective view of the left side of Brook Street, broken by three Lombardy poplars. (*L* 19, p. 61)

She is joking, of course; but the habit of seeing landscape from the painter's viewpoint is clearly there. There is a significance in the number three: '*three* Lombardy poplars'. According to

[1] *Three Essays on Picturesque Beauty* (London, 1792), p. 3.

Gilpin, in his *Essay upon Prints*,[1] when it was a question of combining parts or elements of a picture to form an artistic whole, 'judicious painters have thought three the utmost number that can be allowed' since 'the whole will soon be lost, if the constituent parts become too numerous'. Similarly when, at Netherfield, Mrs Hurst and Miss Bingley each rudely appropriates an arm of Mr Darcy's, leaving Elizabeth to walk by herself along a narrow path, she laughs off Mr Darcy's apologies with a reference to Gilpin:

No, no; stay where you are. – You are charmingly group'd, and appear to uncommon advantage. The *picturesque* would be spoilt by admitting a fourth. (*PP 53*)

Jane Austen shared with her contemporaries a certain contempt for previous ages, when those who modified the landscape for any reason had not considered the view, or, to use a word she favours, the *prospect*. At Donwell Abbey, for instance, there were:

Ample gardens stretching down to meadows washed by a stream, of which the Abbey, with all the old neglect of *prospect*, had scarcely a sight. (*E 358*)

On the other hand, she was aware that the itch to 'improve' landscape and render it more picturesque led to the destruction of much natural beauty. When Mr Rushworth talks of cutting down three fine old trees because 'it opens the *prospect* amazingly' (*MP 55*), Fanny is ready, *sotto voce*, with a quotation from Cowper about fallen avenues.

When Catherine Morland laments her inability to draw or appreciate landscape, Henry Tilney delivers a lecture on the picturesque that relies heavily on Gilpin:

He talked of fore-grounds, distances, and second distances – side-screens and perspectives – lights and shades. (*NA* 111)

[1] (London, 1768) p. 8. F. W. Bradbrook, in *Jane Austen and her Predecessors*, p. 62, quotes appositely from Gilpin's *Observations on the Mountains and Lakes of Cumberland and Westmorland* (London, 1786): 'The doctrine of grouping larger cattle. Two will hardly combine . . . But with three, you are almost sure of a good group . . . Four introduce a new difficulty in grouping' etc.

Gilpin had written of 'two or three *distances* in the landscape',[1] so *distance* would seem to mean what we should now call the middle distance, and *second distance* would be the background. A passage from his account of a tour in the Wye valley[2] illuminates the term *side-screens*. Writing of the Wye, he observes:

> Every view on a river, thus circumstanced (with steep banks), is composed of four grand parts; the area, which is the river itself; the two *side-screens*, which are the opposite banks, and mark the perspective; and the front screen, which points out the winding of the river.

Edward Ferrars cannot boast a knowledge of *the picturesque*, but his disclaimer shows that he, or Jane Austen through him, is aware that Gilpin's terms have been overworked and mis-applied:

> I shall call hills steep, which ought to be bold; surfaces strange and uncouth, which ought to be irregular and rugged; and distant objects out of sight, which ought only to be indistinct through the soft medium of a hazy atmosphere. (*SS* 97)

Marianne Dashwood, a devotee of Gilpin's, has to admit, in answer to Edward's gibes, that 'admiration of landscape scenery is become a mere jargon. Every body pretends to feel and tries to describe with the taste and elegance of him who first defined what picturesque beauty was'. But the true study of picturesque beauty entailed using one's eyes keenly and with discrimination; going for walks, like the Tilneys, 'viewing the country with the eyes of persons accustomed to drawing, and (deciding) on its capability of being formed into pictures, with all the eagerness of real taste' (*NA* 110). This same word *capability* is applied to landscape, houses, etc., in the sense of 'possibility or potentiality for development'; a sense which stems closely from, but is not the same as, the word's original meaning of 'capacity'. We recall the nickname of 'Capability' Brown, given to the eighteenth century landscape designer

---

[1] The third *Essay on Picturesque Beauty*, p. 65.

[2] *Observations on the River Wye, and several parts of South Wales, etc., relative chiefly to Picturesque Beauty* (London, 1782), p. 8.

Lancelot Brown, because of his habit of saying that grounds which he was asked to lay out had *capabilities*. In the novels the word is applied, perhaps ironically, to such a mundane matter as the possibilities of a room at a country inn as a ballroom:

My father and Mrs Weston are at the Crown ... examining the *capabilities* of the house. (*E 253*; also *E 198*)

But it is also used in the more orthodox and exalted context of landscape creation, as when Henry Crawford, who fancies himself in such matters, inspects Sotherton:

Mr Crawford was the first to move forward, to examine the *capabilities* of that end of the house. The lawn, bounded on each side ... (*MP 90*)

In similar contexts, the adjective *capable* occurs. Henry Crawford is full of ideas for the 'improvement' of Edmund's newly acquired living of Thornton Lacey:

The air of a gentleman's residence you cannot but give it ... But it is *capable* of much more. (*MP 243*)

The word *improve* is fairly common, especially in *Mansfield Park*, in the special sense of improving on Nature by modifying the landscape on picturesque principles. Mary Crawford describes her brother as a 'capital *improver*' (*MP 244*); but the 'capital improver' of the day is in fact referred to by name in this novel: Humphry Repton (*MP 53*). The word also occurs in the letters:

Our *Improvements* have advanced very well; the Bank along the Elm Walk is sloped down ... etc. (*L 23*, p. 76)

Certain expressions are unfamiliar because the ideas or objects they suggest are not of our own day. The insistence on rank yields collocations like *gentlemen and half-gentlemen* (*E 197*), and the collective noun *quality*, meaning people of good social standing:

Bold queer-looking people, just fit to be *quality* at Lyme. (*L 39*, p. 142)

With this word *quality* the *NED* compares the word *consequence*, with the special meaning of 'importance in rank or position, social distinction':

> Their fortune . . . was such as to make them scarcely secondary to Donwell Abbey itself, in every other kind of *consequence*. (*E* 136)
> *Consequence* has its tax. (*P* 17)

The phrases *woman of . . . fortune* (*SS* 216) and *gentleman of fortune* (*E* 62) both occur apropos of moneyed people. The latter phrase now carries incongruous suggestions, from the other meaning of *fortune*, of an adventurer.

A word that occurs in a special sense, of rank in society, is *representative*, meaning the head of a family, the chief bearer of the family name, or perhaps the heir who is to have that position in the future. This is a meaning that, as Henry Bradley admitted to Dr Chapman, has been ignored by the *NED*. The word occurs three times in the novels:

> Mary . . . was long in finding among the dashing *representatives* or idle heir apparents . . . any one who could satisfy the better taste she had acquired at Mansfield. (*MP* 469)
> 'Consider, my father's heir – the future *representative* of the family.'
> 'Don't talk to me about heirs and *representatives*,' cried Charles. (*P* 224)

A collocation, on the other hand, that is illustrated in the *NED* from the Book of Common Prayer onwards is *private gentleman*, or *private man*, meaning a gentleman not holding public office:

> To live no longer with the decencies even of a *private gentleman*! (*P* 13)
> My eldest son . . . will perhaps inherit as considerable a landed property as any *private man* in the county. (*NA* 176)[1]

Its antonym *public* occurs in the unusual phrase *going into public*. The *NED* illustrates this 'rare' phrase only from Fanny

---

[1] Cf. Shakespeare:
> What infinite heart's ease
> Must kings neglect that *private men* enjoy
> *Henry V* IV, i, 242.

Burney's *Evelina* (in fact, it also occurs in Richardson). The expression is concerned with the 'coming out' of young ladies into society and, in effect, on to the marriage market. The question of whether Fanny Price was 'out or not out', it will be remembered, had perplexed Mary Crawford (*MP* 48). Girls went 'into public' under the aegis of an older woman, acting as chaperone:

Lady Bertram did not go *into public* with her daughters. (*MP* 35)
The idea of her . . . going *into public* under the auspices of a friend of Mrs Elton's. (*E* 275)

The word *appearance* occurs with a related meaning:

Fanny was now preparing for her *appearance* as of course she would come out. (*MP* 147)
Miss Emma Watson . . . was to make her first public *appearance* in the Neighbourhood. (*MW* 315)

Rank was emphasized in the minor ceremonies of everyday life; in the matter of precedence when going in to dinner, for example. The phrase *to take place of*, meaning, among other things, 'to go before when proceeding into a room etc.', occurs in such contexts. The host led the way with the most important lady visitor, the hostess bringing up the rear. Hence Aunt Norris's warning to Fanny when she is invited out to dinner:

Though Miss Crawford is in a manner at home, at the Parsonage, you are not to be *taking place of* her. (*MP* 221)

No doubt many women of the time would have insisted on such precedence; would have been, to use her own word, *tenacious*:

It would be a great deal better if she were not so very *tenacious*; especially, if she would not be always putting herself forward to take place of mamma. (*P* 46)
Her nephew Henry, whose rights as heir expectant had formerly been so *tenaciously* regarded. (*E* 449)

Both the noun and the verb *place* occur with such connotations of rank in society. Thus when Maria Bertram has come to grief, 'where she should be *placed*, became a subject of most melancholy . . . consultation' (*MP* 464). This means, not merely where she should go, geographically speaking, but to what level in society she might continue, in her disgrace, to aspire. For, in the words of Mr Elton, 'Every body has their level' (*E* 132). And yet, the best characters keep their regard for rank in due proportion. Anne Elliot is too proud 'to enjoy a welcome which depends so entirely upon *place*' (*P* 151).

One final pregnant sense of the word *place* should perhaps be mentioned. It is Henry Crawford's use, when he discusses the improvements he recommends for Thornton Lacey:

> The air of a gentleman's residence . . . you cannot but give it . . . But it is capable of much more . . . You may raise it into a *place*. From being the mere gentleman's residence, it becomes, by judicious improvement, the residence of a man of education, taste, modern manners, good connections. (*MP* 244)[1]

Needless to say, position in the higher ranks of society, whether in the services or professions, depended on birth, money and influence; or, to use a typical word of the time, *interest*. Henry Crawford gets William Price an introduction to his uncle, the Admiral, because 'the Admiral . . . had *interest*' (*MP* 266). When Jane Bennet's engagement to Bingley was known, 'her younger sisters soon began *to make interest* with her for objects of happiness which she might in future be able to dispense' (*PP* 349). This is a slightly different meaning of a claim upon someone else's good offices. Both these meanings seem combined when Lady Catherine, with topsy-turvy priorities, attacks Elizabeth for wishing to marry Darcy when 'honour, decorum, prudence, nay *interest* forbid it' (*PP* 355). In a still different meaning the word expresses Sir Thomas Bertram's pleasure in the projected marriage of Maria and Mr Rushworth: 'It was a connection exactly of the right sort; in the same county, and the same *interest*' (*MP* 40); that is, probably, the same political party, Tory as against Whig, or perhaps the same economic interest, landed as

---

[1] The ramifications of Jane Austen's terminology are endless; the collocation *modern manners* here is intended to contrast with Edmund Bertram's re-definition, already quoted (p. 61n) of what he, as a clergyman, understands by *manners*.

against mercantile. It amounts, as Dr Chapman points out, to the same thing. The participial adjective *interested* occurs in a more pejorative sense of 'self-interested' and therefore 'biassed': '*Interested* people have . . . misrepresented' (*PP* 85); 'Caroline's *interested* wishes'. (*PP* 120).

Without *interest*, promotion in the services or the professions was often slow. Many an underprivileged William Price must have grumbled:

> I begin to think I shall never be a lieutenant . . . Every body gets *made* but me. (*MP* 250)

To be made was used of promotion to the rank of a commissioned officer, or of subsequent promotion in the Navy. Here, as in *Persuasion*, the novelist is drawing on the experience of her own relatives:

> (Captain Benwick) when he came home from the Cape, – just *made* into the Grappler. (*P* 108)
>
> Frank is *made* – He was yesterday raised to the Rank of Commander. (*L* 16, p. 47)

Some similar idea of a necessary condition of promotion in the Army is the meaning of *qualification* in the following context. By means of it, Henry Austen, Jane's brother, became a lieutenant in the Oxford Militia:

> I suppose you have heard from Henry himself that his affairs are happily settled. We do not know who furnishes the *qualification*. (*L* 12, p. 31)

The obsolete use of *embodied*, in the next example, is also a military one; the word means 'formed into a military company':

> Mr Weston . . . satisfied an active cheerful mind and social temper by entering into the militia of his county, then *embodied*. (*E* 15)

The word *qualification* of the last paragraph has also a civilian use now obsolete. This word in the following quotation from *Mansfield Park*, and the word *deputation* in the quotation from *Persuasion*, both relate to the game laws, and to those who were qualified as landowners, and those deputed by authority,

D

to shoot. Both words appear more prominently in Fielding's novels, as befits his more masculine subject-matter:

> His boast of his dogs, his jealousy of his neighbours, his doubts of their *qualification*   and his zeal after poachers. (*MP* 115)
> Would be glad of the *deputation*   certainly, but made no great point of it; – said he sometimes took out a gun, but never killed. (*P* 22)

Small detailed differences are apt to escape our notice: Dr Chapman points out how much more likely seven shillings was to be regarded as a casual unit of expenditure when guineas were a common unit of trade and coinage:

> Poor Nancy had not *seven shillings* in the world. (*SS* 370)
> He treated himself with this *seven shilling* purchase. (*L* 84, p. 334)

References to helping to *break* sugar (*L* 117, p. 437) and to a *new loaf* of sugar (*L* 86, p. 345), large conical pyramids which required breaking, point to a minor domestic difference. Sugar cutters are still to be found in old households. The expression *a dish of tea*, commoner in the eighteenth century, was perhaps dying out. The usual expression is *to drink tea* (*SS* 99); occasionally *to take* (*one's*) *tea* (*E* 209). *A dish of tea* occurs twice only; used once by the unfashionable Mrs Price, and once in *The Watsons*, in what may be a jocular context:

> I could not tell whether you would be for some meat, or only a *dish of tea*. (*MP* 379)
> The entrance of the Tea things . . . was some relief – & luckily Mr and Mrs Edwards always drank a *dish* extraordinary. (*MW* 326)

Tea-board, meaning 'tea-tray', occurs:

> The solemn procession . . . of *tea-board*, urn, and cake-bearers. (*MP* 344)

A word that is now rare in the meaning of preparing food for eating is *to dress;* it is commoner in early Modern English. We can compare Milton's *L'Allegro:*

> Herbs and other country messes,
> Which the neat-handed Phyllis *dresses*.

And in the novels:

> I am afraid Campbell will be here, before there is time to *dress* a steak.
> (*MP* 379)
> I really do not think she cares for any thing but boiled pork: when we
> *dress* the leg it will be another thing. (*E* 177)

Lydia and Kitty Bennet's '*dressing* a sallad' (*PP* 219) seems
less obsolete in view of modern expressions like '*dressed* crab'
and 'salad *dressing*'. Another word with culinary associations is
rout-cakes (*E* 290), illustrated by *NED* quotations from 1807 to
1873. This was a rich cake suitable for *routs* or receptions.

There are references in both *Pride and Prejudice* and *Northanger Abbey* to *spars*, evidently small pieces of lustrous stones,
or geological specimens, to be purchased as ornaments and
souvenirs. The first *NED* quotations for *spars*, used elliptically
for *spar ornaments*, is from Mayhew, dated 1851:

> I may enter his county with impunity, and rob it of a few petrified *spars*
> without his perceiving me. (*PP* 239)
> They . . . laid out some shillings in purses and *spars*. (*NA* 116)

The word *hobby* occurs in the novels in its uncontracted form,
hobby-horse; indulging in one's favourite pastime being compared to riding a horse, originally:

> If he had a *hobby-horse* it was that. He loved a garden. (*NA* 178)
> Sanditon . . . was his Mine, his Lottery, his Speculation & his *Hobby
> Horse*. (*MW* 372)

The word *fish*, adapted from French *fiche*, meaning 'a peg',
from *ficher*, 'to fix', was a small piece of ivory or bone used
instead of money for keeping account in games of chance.
Sometimes these counters were made in the form of a fish:

> Lydia talked incessantly of lottery tickets, of the *fish* she had lost and
> the fish she had won. (*PP* 84)

Like *fish* in being both a French loan-word and an instance of
popular etymology is the word *ridicule* (*E* 453), 'a small

handbag'. The perversion of *reticule* to *ridicule* had already occurred, as the *NED* points out, in French. Another example of popular etymology is *noonshine* (*L 52*, p. 195), beside the less corrupted form *nuncheon* (*SS* 318). Etymologically the word means 'noon-draught' or 'noon-cup' (*OE scenc*, related to the verb *scencan* 'to pour'); the meaning in both these contexts is 'a midday snack'.[1] Obsolete or archaic words to indicate time are *se'nnight* (*NA* 139) for 'week',[2] and *a twelvemonth* (*PP* 128) for 'a year'.

The weather is an important topic in the novels; almost as important as it is among English people in real life; and certain expressions call for comment. Her use of *open* meaning 'free from frost' (*NED open* a. 9b), of weather or a season, is now rare. It was clearly a word that would have been frequently heard apropos of the all-important question of field sports:

> If this *open* weather holds much longer . . . Sir John will not like leaving Barton . . . 'tis a sad thing for sportsmen to lose a day's pleasure. (*SS* 167)
> Fine *open* weather Miss Emma! – Charming season for Hunting (*MW* 357)

We no longer use *floated* for 'flooded':

> The near way . . . quite *floated* by this rain. (*E* 179)

Dirty, meaning 'muddy' now tends to be dialectal:

> The *dirty* month of February. (*MP* 376)
> And very long walks, you know – in summer there is dust, and in winter there is *dirt*. (*E* 356)

The adjective *putrid*, used of disease, which strikes an odd, jarring note in the novels, reminds us how much more poten-

---

[1] Dr Johnson defined *nuncheon* as 'a piece of victuals eaten between meals'. Midday is an unusual time for a meal in the novels, dinner-time being at any time from 4 to 6.30 p.m.

[2] This compound (OE *seofon niht* 'seven nights') was already obsolescent, and perhaps it was somewhat pompous; only characters like Mr Collins and General Tilney have it.

tially dangerous many illnesses were then than now. The *'putrid* sore throat' which Mr Elton was afraid Emma would catch in visiting Harriet (*E* 109), is probably diphtheria; and this, or possibly typhus, is what is feared when Marianne Dashwood's disorder is pronounced 'to have a *putrid* tendency' (*SS* 307). Marianne, like Mr Woodhouse, is attended by an *apothecary*, though when Louisa Musgrove's accident occurs a *surgeon* is called for (*P* 110). Mr Woodhouse's doctor is addressed as *Mr Perry* or *Perry*. *Doctor* as an appellation seems always to refer to Doctors of Divinity: Dr Grant, in *Mansfield Park*, Dr Shirley in *Persuasion*, Dr Davies, chased by Anne Steele and referred to as *the Doctor* in *Sense and Sensibility*, and presumably Dr Hughes, briefly mentioned in *Emma* (*E* 323), are all clergymen.

The sending of letters was a much more expensive and troublesome business than it is today. We take relatively cheap postage and gummed envelopes for granted. A letter from her sailor brother Francis in the Baltic Jane Austen describes as well worth its 2/3d (*L* 85, p. 336). One way of economizing was to get an MP to superscribe the letters, since free postage was one of his perquisites. This was known as *franking* a letter. Both verb and noun occur:

> To see all his letters directed to him with an M.P. – But do you know he says, he will never *frank* for me? (*SS* 113)
> Mr Lushington M.P. for Canterbury . . . If I can, I will get a *frank* from him. (*L* 86, p. 344)

Envelopes were not yet in general use. By the *envelope* of Darcy's letter to Elizabeth – 'an *envelope* containing two sheets of letter paper, written quite through . . . The *envelope* itself was likewise full' (*PP* 196) – Jane Austen appears to mean another larger sheet enclosing the rest. Letters were folded and sealed by means of a wafer, a small disc made of gum and flour, often coloured, which could be moistened and used for sealing letters:

> My sweet little George! . . . I admired his yellow *wafer* very much, and hope he will choose the wafer for your next letter. (*L* 17, p. 51)

No doubt it was the high cost of letter-writing, combined with her own poverty, that led Jane Fairfax normally to 'fill the whole paper and *cross* half' (*E* 157); *crossing* a letter was turning it at right angles and writing across what had already been written. An aunt of mine with a turn for economy used to have this illegible habit.

It is an interesting reflection on the vagaries of fashion that at this time it was short hair that was disapproved of:

> I thought Edward would not approve of Charles being a *crop*. (*L* 18, p. 57)

Crop here clearly means a person having a close-cropped head of hair. *Cropped* is also used of gardens, and means not, as now, 'harvested', but 'trimmed and tidied':

> She hopes you will not omit begging Mrs Seward to get the Garden *cropped* for us. (*L* 66, p. 262)

This is the same verb that she uses figuratively when she writes in her letters of having reduced the size of *Pride and Prejudice*:

> I have lop't and *crop't* so successfully, however, that I imagine it must be rather shorter than S. & S. altogether. (*L* 76, p. 298)

Living as she did at the beginning of the industrial revolution, when mass production and distribution were beginning to make various tradesmen's and inventors' names household words, Jane Austen must be one of the first great writers to refer to manufactured articles by the proper name of, or associated with, their inventors or developers. At Northanger Abbey, we are told, the old open fireplace had been 'contracted to a *Rumford*' (*NA* 162), the name being from Count von Rumford, inventor of the modern type of grate. An apricot tree which Dr Grant disparages is vindicated by Mrs Norris: 'It is a *moor park*, we bought it as a *moor park*' (*MP* 54); so called, Dr Chapman thinks, from Sir William Temple's house of that name. The 'fine old *Constantia* wine' (*SS* 197), which Mrs Jennings has in the house, is, even at this early date, South African wine, from a farm near Cape Town called the Constantia farm. British rule of the Cape began in 1795 as a result of the wars with France. When Sir Walter Elliot compliments his daughter on her improved looks, he asks her whether she uses *Gowland* for her complexion (*P* 146). This is Mrs Vincent's Gowland's skin lotion. A rather earlier development, depending on aristocratic trend-setting rather than industrial enterprise, appears in Miss Bates's *spencer*, meaning 'a short close-fitting jacket or bodice' ('I had got my bonnet and *spencer* on', *E* 173), named after the second Earl Spencer. References to superior tradesmen added both realism and polish. Jane Fairfax's mysterious piano arrived 'from *Broadwood's*' (*E* 215). It is interesting that already the Austens were getting their crockery from *Wedgwood* (*L* 74, p. 290) and their tea from *Twining* (*L* 93, p. 382). Such names were destined to play an increasingly important part in the English language.

How far was Jane Austen an innovator in English? One has to be careful here; a word like *come-at-able* (*E* 20), which looks like a nonce-formation, had in fact been in use for centuries before her day. Similarly *successless* (*E* 168), to our eyes an innovation, was a fairly common eighteenth-century word. Also quite common was the verb *to mizzle* (*E* 12), meaning 'to rain in fine drops, to drizzle'. On the other hand *do-nothing-ness* (*MP* 390) is apparently her coinage, and so, as we shall see (p. 201) are *in-betweens* and the now very common *grown-ups*. Not all her coinages were acceptable. The word *imaginist* is illustrated in the *NED* with this single quotation:

> How much more must an *imaginist*, like herself, be on fire with speculation. (*E* 335)

A *coze*, a clipped form of French *causerie*, influenced, perhaps, by English *cosy*, and meaning 'a pleasant chat', is first illustrated in the *NED* from her novels:

> Miss Crawford . . . proposed their going up into her room, where they might have a comfortable *coze*. (*MP* 257)
> The two Brothers are having a comfortable *coze* in the room adjoining. (*L* 83, p. 326)

A *sweep*, in the sense of 'a curved carriage drive', is also first exemplified in the *NED* (*sweep* n. 16c) from the novels:

They . . . could chuse papers, project shrubberies, and invent a *sweep*.
(*SS* 374)
The great iron *sweepgate* opened. (*E* 332)

Deedily, meaning 'industriously', is perhaps a dialect word; it
is more fully illustrated from the Southern dialects, including
Hampshire, in the *EDD*, than in the *NED*, where this quotation from *Emma* is the first example:

Frank Churchill . . . most *deedily* occupied about her spectacles. (*E* 240)
They are each about a rabbit net, & sit as *deedily* to it . . . as any two
Uncle Franks could do. (*L* 86, p. 344)

It is perhaps a dialectal pronunciation of *seem*, meaning 'how (a
cloak) *seems* or appears', that is intended when she writes in a
letter to a friend, 'I hope you like the *sim* of it.' (*L* 74.1, p. 499)

The word *nidgetty*, meaning 'trifling', apparently, seems to
have been her own invention:

I have been enabled to give a considerable improvement of dignity to
my Cap, which was before too *nidgetty* to please me. (*L* 14, p. 37)

The expressive word *tittuppy*, however, used by John Thorpe to
describe a flimsy and easily overturned gig (*NA* 65), has
several precedents. An equestrian word that *is* first recorded
in the NED from her writing, however, is the verb *to jib*, used
of a horse in harness, meaning 'to refuse to go on':

The horses actually *gibbed* on this side of Hyde Park Gate (*L* 70
p. 276)

This, the NED points out (*jib* v.²), is a comparatively recent
word, of uncertain derivation. It was almost certainly not her
own invention, however; it is next illustrated in the NED in
a figurative sense, from the *Sporting Magazine*, a year later
than this letter, in 1812; and that keen horseman, Sir Walter
Scott, provides two more early examples. The new word was
probably on everyone's lips; but characteristically, she is the
first to record it. Her spelling, apparently, is still allowable.

We have already noticed, and shall have reason to note again
in the second part of this book, that, parallel to the decline of the
word *genteel* (and perhaps the ideas associated with it) from

something truly admirable to false refinement, there has been a decline also, since Jane Austen's day, in the acceptability of certain expressions: phrases, for instance, like *quite the gentleman, of an evening, she had a complaint on her,* and *a gown something the same.*[1] All these were reputable idioms in Jane Austen's time, but are no longer used by those who aspire to the best spoken English. Certain individual words, too, show a like falling off in acceptability. The use, found also in the eighteenth century, of the word *lady* for 'wife' is one example. Sir Thomas Bertram appeared to better advantage 'than his *lady* did' (*MP* 277); Mr Henry Dashwood had 'by his present *lady*' three daughters (*SS* 3). So is the use, apropos of both persons and things, of the word *treasure:*

> She finds Miss Pope *a treasure.* 'Lady Catherine,' said she, 'you have given me *a treasure.*' (*PP* 165)
> That Mrs Whitaker is *a treasure*! (*MP* 105)
> If he have nothing else to recommend him (except his good looks), he will be *a treasure* at Highbury. (*E* 149)

The speakers in the first two instances here (Lady Catherine de Bourgh and Mrs Norris) might lead us to suppose that the word had already taken the downward path; but the last speaker is Emma, and we find the word applied elsewhere to a mare (*MP* 37) and to a letter (*L* 132, p. 461).

In the sense of 'biassed' or 'prejudiced', the adjective *partial* is still very acceptable English; Jane Austen uses the word with this meaning (*PP* 208). More commonly, it occurs in the collocation *partial to* meaning 'fond of', a usage which tends now to be vulgar. It would hardly occur now in serious contexts; certainly not in discussing love affairs, unless one were joking:

> He grew more and more *partial* to the house and environs. (*SS* 101)
> He is really *partial* to Miss Darcy. (*PP* 148)
> Colonel Brandon's *partiality* for Marianne. (*SS* 49)

It is indicative of the word's present status that the last *NED* quotation in this sense is of someone who is partial to sausages!

[1] See Joan Platt, *The Development of English Colloquial Idiom during the Eighteenth Century* in Review of English Studies, II, 70–81, 189–196.

The word *party* meaning 'a person concerned' is also, apart from its special legal uses, now 'shoppy, vulgar or jocular' (*NED party* n. 14):

> Marianne's indignation burst forth as soon as he quitted the room . . . they all joined in a very spirited critique upon the *party*. (*SS* 269)
> Nothing but the belief of your being a *party* concerned (PP 321)

As a last example of a word that has suffered a decline in this way, we might quote her use of the word *line* in the vague sense of a department or sphere of activity:[1]

> An uncle remained – in the law *line*. (*E* 183)
> G. Turner has another situation, something in the cow *line*, near Rumsey. (*L* 96, p. 388)

Modern American speech is suggested by her frequent use of the verb *to quit*, in the sense of 'to leave', and the occasional *to be quit of*, meaning 'to be rid of'. But the two most typical American collocations with this verb, the absolute use and the use with a following gerund (*I quit; quit doing that*) do not occur:

> That your father . . . would *quit* town next morning. (*PP* 323)
> Amidst the various endeavours of different people to *quit* the topic, it fell to the ground. (*SS* 62)
> An escape *to be quit of* the intrusion of Charles Maddox. (*MP* 158)

Once, Emma Woodhouse, of all people, uses the expression *I guess* ('They are known to no human being, *I guess*, but herself' *E* 202), which we now associate with America.[2] But this phrase has, of course, had an honourable place in the language from at least the time of Chaucer.

Two occupation nouns which suggest America now are *attorney* (*PP* 36) and *druggist* (*NA* 200), meaning 'chemist,

---

[1] Perhaps the expression has always been slightly substandard: 'Johnson was at all times . . . prompt to repress colloquial barbarisms; such as . . . *line* for *department* or *branch* as, *the civil line, the banking line.*' Boswell, *Life* III, 196.

[2] *I guess now* is in fact mentioned by Byron, in 1813, as an Americanism. *Letters and Diaries* (ed. Quennell), I, 229.

pharmacist'. The former was the regular word, until 1873, for a legal agent in the courts of Common Law, the counterpart of a solicitor in Chancery. The word has now been superseded in Britain by the general term *solicitor;* but survives in certain special collocations like *Attorney-General, power of attorney. Druggist* is still a regular word for a pharmacist in Scotland as well as in America.

Apropos of American parallels, we might mention here, though it is strictly more a matter of syntax than vocabulary, that she is very fond of a turn of phrase, more common now in American than in British English, whereby *have* is followed by a personal object and an infinitive. The crisp terseness of this idiom is characteristic:

I have been a good deal used *to have a man lean* on me for the length of a street. (*MP* 94)
'Come, Darcy,' said he, 'I must *have you dance*'. (*PP* 11)

Perhaps the most remarkable foreshadowing of later American usage, however, occurs when Jane Austen describes three of her acquaintance as 'three old *Toughs*' (*L* 36, p. 129). This conversion from the adjective is still regarded by the *NED* as American, and the first quotation for it is dated 1866.

Finally, certain derivatives in the novels seem slightly unusual today. She favours the negative prefix *un-* more than we do: *unagreeable* (*MP* 278), *unfrequently* (*MP* 397), *undescribable* (*MP* 405), and *unexpensive* (*P* 97) occur. Contrariwise, she speaks of a character being 'careless and *immethodical*' (*P* 203), and of '*illaudible* sentiments' (*SS* 53). *Accustomary* (*SS* 307, *MP* 266) regularly appears in place of the now usual *customary. Blameable* (*SS* 140, 329) is fairly frequent, where we now tend to say *blameworthy,* or, more probably, *to blame. Complicate* (*P* 215) is an adjective meaning 'complicated', and *dismission* (*PP* 114), once quite a usual noun from the verb *dismiss,* has now been replaced by *dismissal*. The last *NED* quotation for *dismission* is from Macaulay.

II

SENTENCE STRUCTURE

Tenses of the Verb

In the Germanic languages only two tenses were distinguished inflectionally: the present and the preterite. Already in Old English the auxiliary verbs *willan*, *sculan*, *habban* and *beon* were being developed to supply this deficiency in tense inflections. But in Old English it was still quite usual to express future time by a present tense; and it is partly a survival from this state of affairs that we can still occasionally use the present tense with future meaning, as in 'Tomorrow *is* Tuesday'. Indeed, the present tense is usual to express future time in temporal clauses. Compare 'When I go' with French 'Quand j'irai'.

Jane Austen quite often uses the present tense with future meaning in main clauses, particularly if she wants to suggest something previously arranged or inevitable.[1] This use, which is sometimes known as the dispositional present, is still a recognized part of our tense structure. But, as Barbara Strang points out (*Modern English Structure*, p. 146), an appropriate time-indicating word is present, usually, in the sentence nowadays: 'I *leave* for London *tomorrow*'. The frequency of this present without any such adverb modifier in the novels contributes to the tendency to be authoritative and dispositional which is one of the salient characteristics of Jane Austen's prose. We might well use the emphatic and compulsive *is to* if we were paraphrasing some of these examples:

> You are prepared for the worst, I see . . . Harriet Smith *marries* Robert Martin. (*E* 470)
> My dear Edmund, there is no idea of her going with us. She *stays* with her aunt. (*MP* 78)

---

[1] When the possibility of arrangement is excluded, it has never been possible to use the present tense in this way: * 'I break my leg tomorrow' is not English.

You are mistaken Elinor; you are very much mistaken. A very little trouble on your side *secures* him. (*SS 223*)
If the weather permits, Eliza & I *walk* into London this morning. *L* 69, p. 270)

The apparent present tense of the verb *to see* occurs in vulgar usage for a past tense. I say, the apparent present, because in fact this dialectal form probably derives historically from an otherwise obsolete preterite singular, *OE seah*. Only servants in the novels have this usage:

I *see* Mr Ferrars myself ma'am (Thomas, the manservant). (*SS* 354)
It is a pleasure to see a lady with such a good heart for riding! . . . I never *see* one sit a horse better (coachman). (*MP* 69)

There are certain contexts where a perfect tense, with the auxiliary *have*, rather than a preterite, is now preferred. Two of these tenses have been defined as the resultative perfect, denoting a past action, connected, through its result, with the present moment; and the perfect of experience, expressing what has happened, once or more than once, within the speaker's or writer's experience.[1] These are distinctions, however, which developed slowly through the centuries, and while Jane Austen's usage is generally that of present English, occasionally the simple preterite is found where we should expect the perfect, either (a) resultative, or (b) of experience:

(a) Julia is with the cousins, who live near Bedford Square; but I *forgot* their name and street. (*MP* 434)
(b) It is as pretty a letter as ever I *saw*. (*SS* 278)
I never *was* at his house. (*SS* 111)
Till this moment, I never *knew* myself. (*PP* 208)

Another slight difference in matters of tenses which gives a period flavour to Jane Austen's writing concerns the use of perfect and pluperfect auxiliaries. In Old English, intransitive

---

[1] Examples of the resultative perfect and the perfect of experience are, respectively, 'I have lost my wallet and cannot pay' and 'I have been to Paris twice'; F. R. Palmer, in *A Linguistic Study of the English Verb* (p. 74), prefers to explain the resultative perfect in terms of 'current relevance'; the result, after all, may be nil; as in a sentence like 'I've written, but they haven't replied'.

verbs, often verbs of motion, had formed their perfect and pluperfect tenses with the verb *to be*, while *have* had been used with transitive verbs. Throughout Middle English, as Mustano-ja observes (*Middle English Syntax*, p. 501), *have* became steadily more common with all verbs as a perfect auxiliary, at the same time that *to be* was increasingly associated with the passive voice. Today perfects and pluperfects formed with *is* and *was* are rare; they were less rare in the novels. In particular, what are sometimes known as mutative verbs, those which indicate a transition from one place or condition to another, verbs of motion and verbs like *become, grow,* etc., are often constructed by Jane Austen with the verb *to be*:

It was plain that he *was* that moment *arrived*. (*PP* 252)
So, you *are come* at last! (*P* 37)
Miss Tilney *was walked* out. (*NA* 91)
You have heard of his leaving the —shire, and of his *being gone* into the regulars. (*PP* 337)
He *was sailed* within four days. (*MP* 388)
Anne herself *was become* hardened to such affronts. (*P* 34)
He *was grown* so steady, and such an excellent correspondent, while he was under your care. (*P* 67)
That it would not be safe for her, – that she *was* not enough *recovered*. (*PP* 59)
I am so glad we *are got* acquainted at last. (*SS* 116)

This feeling for the result of a motion rather than the movement itself, accounts for the combination of *had* and *been* here :

Lady Russell *had not been arrived* five minutes the day before, when a full account of the whole had burst on her. (*P* 124)
Mr Rushworth *had been gone*, at this time, to Bath. (*MP* 450)
The others *have been gone on* to Scarborough, these three weeks.[1] (*PP* 342)

When the action itself, rather than the state resulting from the action, is emphasized, the auxiliary *have* occurs with verbs of motion, as in present English:

It would have been strange if I *had* not *gone*. (*P* 39)
He said he should not stay out long; but he *has* never *come* back. (*P* 37)

---

[1] So George III, to Fanny Burney:
    How long *have* you *been come* back, Miss Burney?
                                        Fanny Burney's *Diary* II, 317.

The most interesting and idiosyncratic feature of tenses in the novels, however, is the use of expanded tenses. Jane Austen's employment of these has been discussed in a recent article by Edith Raybould in a *Festschrift* to Dr Karl Brunner (1957). In her view many expanded tenses found in the novels, and the frequent expanded infinitives in the later novels in particular, have a modal function. Whereas verbs with simple infinitives following them express an intention likely to be followed up by an event, verbs followed by expanded infinitives tend to express a point of view or an emotional inclination that is not sure of realization. Compare, for instance:

This was the principle on which Anne wanted her father *to be proceeding*, his friends *to be urging* him. (*P* 12)

where Anne Elliot's wishes for her father could never be fulfilled, and the tentativeness is conveyed by the expanded form; and on the other hand:

Admiral Croft . . . only wanted a comfortable home, and *to get* into it as soon as possible. (*P* 22)

Here the Admiral's intention is followed up by action; he does take over Kellynch Hall; consequently the simple, unexpanded infinitive is preferred. This point of Miss Raybould's seems to me partly valid, so far as the expanded infinitives are concerned, though not all the examples support it; but the increasingly frequent use of these tenses in the later novels seems to call for further explanation.

As Miss Raybould points out, many instances are far removed from present-day usage; especially those in which the durative aspect of the verb, now normally conveyed by the expanded tense, is severely limited, implicitly or explicitly, by some circumscribing of the time in the context. In the first instance here, for example, the use of the expanded tense to describe Jane Fairfax falling overboard from a ship would only be likely today if we were re-showing the whole incident in slow-motion photography!

A water-party; and by some accident she *was falling* overboard. He caught her (*E* 218)

Sir Thomas . . . had sought no confidant but the butler, and *had been following* him almost instantaneously into the drawing-room. (*MP* 180)

If two moments, however, can surround with difficulties, a third can disperse them; and before she had opened the letter, the possibility of Mr and Miss Crawford's having applied to her uncle and obtained his permission, *was giving* her ease. (*MP* 437)

I am writing what will not be of the smallest use to you. I *am feeling* differently every moment. (*L* 103, p. 408)

And the next moment she *was hating* herself for the folly which asked the question. (*P* 60)

She saw on looking up that Colonel Fitzwilliam *was meeting* her. (*PP* 182)

This last phrase *was meeting* would now imply iteration, or a prolonged repetition of separate acts; an implication the expanded tense does have elsewhere, as in 'The two families *will be meeting* every day in the year' (*MP* 27). It is also worth noting that two of the verbs expanded here, viz. *hate* and *feel* (in the sense of an emotion applicable to a particular situation, as opposed to *feeling better*, etc.), are almost never expanded in present English. See Martin Joos *The English Verb*, p. 115.

What is particularly interesting is that in this wider use of expanded tenses, Jane Austen is clearly an innovator; I cannot find precedents for these frequent expansions, even in Fanny Burney, to whose usage she owes so much. She clearly felt that expanded tenses gave increased actuality, that they heightened the emotion, excitement, or irritation of a situation:[1]

Every sentence that he uttered *was increasing* her embarrassment. (*PP* 252)

I hope you will not *be* cruelly *concealing* any tendency to indisposition. (*MP* 411)

A question of force and interest to rise over every other, to be never *ceasing*, alternately *irritating* and *soothing*. (*NA* 231)

There was a restlessness, which showed a mind not at ease. He *was looking* about, he *was going* to the door, he *was watching* for the sound of the other carriages. (*E* 320)

With such emotional usage in mind, we can explain many of the expanded tenses in *Persuasion*, for example, by considering the

---

[1] The use of expanded tenses to express annoyance is a marked feature of present English. Compare 'Segovia *played* the guitar' with 'That boy *has been playing* the guitar all evening!' See Palmer, *op. cit.* p. 94.

nature of the heroine's love. Anne Elliot claims for herself, and for her sex, 'the privilege . . . of loving longest, when existence or when hope is gone' (*P 235*). In her steadiness and maturity, she is very different from a younger, more impressionable temperament like, for instance, Catherine Morland. People like Anne feel more deeply, and change their feelings more slowly and reluctantly. Her love for Wentworth had remained dormant and unfulfilled for over seven years. Expanded tenses express this depth of feeling:

> Soon, however, she began to reason with herself, and try *to be feeling* less. Eight years, almost eight years had passed, since all had been given up. How absurd *to be resuming* the agitation which such an interval had banished into distance and indistinctness! (*P* 60)

A further consideration is that the expanded tenses can still merge, and in the novels frequently do merge, into another construction: the verb *to be* with a participle as predicative adjective. We can compare, in present English, 'She is trusting us' (expanded verbal form) with 'She is so trusting' (adjectival form); in practice the two constructions are not always as clearly differentiated as this. Here are two sentences chosen out of many in which the adjectival and verbal constructions seem to merge:

> This event (the birth of a son to cut off an entail) had at last been despaired of, but it was then too late *to be saving*. (*PP* 308)
> She was . . . ashamed of every sensation but the one revealed to her – her affection for Mr Knightley. Every other part of her mind *was disgusting*. (*E* 412)

One of the reasons why this second sentence sounds so out of key to our modern ears, is semantic: *disgust*, as we have seen, often means merely 'distaste' in the novels. But we also misconstrue the sentence if we are not aware that this may well not be, as it would be in Modern English, an adjectival construction. If pressed to do so ungenteel a thing as to analyse what she meant here, Jane Austen would probably have construed this as verbal: 'was giving her feelings of self-disapproval'. The omission of the object, *her*, of a normally transitive verb is very characteristic. See below, p. 153.

The first type of merging is the more common, i.e. the expanded tense with adjectival overtones. The following sentences suggest, by co-ordination with adjectives and by other means, the prominence of the adjectival construction in the writer's mind:

> When I am in company with him, I will not *be wishing*. In short, I will do my best. (*PP* 145)
> He *was* . . . wholly reconciled and *complying*. (*E* 443)
> He *was* always agreeable and obliging, and *speaking* pleasantly of every body. (*E* 139)
> As you say, one's mind ought to be quite made up – One should not *be hesitating*. (*E* 53)

Contrariwise, even though the adverb of degree formally disqualifies the next two instances from being expanded tenses, both still seem influenced by the verbal construction:

> He is . . . *very smiling*, with an exceeding good address. (*L* 87, p. 353)
> Mrs Price was greatly obliged, and *very complying*. (*MP* 401)

I have dwelt on this influence of the adjectival construction, because I believe it partly accounts for the large number of expanded tenses used by Jane Austen to describe a settled state of mind; a state very different from the iterative aspect which is now inseparable from our own associations with the expanded tenses in contexts descriptive of human feelings:

> She *was* humble and *wishing* to be forgiven. (*MP* 462)
> Had he learnt to love her because he believed her *to be preferring* him, it would have been another thing. (*P* 182)
> I had supposed him *to be despising* his fellow-creatures in general. (*PP* 80)
> As Elinor *was* neither musical, nor *affecting* to be so. (*SS* 250)

As Miss Raybould points out, the use of the expanded tenses seems in any case to have been increasing during the decades at the turn of the eighteenth–nineteenth centuries; and it was then that a development took place which now seems to us inevitable: namely the passive form of these tenses. Grammarians of the day, however, set their faces against expanded forms of the passive, such as 'The house *is being built*'. Down to the end of the eighteenth century the form for this would have been 'The house *is building*', or possibly the earlier *'a-building'*; i.e. the active form could also convey a passive meaning. The colloquial expression 'Nothing *doing*', meaning 'Nothing *being done*' is a survival from this state of affairs. Jane Austen's avoidance of the passive form, and fairly frequent use of the active form of the expanded tenses in a passive sense, gives a slightly un-modern quality to several of her sentences:

> She only came on foot, to leave more room for the harp, which *was bringing* in the carriage. (*P* 50)
> The clock struck ten while the trunks *were carrying* down. (*NA* 155)
> An enormous roll of green baize . . . *was* actually *forming* into a curtain by the housemaids. (*MP* 130)
> Our Garden *is putting* in order. (*L* 49, p. 178)

I have found no instances of the expanded passive form; and this is remarkable because, as we shall see, Jane Austen favours the passive voice, and because the passive of gerunds, on the other hand, is quite common.

Other grammarians have noted Jane Austen's curious and rather frequent use of the expanded present participle; a construction which, even with our present increasing use of expanded forms, is still hardly possible:[1]

> I must say it is very unfeeling of him, to be running away from his poor little boy; talks of his *being going* on so well. (*P* 56)
> It would rather do her good after *being stooping* among the roses. (*MP* 73)
> Their *being going* to be married. (*SS* 182)
> To be driven by him, next to *being dancing* with him was . . . the greatest happiness in the world. (*NA* 157)
> And exclaimed quite as much as was necessary (or *being acting* a part, perhaps rather more). (*E* 145)
> And the concert *being* just *opening* she must consent for a time to be happy in an humbler way. (*P* 186)

This use of *being* with a present participle has its precedents in earlier English. The quasi-conjunctive use of *being* meaning 'since' or 'because' (still found in substandard English) is probably an influence in the seventeenth and eighteenth

---

[1] Palmer (*op. cit.* p. 58) asterizes expanded participles like **being taking* to indicate that such usage is not possible today.

century quotations below, and in at least the last two examples
from Jane Austen quoted above:

> And *being* (we are, as I perceive) *going* some considerable way together,
> I will give you an account of the whole of the matter. Bunyan, *Pilgrim's
> Progress* (World's Classics), I, 174.
> I am on a ramble from home . . . my wife and self *being performing* our
> triennial visitations. 1748, *Verney Letters of the Eighteenth Century*
> II, 239.

Jane Austen has only one example of *being* meaning 'because'
(or 'although'). It occurs in her letters:

> I am tired of Lives of Nelson, *being that* I never read any.[1] (*L* 86, p. 345)

Miss Raybould points out that Jane Austen's use of expanded
tenses is most marked in the infinitives and the preterite. Their
commonest occurrence today, at least in conversation, is
probably in the present tense, often covering future as well as
present time. Here, on the other hand, Jane Austen often prefers
the unexpanded tense:

> Grandmama hopes the white Turkey *lays*. (*L* 22, p. 73)
> But where is her all-conquering brother? . . . I *die* to see him. (*NA* 57)
> 'I *walk*. I prefer walking.'
> 'But it *rains*.' (*P* 177)
> Quite unnecessary! – a great deal too kind! But Edmund *goes*; – true – it
> is upon Edmund's account. (*MP* 222)

Again, the interrogative and negative form with *do* is used by
her where now an expanded tense is normal. The interrogative
do form now tends to be confined to the expression of customary,
not particular, action:

> I . . said it *did not rain* and I must go. (*E* 179)
> Well, my dears, how *does* your book *go* on? (*E* 78)
> Mrs Perry and the children, how are they? *do* the children *grow*?
> (*E* 101)[2]

[1] For earlier examples, see Margaret Williamson, *Colloquial Language
of the Commonwealth and Restoration*. Pamphlet of the English Association
LXXIII, pp. 15–16.

[2] Compare the nursery rhyme 'Mary, Mary, quite contrary, how *does*
your garden *grow*?' With the decline in Bible-reading and church-going,
it is chiefly by such rhymes that a sense of archaic constructions is preserved for the young.

It is perhaps worth recording the negative fact that the most recent development of expanded tenses, viz., the use with adjectives ('He *is being clever*' as an expansion of 'he *is clever*') does not occur in the novels. According to Jespersen (*MEG* IV 14.7.3), this usage is rare until the last decade of the nineteenth century. Nevertheless, by gerundial usage like the following, Jane Austen does approach the modern construction:

She was so happy herself, that there *was* no *being severe*. (*E* 444)

Auxiliaries: do

Originally, the verb *to do* meant 'to put'. Much of its original force survives in the archaic words *don* and *doff*, meaning 'to put on' and 'take off' (clothes). Something of its etymological force also survives in Jane Austen's rather frequent expression *to do away*, where we now prefer *do away with*, or some synonymous expression like *dispel*:

All Elizabeth's anger against him had been *done away*. (*PP* 261)
Mr Collins's letter had *done away* much of her ill-will. (*PP* 64)
Nothing could *do away* the knowledge of what the latter had suffered. (*SS* 349)

Much more important than any original meaning this verb had, however, has been its development in various periphrases. In particular, *do* is regularly used with all except a few of the commoner auxiliary verbs, to make up the negative and interrogative form. This is a development of late Middle and early Modern English. For at least four centuries the simpler form of the negative with *not* (*I know not*), and the simpler form of the interrogative with inversion (*Know you? Know you not?*) were in competition with the periphrastic forms of negative and interrogative with *do* (*I do not know. Do you know? Don't you know?*). It is the latter forms, of course, which have survived.

Jane Austen's employment of the last vestiges of the older simple forms without *do* gives her writing at times a slightly old-fashioned quality. The non-periphrastic negative form of the verb *to know* is fairly common, though the modern pattern *I do not know* is also frequent. As Jespersen observes (*MEG* V

23.1.3), the simpler form had probably been normal colloquial usage in the seventeenth and eighteenth centuries:

> What he means to do, I am sure I *know not*. (*PP* 276)
> His brother and sister *knew not* what to think. (*NA* 209)

With other verbs, too, the non-periphrastic negative occurs; particularly in dramatic passages. Marianne Dashwood's 'sensibility' tends also to be expressed by this more old-fashioned and dramatic form:

> He was as generous, she *doubted not*, as the most generous of his sex. (*PP* 311)
> But her eyes were closed; she *breathed not*. (*P* 109)
> He bore her directly into the house . . . and *quitted not* his hold till he had seated her in a chair. (*SS* 42)
> I *care not* who knows that I am wretched. (*SS* 189)
> I *value not* her censure. (*SS* 68)
> Elinor, in quitting Norland, . . . *cried not* as I did. (*SS* 39)

The old inverted interrogative form occurs most commonly with the verbs *say* and *come*. We are dealing here with a surviving minority construction that is still not quite obsolete with these two verbs:[1]

> Well girls . . . What *say you* to the day? (*PP* 342)
> Well, sir, and *what said* Mrs Smith? (*SS* 323)
> Good God! . . . how *came you* here? How *came you* up that staircase? (*NA* 194)
> How *came she* to think of asking Fanny? (*MP* 217)
> How *comes this* about; here must be some mistake. (*MP* 312)

With other verbs, very occasionally, in dramatic passages, the old inverted interrogative is found:

> What *felt Elinor* at that moment? (*SS* 129)

---

[1] For example, in the traditional question of the High Court judge to a jury: 'Members of the jury, how *say you*? Guilty or not guilty?' For the same pattern with *come* we have a survival in the colloquial 'How *come*?' meaning 'How did it happen?' Again, we can compare George III, talking to Fanny Burney: 'How *came you* – how *happened it*? – what? – what?' (*Diary* II, 320). Two negative contexts where the old non-periphrastic constructions have been preserved, like flies in amber, are the lovers' gambit 'She loves me, she *loves me not*', and the plant name '*forget-me-not*'.

When the negative adverb *not* is replaced by an adverb phrase such as *by no means*, Modern English does not employ the *do* auxiliary. Here Jane Austen's practice differs:

> You are giving it a turn which that gentleman *did by no means* intend. (*PP* 49)
> The morrow, though differing in the sort of evil, *did by no means* bring less. (*MP* 192)
> As Miss Bertram's inclination for so doing *did by no means* lessen. (*MP* 98)

The modern *did not by any means* (*E 113*) occurs also.

Elsewhere than in negative and interrogative sentences, the auxiliary *do* occurred quite frequently to make an alternative form of tenses in the early Modern English period. The poets in particular enlisted the auxiliary to eke out their metre. As Pope put it in the *Essay on Criticism* (1. 246):

> Expletives their feeble Aid *do* join
> And ten low Words oft creep in one dull line.

Today, however, when the sentence is not negative or interrogative, the use of *do* indicates emphasis. We may compare the now archaic usage of Ariel's song in *The Tempest*, 'On the bat's back I *do fly*', with unstressed, or perhaps semi-stressed *do*, and the modern 'I *do like* to be beside the sea-side', where the statement is emphatic and the vowel of *do* is stressed. Jane Austen's usage with emphatic *do* is much like our own: when *do* occurs in positive sentences (provided there is no inversion), it normally has extra emphatic force, serving to underline a statement or reinforce an imperative:

> So I said to Sir John, I *do think* I hear a carriage. (*SS* 106)
> How you *did tremble*! (*MP* 69)
> If any one faculty . . . may be called more wonderful than the rest, I *do think* it is memory. (*MP* 208)
> '*Do come* now,' said he, 'pray come'. (*SS* 119)

Occasionally, however, *do* appears where little or no emphasis seems called for:

Highbury . . . to which Hartfield, in spite of its separate lawn and shrubberies and name, *did* really *belong*. (*E* 7)

That she was not immediately ready, Emma *did suspect* to arise from the state of her nerves. (*E* 240)

The proviso mentioned in the last paragraph calls for comment: this is the use of *do* in an expansion of verbal inversion, following an initial adverb. This is still common, if somewhat literary, present English usage. Old English, like present-day German, had regularly inverted the subject and verb after an initial adverb or adverb phrase. This simple inversion following an adverb survived in the poetry of Jane Austen's time; in Wordsworth's *Westminster Bridge* sonnet, for example:

> Ne'er *saw I*, never felt, a calm so deep.

In the novelist's own sentences, however, the verb *do* is the one which is inverted after the adverb, and the main verb takes up its modern position following the subject. This probably accounts for the verb *do* here: it effectively resolves a conflict between the traditional feeling for inversion and the increasing need, in an inflectionless language, for a fixed word-order: subject, verb, object:

> With much uneasiness *did she* thus *leave* them. (*NA* 148)
>
> Already *did Catherine reproach* herself with having parted from Eleanor coldly. (*NA* 235)
>
> The mischief of neglect and mistaken indulgence towards such a girl – Oh! how acutely *did she* now *feel* it. (*PP* 280)

In sentences like these, most modern writers would no longer use any form of inversion; they would achieve a similar effect by some such introductory phrase as 'It is', or 'It was', and a following clause: 'It was with much uneasiness that she left them'.

The preceding adverbial phrase probably accounts for the position of *did* in the following sentences, though there is no inversion. Dr Craik (*Jane Austen: The Six Novels*, p. 110) suggests that the first example here is a conscious archaism of Mary Crawford's:

Cannot you imagine with what unwilling feelings the former belles of the house of Rushworth *did* many a time *repair* to this chapel? (*MP* 87) With the advantage of knowing half the scenes by heart already, he *did* now with the greatest alacrity *offer* his services for the part. (*MP* 132)

It was, and still is, possible (though it tends now to be old-fashioned) to invert the auxiliary *do* and its subject at the beginning of a sentence as an alternative way of forming a conditional clause; but this is possible with other auxiliaries also; see below, p. 130

A survival from a former use of *do* with full meaning, viz., 'to fare, prosper' is the modern conversational formula '*How do you do?*' This is used more flexibly by Jane Austen, in the past as well as in the present, and with various subjects besides the second personal pronoun:

How do you do, my dear? *How does Mrs Dashwood do?* (*SS* 106)
And now, *how do you all do?* (*L* 92, p. 377)
She always curtseys and asks me *how I do*. (*E* 9)
After enquiring of her *how Mr and Mrs Gardiner did*. (*PP* 335)

Auxiliaries: May, Must, Used to

Of the auxiliary verbs *may*, *must*, and *used to*, the following usage is sufficiently different from our own to call for comment.

The past tense of *may* (i.e. *might*) is used where now *may have* would be preferred. This was regular eighteenth century usage, and comes very naturally from the middle-aged Mrs Norris:

The boy looked very silly and turned away without offering a word, for I believe I *might* speak very sharp. (*MP* 142)

Quoting its last example of this usage from Borrow, the *NED* (*may* v.[1], 5c) comments that the collocation that has superseded this (here *I may have spoken*) is more logical, since the subjective possibility is a matter of the speaker's present. The doubt of whether she may have spoken sharply is in Mrs Norris's mind as she considers the matter in the present. So also in the following:

They think Charles *might* not *be* learned and bookish enough to please
Lady Russell, and that therefore, she persuaded Anne to refuse him.
(*P* 89)
He has changed his hour of going, I suppose, that is all – or I may be
mistaken; I *might* not *attend*. (*P* 223)
I gave him a lock of my hair set in a ring when he was at Longstaple
. . . Perhaps you *might notice* the ring when you saw him? (*SS* 135)

A frequent alternative expression for *I hope he will* (*not*) is *I
wish he may* (*not*).[1] The latter expression outnumbers more
modern collocations like *I hope it will* (*PP* 302) and *I hope it
may* (*L* 87, p. 352):

> *I wish I may not* sink into 'poor Emma' with him at once. (*E* 464)
> *I wish you may not* be fatigued by so much exercise. (*MP* 68)
> Mary tells me that Eliza means to buy it. *I wish she may*. (*L* 91, p. 372)
> *I wish there may not be* a little sulkiness of temper. (*MP* 13)

Must is employed widely as a preterite, a use which is today
very much restricted. *Must* now occurs as a preterite only in
indirect speech, or in a colloquial use that the *NED* calls
'satirical or indignant'. One of the *NED* quotations for this
(*must* v.[1], 3e) is 'The fool *must* needs *go* and quarrel with his
friend'. There are sometimes overtones of this kind in Jane
Austen's employment of *must* as a preterite, as, for example, in
the first quotation below; for the most part, however, we
should substitute in these instances some such collocation as
had to or *was bound to* for *must*, thus indicating the past tense
more explicitly:

> Yet, whenever she did speak, she *must be* vulgar. (*PP* 384)
> He had an affectionate heart. He *must love* somebody. (*P* 167)
> The Grappler was under orders for Portsmouth. There the news *must
> follow* him, but who was to tell it? (*P* 108)
> There was a little awkwardness at first in their discourse on another
> subject. They *must speak* of the accident at Lyme. (*P* 124)

[1] For the idiom, we can compare the song *The Blue Bells of Scotland*,
which, like some other nominally Scottish songs, was composed in England, in this case at the time of the Napoleonic Wars ('He's gone to fight
the French for King George upon the throne'). The last stanza runs:
'Suppose and suppose that your Highland lad should die . . . But it's Oh!
in my heart, *I wish he may not* die'.

We may compare Wordsworth's usage in his sonnet *On the Extinction of the Venetian Republic*:

> And, when she took unto herself a Mate,
> She *must espouse* the everlasting Sea.

Must is a favourite auxiliary of Jane Austen's; particularly in contexts where she wishes to state the proper feelings it is imperative to have, as, for instance, in circumstances of bereavement:

> The great Mrs Churchill was no more. It was felt as such things *must* be felt. (*E* 387)
> The loss of such a Parent *must* be felt, or we should be Brutes. (*L* 40, p. 145)
> He went to inspect the Gaol . . . & took me with him. I . . . went through all the feelings which People *must* go through . . . in visiting such a Building. (*L* 90, p. 365)

It is remarkable, as it is also thoroughly characteristic, how frequently such expressions of compulsion and disposition occur. Like Fanny Price at Portsmouth, Jane Austen often seems to be pining, at least subconsciously, for a more ordered world. Constructions like the dispositional present, which we have already mentioned, the auxiliaries *must* and *must have*, and particularly the *is to* construction, with the adjectival infinitive which has a similar compulsive import (below p. 140), all point to the moral imperatives and social decorums that are never far away. A two-word sentence which C. S. Lewis throws out, in 'A Note on Jane Austen' (*Essays in Criticism* IV, 370) seems absolutely to characterize much in her subject-matter, her style, and consequently her sentence structure. The sentence is 'Compulsion waits'. I quote it in context from Lewis's article:

> If charity is the poetry of conduct and honour the rhetoric of conduct, Jane Austen's 'principles' might be described as the grammar of conduct. Now grammar is something that anyone can learn; it is also something that everyone must learn. Compulsion waits.

Returning, however, to *must have*, another auxiliary collocation to express such compulsion, we note that her usage here differs from our own. We use *must have* rather like *may have*, to speculate about or pontificate about the past in present time. 'He *must have been* a beautiful baby' is a present-day assertion about past glory. *Must have* in the novels, however, indicates necessity in the past; 'should have' or 'was bound to have' are often possible modern glosses:

> If he had at all cared about me, we *must have met* long, long ago. (*PP* 148)
> You have said so much against him that I could not wish either for the obligation, or the Intimacy which the use of his Carriage *must have* created. (*MW* 341)
> You would have thrown yourself out of all good society. I *must have* given you up. (*E* 54)
> In her mother she lost the only person able to cope with her. She inherits her mother's talents, and *must have been* under subjection to her. (*E* 37)

The last two instances here illustrate usage quite at variance with present English. The first means, 'I should have been forced to give you up'; the second, not, as it would mean today, 'It is certain that she was under her mother's control', but 'She would have been under her mother's control (if her mother had lived)'. Uncommonly, however, the modern meaning of present supposition or certainty about the past does occur:

> 'The last time I saw her, she had a red nose, but I hope that may not happen every day.'
> 'Oh! no, that *must have been* quite accidental.' (*P* 142)

To express the frequentative or habitual aspect of the verb in the past tense, a regular modern collocation is *used to*: 'I used to ride to school every day on a bicycle'. Jane Austen's usage here is rather different, in that she prefers the more explicit 'I was used to':

> The sister with whom she *was used to be* on easy terms. (*MP* 162)
> She *was* so totally *unused to have* her pleasure consulted. (*MP* 280)
> If you *had been* as much *used* as myself *to hear* poor little children first learning their letters. (*NA* 110)

Occasionally, but not so frequently, the modern phrase occurs:

'Is not she looking well?' said he. . . . 'Better than she ever *used to do*?'
(*E* 477)
Madame B. always markets for him as she *used to do.* (*L* 85, p. 338)

In one respect Jane Austen's use of this auxiliary is very
modern: she favours the negative preterite form *did not use*, a
collocation which, I suspect, has long flourished colloquially in
spite of being disapproved by purists who favour *used not.* As
Barbara Strang puts it (*op. cit.* p. 158): 'With *use(d) to*
prescription has taken the form of supporting the *do*-less forms
against the form with *do.* It is my impression . . . that in this case
the open-class pattern (with *do*) is, as with *need* and *dare*, most
usual, at least in colloquial use and in the speech of the young.'
It is gratifying to find that the more fashionable of Jane
Austen's characters are abreast of modern youth here. Captain
Wentworth remarks to Anne Elliot: 'You *did not use* to like
cards' (*P* 225), and Mary Crawford writes: 'I *did not use* to
think her wanting in self possession' (*MP* 393).

Auxiliaries: Will and Shall

One of the first to formulate the time-honoured schoolmaster's
distinction between the use of *shall* and *will* was Robert Lowth
in *A Short Introduction to English Grammar* (1762), p. 58:

> *Will* in the first person singular promises or threatens, in the second
> and third person only foretells; *shall*, on the contrary, in the first
> person simply foretells, in the second and third persons commands or
> threatens.

The inadequacies of this rule to cover the finer points of
English usage, and to keep pace with the increasing use of *will*
instead of *shall*, have often been pointed out. It seems to be
generally applicable, however, to Jane Austen's usage. Note in
these passages the reversal of the normal *shall, will* auxiliaries
to express extra determination:

> We *will know* where we have gone – we *will recollect* what we have seen,
> Lakes, mountains, and rivers, *shall* not *be jumbled* together in our
> imaginations. (*PP* 154)
> If Jane does not get well soon, we *will call* in Mr Perry. The expense
> *shall* not *be thought* of. (*E* 162)

Henry Sweet, in *A New English Grammar*, II, 94, suggested an emendation of the rule regarding the first plural with *shall*:

> Such combinations as *you and I, we two, we three, we all,* take *will* instead of *shall*; '*we shall* get there first' but '*you and I will* get there first'.

Sweet's emendation is on the whole right for modern colloquial English; but Jane Austen more often uses *shall* for the pure future, whenever the subject amounts to a first person plural, however compounded:

> We can finish this some other time, you know. *You and I shall* not want opportunities. (*E* 453)
> Here we separate, but *Harville and I shall* soon be after you. (*P* 236)
> Coachman, you had better not go, *your Lady and I shall* be very safe. (*MP* 189)
> *We three shall* be able to go . . . in my chaise. (*SS* 153)

The original obligatory force of *OE sculan* 'to owe, be in debt', ancestor of auxiliary *shall*, survives quite strongly in the following contexts, which express the kind of obligation or disposition dependent on the will of the speaker. Commands and promises have always tended to be expressed in English by *shall*, though now *will* is constantly encroaching:

> If you please, *you shall send* it all to Mrs Goddard's. (*E* 235)
> Till it is absolutely settled . . . *he shall know* nothing of the matter. (*MP* 293)
> 'Here comes Marianne,' cried Sir John. 'Now, Palmer, *you shall see* a monstrous pretty girl.' (*SS* 108)
> When you are tired of eating strawberries in the garden, there *shall be* cold meat in the house. (*E* 355)

In clauses expressing indefinite futurity, Jane Austen's usual practice, like our own, is to use the present tense. In more formal contexts, where a need to express the tense explicitly is felt, *shall*, not *will*, is, according to Fowler (*MEU shall* 4), correct usage. Sir William Lucas is being formal, not to say pompous, in this passage:

> I must hope to have this pleasure often repeated, especially when a certain desirable event . . . *shall take* place. (*PP* 92)

Auxiliaries: Would and Should

The commonest use of *should* and *would* by Jane Austen is in the reporting of speech. Here she frequently uses *should* and *would* precisely according to whether direct speech would have been *shall* or *will*:

You told Mrs Bennet this morning that if you ever resolved on quitting Netherfield *you should* (= *I shall*) be gone in five minutes. (*PP* 49)
The child to be born at Randall's must be a tie there . . . and Mrs Weston's heart and time *would* (= *will*) be occupied by it. *They should* (= *we shall*) lose her. (*E* 422)
She must suppose her return *would* (= *will*) be unwelcome at present, and that *she should* (= *I shall*) be felt as an incumbrance. (*MP* 436)

In instances like the following, the relationship between *shall/will* and *should/would* is even more apparent, since the quotation marks of direct speech are included in the reporting. We shall discuss this again later (p. 204):

She felt a moment's regret. But '*they should* (= *we shall*) meet again. *He would* (= *I will*) look for her'. (*P* 185)
Mary deplored the necessity for herself. 'Nobody knew how much *she should* (= *I shall*) suffer. *She should* (= *I shall*) put it off as long as she could.' (*P* 48)

Should and *would* frequently occur, also, in contexts of condition. Here, as Jespersen (*MEG*, IV, 19.2.2) points out, 'In strict (Southern English) language a distinction is made . . . between *I should* and *I would*, the former eliminating and the latter emphasizing the idea of will'. He quotes a passage from Johnson's *Rasselas* to illustrate this 'orthodox' use of *should* and *would*. It is a distinction frequently to be observed in the novels also:

I *should have* made a good likeness of her, if she *would have* sat longer. (*E* 45)
'If I were to see you at it (drinking) I *should take* away your bottle directly.' The boy protested that *she should not*; she continued that *she would*, and the argument ended only with the visit. (*PP* 20)

More commonly than in present English, *should* is employed as a periphrastic expression of the subjunctive. A surviving sense of doubt formerly conveyed by a subjunctive inflection is suggested by the following use of *should* in noun clauses governed by an expression indicating uncertainty. We tend to prefer a simple indicative in such contexts today:

> It is not likely that money *should be* very abundant. (*PP* 282)
> It is not likely you *should* ever *have observed* him. (*E* 29)
> It is not unlikely that he *should be* at Mrs Goddard's today. (*E* 60)
> I rather wonder that Eleanor *should* not *take* it for her own. (*NA* 196)

There are four contexts in which *should* occurs where *would* is now normal: (1) where we now usually say *It would seem*, Jane Austen follows earlier usage with *it should seem*:

> And yet *it should seem* by her manner of talking, as if she wanted to persuade herself. (*PP* 148)
> *It should seem* that they must either be very busy for the Good of others, or else extremely ill themselves. (*MW* 412)
> There was such an affability in her behaviour as really *should seem* to say, she had quite took a fancy to me (Lucy Steele). (*SS* 239)

(2) After the indefinite pronoun *one*. Jespersen (*MEG*, IV, 20.34) considers that this is virtually a synonym for *I* in her usage. The *NED* (*shall* 19c) quotes only one example of *one should*, dated 1862, and describes it as 'abnormal'. But it is normal in the novels, though *one would* also occurs (*SS* 291):

> Although there doubtless are such unconquerable young ladies of eighteen (or *one should* not *read* about them). (*MP* 231)
> And you know *one should* not *like* to have dear Sir Thomas . . . find all the varnish scratched off. (*MP* 77)
> If the servant had not been in mourning, *one should have known* him by the livery. (*P* 106)

(3) Where, according to Sweet's rule, the first person plural is of a composite origin (*you and I*, etc.) we prefer *would* to *should*. As with *shall*, Jane Austen prefers the *sh*-form

> It was dirty, indeed, but what did that signify? I am sure John and I *should not have* minded. (*NA* 90)

(4) The overtones of obligation present in the original *OE* verb *sculan* are seen in the use of *should* with interrogatives,

where modern usage tends to have *would*. We can compare the
literary-archaic use of *Who shall say?* i.e. 'Who is to say?':

> And that is not very likely to be, Sir Thomas. Who *should invite* her?
> (*MP* 285)
> Well . . . it is all very right; who *should do* it but her own uncle?
> (*PP* 306)
> 'But you are not going to walk to Highbury alone?'
> 'Yes – what *should hurt* me? – I walk fast.' (*E* 362)

If the compulsive force of *should* comes out in the foregoing
examples, the original volitional force of *would* is apparent in
the following emphatic usage, which is still possible in present
English, though we should perhaps hesitate to use it in the
passive, as in the last two sentences below:

> It was hardly right; but it had been so strong an idea, that it *would
> escape* her. (*E* 231)
> Bid her not mind it . . . for Mrs Hodges *would be* cross sometimes.
> (*E* 239)
> She met him with a hand that *would be taken* and a voice that expressed
> the affection of a sister. (*SS* 242)
> It made her uncomfortable for a time, – but yet there were enjoyments
> in the day and in the view which *would be felt*. (*MP* 409)

The phrases 'I would rather' and 'I had rather' occur in
similar contexts and are understandably blended. In present
English both phrases are often abbreviated to the same unstressed form 'I'd rather'. There is some confusion and merging
in the following:

> 'And I *would rather* be overturned by him, than driven safely by
> anybody else.'
> '*Had you*?' cried he, 'I honour you.' (*P* 85)
> I *would* not wish to do anything mean . . . One *had rather* . . . do too
> much than too little. (*SS* 9)

In the next, where Catherine Morland's confusion is conveyed
by rather loose grammar, *had* is followed by *have been*, as if it
were *would*. This, according to Jespersen (*MEG*, IV, 19.9.4)
is 'in recent times chiefly found in renderings of vulgar speech':

> But I *had* ten thousand times rather *have been* with you; now had not I,
> Mrs Allen? (*NA* 93)

E

Conversely, *would* is found without *have* in this remark of
Harriet Smith's, when she too is flustered. Dr Chapman's note
is: 'Mrs. Goddard (Harriet's instructress) no doubt had done
her best!'

> Oh! Miss Woodhouse, I *would* rather *done* any thing than have had it
> happen. (*E* 179)

Auxiliaries: Inversion

Inversion of an auxiliary verb in lieu of an introductory
conditional conjunction was commoner in the early nineteenth
century than it is today:

> *Did Henry's income depend* solely on this living, he would not be ill
> provided for. (*NA* 176)
> She would gladly have been there too, *might she have gone* in uninvited.
> (*MP* 65)
> It would be a very eligible . . . plan, *would any one advance* him Money.
> (*L 5*, p. 13)

We have seen that an initial adverb often results in the use of
did followed by the subject. A similar inverted order occurs
with other auxiliaries also:

> Only ten days ago *had he elated her* by his pointed regard. (*NA* 230)
> Either in the morning or evening of every day . . . *have we seen* either
> Mr Weston or Mrs Weston. (*E* 94)
> They talked much, and with much enjoyment; but again *was Catherine
> disappointed*. (*NA* 35)
> For in a small house, near the foot of an old pier of unknown date, *were
> the Harvilles settled*. (*P* 96)

The relative frequency of inversion, compared to present-day
English, makes the following quotations remarkable: there is
no inversion here after *not only*, where it is obligatory in present
English:

> I was told, that not only *your sister was* on the point of being most
> advantageously married, but that you . . . would . . . be soon afterwards
> united to my nephew. (*PP* 353)
> Tell me that not only *your house will remain* the same, but that I shall
> ever find you . . . unchanged. (*SS* 74)

The Gerund

In a valuable and perceptive essay on the English language in Sir Ernest Barker's anthology *The Character of England* (p. 299), C. T. Onions writes:

> The frequency – one might almost say the ubiquity – of the gerund (the verb-noun in *-ing*) is very remarkable (as a characteristic of the English language) . . . The English gerund may be the subject of a sentence or the predicative noun, it may be the object of a verb or a preposition, and may be qualified by a possessive or an adjective or modified by an adverb, or used like a noun in the attributive position.

Attempts have been made by grammarians from the eighteenth century onwards to set limits to this versatility of construction. Robert Lowth, in his aforementioned grammar of 1762 (p. 111, footnote) wrote:

> A word which has an article before it, and a Noun, with the Possessive Preposition *of*, after it, must be a Noun, and if a Noun, it ought to follow the construction of a Noun, and not have the regimen of a Verb. It is the Participial Termination of this sort of words that is apt to deceive us, and make us treat them as if they were amphibious species, partly Nouns, and partly Verbs.

Lowth quotes from the Book of Common Prayer of 1662 examples where the 'amphibious' nature of the gerund is too much in evidence:

> God, who didst teach the hearts of Thy faithful people, *by the sending to them the light* of Thy Holy Spirit. (*Whitsunday Collect*)
> Sent to prepare the way of Thy Son our Saviour *by preaching of repentance*. (*Collect for Saint John Baptist's Day*)

The only possible variations of construction in late eighteenth century, and in present-day English, ought to have been, if the proscriptive grammarians had had their way, *by the preaching of repentance* (nominal) and *by preaching repentance* (verbal). In practice, the other two permutations, which Lowth here condemns, have tended to survive; particularly the first. Jane Austen has many instances like the first of Lowth's 'errors' (definite article with no *of*), though none of the second (*of* with no definite article):

There can hardly be a more unpleasant sensation than *the having any thing returned* on our hands, which we have given. (*MP* 263)
The looking over his letter again . . . had such a softening tendency. (*E* 55)
Have you ever mentioned *the leaving off Tea* to Mrs K? (*L* 70, p. 277)

The gerund preceded by *a*, from an earlier *on*, is still not quite obsolete by Jane Austen's day, and occurs very occasionally, not merely in conversation; but the last vestiges of this construction seem to be confined to contexts of field sports:[1]

I had no notion but he would go *a shooting* or something or other. (*PP* 374)
Charles Musgrove and Captain Wentworth being gone *a shooting* together. (*P* 83)

Bearing in mind the statement by Onions, just quoted, we may say that in her fondness for the gerund, as in so many other ways, Jane Austen is a typically English writer. If anything, the gerund is more frequent in the novels than in most present-day prose; and in this respect, too, she is typical. Mrs Piozzi, formerly Dr Johnson's great friend Mrs Thrale, observed in her *British Synonymy* (I 234) of 1794:

'Tis the age for verbal nouns to increase their consequence, and from mere participles – so called, as every one knows, because they participated of both natures – are going forward to become substantives completely, and signifying things as well as actions; taking up their plural number of course, and ranking with the nouns as if originally of their family.

We find Jane Austen using the gerund in the plural in this way, and at the same time attaching an adverb:

You must not be always walking from one room to the other and doing the *lookings on*, at your ease, in this way. (*MP* 166)
The difference which Randalls . . . makes in your *goings-on*, is very great. (*E* 312)

[1] In most contexts, it was archaic enough, by 1778, for Fanny Burney's Evelina to see it as an eccentricity: 'We have been *a shopping*, as Mrs Mirvan calls it'. (*Evelina* p. 27)

She can form compounds, too, with a gerund preceded by its object; rather more widely than our own limited and stereotyped compounds such as *homecoming, leave-taking*:

> After a period of *nothing-saying* amongst the party. (*P* 189)
> The *nothing-meaning* terms of being 'elegantly dressed and very pleasing'. (*E* 270)
> I fancy you must have a little *cheek-glowing*[1] now & then Miss Emma. (*MW* 358)

Gerunds with plural inflections are also more frequent:

> It must be my uncle's *doings*. (*PP* 304)
> Instead of going on with their *buyings*, they began whispering. (*E* 178)
> A flutter of spirits which required all the *reasonings* and *soothings* and attentions of every kind. (*E* 267)

As to the vexed grammatical question of whether to put the subject of the gerund into the possessive case or not, in sentences like 'Forgive John/John's interrupting you', her usage fluctuates. She generally, but not always, uses a possessive:

> I told him of *the church's* being so well worth seeing. (*P* 131)
> *Mr Collins's* fancying himself in love. (*PP* 124)
> I talked of *it's* [*sic*] being bad weather for the Hay. (*L* 130, p. 459)
> He . . . earnestly tried to prevent *any body's* eating it.[2] (*E* 19)

The following are some of the much rarer instances with no possessive:

> Deriving some accession of pleasure from *its writer being* himself to go away. (*MP* 266)
> He had no doubt of *it being* highly agreeable to Fanny. (*MP* 368)
> Perry had many doubts about *the sea doing* her any good. (*E* 101)

[1] The equivalent, as the context makes clear, of the modern 'Your ears were burning', said of a person being talked about *in absentia*. Cf. Dorothy Osborne's letters: 'Sure if there bee any truth in the olde observation, your *Cheeks glowed* notably' (12th August 1653).
[2] The insistence on the genitive in the last instance here seems to show that she was aware of the 'rule'; not the least of the objections to which is that it is not always enforceable – with a demonstrative, for example, which has no genitive case: 'Time . . . must be allowed for *this being* thoroughly done'. (*E* 142)

Though, as I have noted above (p. 115), I have not found any examples of the expanded tenses in the passive, of the type 'The house is being built', there are several instances of the gerund in the passive form. From here to the expansion of the *-ing* form after the verb *to be* is only a small step, though one that was not taken:

> The claims of her cousins to *being obliged* were strengthened by the sight of present upon present. (*MP* 153)
> Miss Bates might be heard from that moment . . . till her *being seated* at table. (*E* 328)
> For as to Frank, it was more than *being* tacitly *brought* up as his uncle's heir. (*E* 17)

This last sentence is also a pattern for others in its use of a gerund as a direct predicative, where we might well now prefer some such abstract 'buffer' as 'a question of' before the gerund:

> The sun was by now two hours above the horizon, and it would be only *her retiring* to dress half an hour earlier. (*NA* 193)
> It is only *protesting* it to be very beautiful, & you will soon think it so. (*L* 25, p. 84)

Equally characteristic of a certain directness in style is the use of a gerundial construction where a twentieth-century writer might well have a more abstract circumlocution with an appositive noun clause – 'The fact that . . .' etc.:

> *The living* in incessant noise was . . . an evil which no superadded elegance could have entirely atoned for. (*MP* 391)
> *Lydia's being settled* in the North . . . was a severe disappointment. (*PP* 313)
> *Colonel Fitzwilliam's occasionally laughing* at his stupidity, proved that he was generally different. (*PP* 180)

We should now use the infinitive after the verb *fail*, where Jane Austen has the *-ing* form:

> I cannot in decency fail *attending* the club. (*NA* 210)
> And how often . . . Miss De Bourgh drove by in her phæton, which he never failed *coming* to inform them of. (*PP* 168)
> Lord Byron's 'dark blue seas' could not fail *of being* brought forward by their present view. (*P* 109)

Finally, there is one very English use of the gerund which is also a favourite construction of hers: this is its occurrence in negative contexts after *there is*, to express the idea of impossibility:

There is no entering much into the solicitudes of that family. (*L* 66, p. 262)
After all that romancers say, *there is no doing without* money. (*NA* 146)
'*There is no saying*, indeed,' replied Harriet . . . 'But there may be pretty good guessing.' (*E* 33)

The Infinitive

The infinitive is quite often used absolutely with exclamatory force. As Mustanoja puts it (*op. cit.* p. 539): 'Impulsiveness leads one to disregard form: in a state of excitement the speaker has no time or patience to choose the proper tense, mood, person, etc., an expression of the mere verbal idea being sufficient to meet the needs of the moment'. Here are a few of the many examples of exclamatory infinitives in the novels:

These rooms ought to belong only to us. . . . An ancient family *to be so driven* away! (*P* 126)
It is all very strange. So suddenly *to be gone*! (*SS* 77)

Edmund Bertram is particularly prone to exclamatory infinitives, as he is astonished alternately at the charms, and the corruption, of Mary Crawford:

I could not answer, but I believe my looks spoke. She felt reproved. Sometimes how quick *to feel*! (*MP* 454)
To hear the woman whom – no harsher name than folly given! So voluntarily, so freely, so coolly *to canvass it*! (*MP* 454)

The accusative-and-infinitive construction is also common:

He fancied *every body to be living* in Uppercross. (*P* 130)
Lady Russell determined *him to be unworthy* of the interest he had been beginning to excite. (*P* 133)
When he found *her prefer* a plain dish to a ragout. (*PP* 35)
When you have studied the character, I am sure you will feel *it suit* you. (*MP* 135)

With sentences like the last, where a non-prepositional accusative occurs, it is not always possible to say whether an accusative-and-infinitive construction or a noun clause (with a verb in the subjunctive, if singular) is intended:[1]

> You persist, then, in supposing *his sisters influence* him. (*PP* 136)
> Martha does not find *the key*, which you left in my charge for her, *suit* the keyhole. (*L 56*, p. 218)

I think it likely that Jane Austen herself would not have been aware of which construction she was using; the following two anacoluthic sentences have the mark of the noun clause (*that*) and the mark of the infinitive (*to*) both present together:

> She . . . determined . . . *that* as Mrs Willoughby would at once be a woman of elegance and fortune, *to* leave her card with her as soon as she married. (*SS* 216)
> Elizabeth . . . determined, *that* if he persisted in considering her repeated refusals as flattering encouragements, *to* apply to her father. (*PP* 109)

Dr Chapman emends the text in the last example here, by omitting the word *that*, found in all the first three editions, but has some compunction in so doing, citing as a parallel anacoluthon the first quotation above. This very understandable contamination does in fact occur sporadically in Middle and early Modern English.[2]

Jane Austen's infinitive often overlaps the functions of the modern gerund. We have seen (p. 124) that her characteristically passive expression *to be used to*, much commoner in her writing than the modern *used to*, is followed by an infinitive. When we do use her more explicit expression, we now follow with a gerund. Again, a gerund would be preferred today in contexts like these:

---

[1] This type of ambiguity is still occasionally possible: a parallel instance occurs in the Christmas carol, *Good King Wenceslas*:

> Mark my footsteps, good my page,
> Tread thou in them boldly;
> Thou shalt *find* the winter's rage
> *Freeze* thy blood less coldly.

[2] See my article on 'Contamination in Late Middle English' in *English Studies* XXXV (1954), pp. 17-20.

He can have no objection . . . *to oblige* us for one half hour. (*PP* 26)
If you should have no objection *to receive* me into your house. (*PP* 63)
But at length (Wickham) was reduced *to be* reasonable. (*PP* 323)
There was a charm . . . in his sincerity . . . which Miss Crawford might
be equal *to feel*. (*MP* 65)
She . . . had been misled . . . *to suppose* that a much longer visit had been
promised. (*NA* 221)
His persisting *to act* in direct opposition to Jane Fairfax's sense of
right. (*E* 446)
She could not imagine Harriet's persisting *to place* her happiness in the
sight . . . of him. (*E* 143)

(This last by the side of the modern gerundial construction
'persisted *in considering*', *PP* 109).

The infinitive occurs as the subject and object of the sentence,
much as in present English. As the complement of the verb *to
be*, also, it occurs freely:

All that could be done was, *to sit down* at that end of the counter. (*SS*
220)
I thought it would be only *ask* and *have*. (*MP* 58)

Very common, and characteristic of Jane Austen, is a rather
different predicative usage, viz., the *is to* construction with
various overtones. These constructions, of the type, 'John *is to*
come home at once', are common, of course, in present English;
but she uses them more widely. It is easy to find parallels today
for the use in the sense of what is preordained or pre-arranged,
either (a) by the will of Providence, or (b) by the will of man.
In the latter case the *is to* construction is often the equivalent
of a command, or negatively, of a prohibition:

(a) Elinor *was to be* the comforter of others in her own distresses, no
less than in theirs. (*SS* 261)
(b) Twice every year these annuities *were to be* paid. (*SS* 11)
No officer *is* ever *to enter* my house again. (*PP* 300)

In other contexts, the idea of mutual arrangement is expressed
by this construction; again, parallels in present English are not
difficult to find:

The remaining five *were* now *to draw* their cards. (*SS* 145)
His staying was made of flattering consequence, and he *was to meet* Mrs
Rushworth there. (*MP* 467)

As Joos points out (*op. cit.*, p. 22) the import of the *is to* construction today is that of 'a practical determining of subsequent events'.

It is in contexts where such ideas of arrangement and compulsion are weakened that we find sentences more divergent from present idiom; 'is about to' or 'is likely to' often seems the best gloss. But again, as with the dispositional present, one has the feeling, in the discrepancy between the choice of idiom and the context, that Jane Austen is seeking a greater neatness of arrangement and a more compelling sense of certainty than is possible in this untidy and changeable world:[1]

> The balmy air, the sparkling sea, and your sweet looks . . . afforded sensations which *are to raise* ecstacy even in retrospect (Henry Crawford). (*MP* 415)
> It is not time or opportunity that *is to determine* intimacy; it is disposition alone (Marianne Dashwood). (*SS* 59)
> I believe I have now told you everything. It is a relation which you tell me *is to give* you great surprise. (*PP* 325)
> You *are to deal* ma'am; shall I deal for you? (*MP* 283)
> The little boy is very like Dr Cooper, and the little girl *is to resemble* Jane, they say. (*L* 2, p. 5)
> Though heavy and feverish . . . a good night's rest *was to cure* her entirely. (*SS* 306)

This last example well illustrates the difference between the novelist's usage here and our own; in present English this could only mean 'a good night's rest was destined to (and did) cure her'. In fact, however, these were the first symptoms of a 'putrid fever' that nearly caused the death of Marianne Dashwood. Here we have the author reporting, with her typically

[1] I do not think I am reading present-day overtones of compulsion too unwarrantably into these sentences; for one thing, the frequent use of this construction in wide contexts is not, apparently, typical of Jane Austen's contemporaries and predecessors. There is only one other writer who would appear to have it at all frequently: that other moralist and law-giver, Dr Johnson. Boswell reports statements like:
We have done with civility. We *are to be* as rude as we please. (Boswell's *Life* III, 273)
A man who gives the natural history of the oak, *is not to tell* how many oaks have been planted in this place or that. (*Ibid.* III, 273)
You are to consider what is the meaning of purging in the original sense. (*Ibid.* III, 39)

subtle use of *erlebte Rede* (below, p. 204), the words Marianne Dashwood used: 'A good night's rest *is to* (i.e. is likely to) *cure* me entirely'.

Palmer (*op. cit.*, p. 142) asserts that the best way to consider the *is to* construction is as the equivalent of a modal auxiliary. It follows the pattern of modals in having no **to be to, – ing* form, or past participle in present English; and also in having no explicit future tense, as *He *will be to go*. These facts of the present language do not necessarily apply to the early nine-teenth century, however; the participial *being to* form, for instance, is quite common in the novels:

> This same Miss Musgrove, instead of *being to* marry Frederick, is to marry James Benwick. (*P* 171)
> If it had not been for this particular circumstance of her *being to* come here so soon. (*E* 159)
> Congratulations on their travelling so far . . . without any expense, and on Colonel Brandon's *being to* follow them. (*SS* 301)

Rarely, also, a tense explicitly relating to future time occurs:

> She could not sympathize in his wish that the Count and Agatha *might be to act* together. (*MP* 138)
> *You will be to visit* me in prison with a basket of provisions. (*MP* 135)

The negative of the *is to* construction is also used with differ-ent import from present English. Today, *he is not to* means 'he may not', a meaning found in the novels, as we have seen; but it also means, in certain contexts in the novels, 'he is not bound to', a mere negativing of a compulsion rather than a prohibition in the contrary direction. This meaning is now conveyed by 'he has not to'[1] or more usually, and increasingly, by 'he does not have to'. Emma uses *is not to* in this sense, in the early part of the novel, where she is asserting her independence of Mr Knightley:

> A woman *is not to marry* a man merely because she is asked. (*E* 54)
> This is an alliance which . . . must be agreeable to them, provided . . .

---

[1] This construction occurs: 'It was true that she *had not to* charge herself with being the sole and original author of the mischief'. (*E* 402)

they have common sense; and *we are not to be addressing* our conduct to
fools. (*E* 75)
She is not to pay for the offence of others, by being held below the level
of those with whom she is brought up. (*E* 62)

The too assertive form indicates a want of confidence under-
neath. But there is no such saving misgiving when Mr Collins
blandly misinterprets Elizabeth's rejection of his offer of
marriage as female caprice:

I am not now to learn . . . that it is usual with young ladies to reject the
addresses of the man whom they secretly mean to accept. (*PP* 107)

Jane Austen is also very fond (more fond, in fact, than most
modern writers), of the infinitive as adjective phrase describing
a noun. It is a construction not unconnected with the previous
one; supply *that is*, or *that was* in sentences like the following,
and the result has the same authoritative and dispositional
quality that so many of her sentences have:

The following day brought news from Richmond *to throw* every thing
else into the back-ground. (*E* 387)
It is an attachment *to govern* his whole life. (*MP* 424)
How Henry would think . . . was a question of force and interest *to rise*
over every other, *to be* never *ceasing* alternately irritating and soothing.
(*NA* 231)

As an abbreviation of an adverb clause, the infinitive had a
wider range of usage in the early Modern English period than
today. Shakespeare, for instance, could use it as equivalent to a
conditional or a time clause:

To pay five ducats, five, I would not farm it. (*Hamlet* IV, iv, 20)
O my father, I have broke your hest *to say so*. (*Tempest* III, i, 37)

In present English the adverbial range of the infinitive has
been restricted, broadly speaking, to its use as an abbreviation
of clauses of purpose. On the whole Jane Austen's usage is as
restricted as modern usage tends to be; a few examples, however, have conditional or consecutive overtones:

Do not stay at Portsmouth *to lose* your pretty looks. (*MP* 416)
Could you be comfortable yourself, *to be spending* the whole evening
away from the poor boy? (*P* 56)

I caught a small cold in my way down & had some pain every evening –
not *to last* long, but rather severer than it had been lately. (*L* 84, p. 332)
Miss Frances married, in the common phrase, *to disoblige* her family.
(*MP 3*)

There is, of course, a more explicit form of consecutive
expression with the infinitive preceded by *so . . . as;* for example,
'Be *so* good *as* to open the door'. The correlative *as* before the
infinitive is now obligatory in such contexts, and this was the
rule by the end of the eighteenth century, though earlier it was
often absent. In 1762 Lowth (*op. cit.*, p. 152) had condemned
Swift's expression 'They are *so bold to pronounce*', contending
that *as* had been 'erroneously omitted'. Generally, the omission
of *as* in the novels is intended to convey vulgar usage; in the
two following instances, that of Lucy Steele, and Mrs Cole
respectively:

Mrs Ferrars and your sister were both *so good to say* more than once,
they should always be glad to see me. (*SS* 240)
Hoping that some of our good neighbours might be *so obliging* occasionally *to put* it to a better use. (*E* 216)

Two pages later than the first quotation above, as if to illustrate her own better usage, Jane Austen employs the construction with *as:*

She soon afterwards felt herself *so* heroically disposed *as to determine*
. . . to leave the others. (*SS* 242)

It is surprising, therefore, to find the sensitive and fastidious
Marianne Dashwood saying:

This woman . . . may have been *so* barbarous *to bely* me. (*SS* 189)

This may be an error; no doubt Dr Chapman is right to see an
erroneous omission of the first correlative *so* here:

By teaching them to repress their spirits in his presence, *as* to make their
real disposition unknown to him. (*MP* 463)

The use of the infinitive with wider adverbial overtones is a
characteristic of early, as opposed to late, Modern English;

and another typically early Modern English use of the infinitive is that of the past form to indicate an abortive *hope*, *aim* etc., or any expectation or possibility that is not realized. It is therefore worth noting the negative fact that, compared with her predecessor, Fanny Burney, who has five instances, for example, in the first thirty pages of *Evelina*, Jane Austen has very few of these past infinitives:

> The two ladies might have found it impossible *to have lived* together so long, had not a particular circumstance occurred. (*SS* 15)
>
> I expected *to have found* Edward seated at a table writing . . . but I was first. (*L* 93, p. 380)
>
> I wish you had been there . . . *to have given* him one of your set downs. (*PP* 13)

The contemporary grammarian, Lindley Murray, condemned such infinitives in his *English Grammar* of 1805 (I 277):

> 'Last week I intended to have written' is a very common phrase; the infinitive being in the past time, as well as the verb which it follows. But it is evidently wrong; for how long soever it now is since I thought of writing, 'to write' was then present to me.

One of the more noticeable features of Jane Austen's conversations is the curious ellipsis of the verb *to be* after auxiliaries. In each case the auxiliary that lacks the infinitive can be referred back to a previous part of the verb *to be;* but it is obligatory today to include *be* in such contexts:

> 'He is very handsome indeed.'
>
> 'Handsome! – Yes I suppose he *may*.' (*NA* 135)
>
> If you were never . . . struck by her manners before . . . I think you *will* today. (*E* 194)
>
> I wish our opinions were the same. But in time they *will*. (*E* 471)
>
> 'I dare say she was very much attached to him.'
>
> 'Perhaps she *might*.' (*E* 271)
>
> The children are . . . not under such good Order as they *ought* & easily *might*. (*L* 137, p. 473)
>
> But perhaps it may be impossible; unless a Brother can be at home at that time, it certainly *must*. (*L* 69, p. 268)

Have is, less commonly, omitted in a similar way:

You have every body dearest to you always at hand, I, probably, never *shall* again. (*E* 294)

Have you never been there? No, you never *can*. (*MP* 56)

It is significant that these elisions occur either in her letters or in the conversations of her characters. There are precedents for such omission – for example in Richardson:

I cannot but renew my Cautions . . . Yet there may not be . . . any thing in it. But when I reflect, that there possibly *may*, and that if there *should*, no less depends upon it than my Child's . . . Happiness. (*Pamela* I, 14)

The infinitive omitted like this (and, with most verbs other than *to be* such omission is common), is sometimes said to be a latent infinitive. In certain contexts, where the auxiliary takes a prepositional infinitive, (with *ought* and *used*, for example) latent infinitives may have their presence marked today by the preposition *to*. Visser, in his *Historical Syntax of the English Language* (II 1061), has traced the history of this *to*. It is found very occasionally from the fourteenth century; but it has only become common from the second half of the nineteenth century. Jane Austen does not have it in contexts where it is now usual; as in the following:

Nobody would attend as they *ought*. (*MP* 165)

If I write, I will say whatever you *wish* me. (*MP* 59)

She did not do any of it in the same way that she *used*. (*E* 178)

A man does not recover from such a devotion of the heart to such a woman! – He *ought* not – he does not. (*P* 183)

The Present Participle

A notable feature of the novels, and one which the novelist inherits from eighteenth-century writers like Richardson and Boswell, is her use of a present participle to indicate parenthetically the attendant circumstances of direct speech. It is not now usual to do this unless the subject of the present participle is explicitly mentioned. Much, one feels, has been lost in the discontinuing of this trick of style. Its grammar may be shaky, but it imparts an eye-witness quality to the scene, and prevents

the dialogue from being broken up by too much particulariza-
tion:

> 'However, I will not disturb you (*seeing* her preparing to write). You
> know your own concerns best.' (*SS* 287)
> 'Why should you dare say that? (*smiling*) – Do you want to be told . . .'
> (*MP* 197)
> 'I will look another way. I hope this pleases you, (*turning* her back on
> him,) I hope your eyes are not tormented now. (*NA* 147)

Generally in her punctuation Jane Austen does not separate
by a comma the noun from its attributive participial phrase, so
that the phrase often seems as though it is going to be absolute;
but in fact there is generally no other subject than the noun
which the participle describes. This, as G. H. Vallins illustrates
in *The Pattern of English* (p. 68), was regular early Modern
English punctuation. However, it was punctuation that was
growing old-fashioned by the first decades of the nineteenth
century; the contemporary grammarian Lindley Murray (*op.
cit.* I 395) advocated modern punctuation in such contexts:
'When participles are followed by something that depends on
them, they are generally separated from the rest of the sentence
by a comma: as, "The king, approving the plan, put it in
execution".' I append a few of the many instances of earlier
punctuation in the novels:

> Elizabeth immediately recognizing the livery, guessed what it meant.
> (*PP* 260)
> But William determining, soon after her removal, to be a sailor, was
> invited to spend a week with his sister. (*MP* 21)

Nevertheless, absolute constructions do occur:

> The younger Miss Thorpes being also dancing, Catherine was left to
> the mercy of Mrs Thorpe. (*NA* 52)

Jane Austen's use of participles is at times rather loose. Here,
if anywhere, H. W. Garrod's somewhat cavalier dismissal of her
English ('It is not good writing – it is not even grammatical
writing')[1] has some slight justification. Usually, however,

---

[1] 'Jane Austen: A Depreciation' in *Transactions of the Royal Society of
Literature* VIII, 21–40.

there is no obscurity; the phrase 'easy-going grammar', by which H. C. Wyld, in his *History of Modern Colloquial English* (p. 163) characterized the language of the seventeenth-century letter-writers of the Verney family, seems appropriate at times to her style also:

> Having introduced him, however, and being all re-seated, the terrors that occurred of what this visit might lead to, were overpowering. (*MP* 399)
> She moved from one posture to another, till growing more hysterical, her sister could with difficulty keep her on the bed. (*SS* 191)
> The happiness with which their time now passed . . . every meal a scene of ease and good-humour, walking where they liked and when they liked. (*NA* 220)

The carelessness of the next, however, is deliberate; the letter-writer is Lucy Steele:

> My paper reminds me to conclude, and begging to be most gratefully and respectfully remembered to her, and to Sir John. (*SS* 278)

This is the conclusion of what Mrs Jennings describes as 'as pretty a letter as ever I saw. It does Lucy's head and heart great credit'. We are, of course, under no obligation to endorse this opinion; but it is not difficult to find similar inelegantly concluded letters by earlier writers of the seventeenth and early eighteenth centuries whose gentility is unquestioned. By the early nineteenth century, however, the grammarians had made their influence felt. To be blatantly ungrammatical in the novels is to be ungenteel.[1]

As we have noted when discussing expanded tenses, the active participle can have a passive meaning:

> The inclosure of Norland Common, now *carrying* on, is a most serious drain. (*SS* 225)
> A . . . Carriage . . . lately arrived, & by the quantity of Luggage *taking* off, bringing . . . some respectable family. (*MW* 406)

[1] See my article 'Lucy Steele's English' in *English Studies* (Anglo-American Supplement, 1969), pp. lv–lxi.

Jane Austen is fond of using a present participle as an adjective:

A *talking* pretty young woman like Miss Crawford. (*MP* 47)
He is a clever man, a *reading* man. (*P* 182)
She was in *dancing, singing, exclaiming* spirits. (*E* 475)
Many young men . . . drove about town in very *knowing* gigs. (*SS* 103)
A very kind and *feeling* letter. (*L* 59, p. 229)
Such *thinking*, clear, considerate Letters. (*L* 93, p. 382)

One other noteworthy feature of the present participle[1] in the novels, is the inclusion of the possessive adjective as its subject when the participle has the same reference as the subject of the sentence. Such redundancy is not usual in present English:

Anne had never entered Kellynch since *her quitting* Lady Russell's house. (*P* 123)
She had lost ground as to health since *her being* in Portsmouth. (*MP* 409)
By *her taking* so much notice of you . . . she has given you a sort of claim on her future consideration. (*SS* 227)

In all these three examples, *her* refers to the subject of the sentence. In present English, it would only be included if another female were being referred to.

The Past Participle

All the eighteenth and early nineteenth century grammarians publish lists of confusable past tense and past participle forms of verbs. Forms of past tense and past participle had not yet settled down, and it is one of the achievements of the much-maligned eighteenth century grammarians that these forms were gradually stabilized; their confusion had been very characteristic of early Modern English. Lowth (*op. cit.* p. 90) writes:

We should be immediately shocked at 'I have knew, I have saw, I have gave' etc.: but our ears have grown familiar with 'I have wrote, I have drank, I have bore' etc., which are altogether as barbarous.

[1] If, indeed, *participle* is the right word in the circumstances; the inclusion of *her*, the possessive adjective, makes the form in *-ing* less participial and more gerundial.

The first type of 'barbarity' Jane Austen puts into the mouths
of servants or vulgar characters, her Lucy Steeles, and the like;
the second, less blatant type she is capable of herself, particularly with strong verbs of the third class, such as *drank/drunk*,
began/begun and so on:

It would have been such a great pity to have *went* away before your
brother and sister came (Lucy Steele). (*SS* 217)
She had quite *took* a fancy to me (Lucy Steele). (*SS* 239)
I should have *gave* it all up in despair (Lucy Steele). (*SS* 240)
He had got upon his horse and *rid* out into the country (Anne Steele).
(*SS* 273)
So I just *run* upstairs and put on a pair of silk stockings and came off
(Anne Steele). (*SS* 274)
I am determined to *set* for it (a picture) (Lucy Steele). (*SS* 132)

In her own narrative, and in the speech of characters of
unquestioned gentility, we find:

Marianne . . . *sunk* into her chair. (*SS* 177)
A thousand inquiries *sprung* up. (*SS* 347)
The soup would be sent round in a most spiritless manner, wine *drank*
without any smiles. (*MP* 52)
Fanny *shrunk* back to her seat. (*MP* 380)
Much was said, and much was *ate*. (*MP* 84)
The wedding cake . . . was all *eat* up . . . still the cake was *eaten*. (*E* 19)
When Lady Catherine and her daughter had played as long as they
chose, the tables were *broke* up. (*PP* 166)

(Here the third edition, of 1817, according to Chapman's note,
is emended to *broken*).

It would have *broke* my heart (Marianne Dashwood). (*SS* 18)
He will be *forgot* (Jane Bennet). (*PP* 134)

As with present participles, past participial reference is sometimes loose:

Equally formed for domestic life, and attached to country pleasures,
their home was the home of affection and comfort. (*MP* 473)

The Passive Voice

In his Cambridge lectures *On the Art of Writing* (p. 137) Sir
Arthur Quiller-Couch advises aspiring writers to use 'the

active voice, eschewing the stationary passive with its little auxiliary *is's* and *was's* and its participles getting into the light of your adjectives'. This may be good counsel for young writers, but it is not the kind of advice that the great authors of the past have necessarily followed. In fact, one of the characteristics of written English has always been a frequent use of the passive voice. There is no doubt that the passive voice is more extensively used in English than in any of the cognate languages. For one thing, we have no universally accepted indefinite agent pronoun, corresponding to French *on* and German *man*. On the one hand the indefinite *you* is too colloquial for many contexts; while on the other, the pronoun *one*, modelled on the French *on*, has never become acclimatized.[1]

The alternative is a frequent use of the passive voice. A further reason for this frequency is the fact that in English, unlike most languages, it is possible for what would have been the indirect object of an active sentence to become the subject of the passive voice. Jane Austen forms such sentences freely:

I . . . am promised that everything in their power shall be done. (*NA* 121)
He had been bid more for his wool than any body in the country. (*E* 28)

Still more common, in fact one of the distinctive features of her English, is the transforming of a word which in the active sentence would have been the object of a preposition, into the subject of a verb in the passive. The preposition is thus left dangling at the end:

The disgrace of his first marriage *might, perhaps, . . . have been got over*. (*P* 8)
He *was . . . never run away with* by spirits or by selfishness. (*P* 147)
James *was talked to*, and given a charge to go very slow. (*E* 128)
She was too much beloved *to be parted with*. (*E* 164)

[1] '*One* can't help growing older,' ventured Alice in conversation with Humpty Dumpty. '*One* can't perhaps,' was the reply, 'but *two* can. With proper assistance you might have left off at seven.' Humpty Dumpty's instincts here in misunderstanding the indefinite *one* are very English. See *Through the Looking Glass*, chapter VI.

There is a further complication, and a still more idiomatically English solution, when one of the objects in the prototype active expression is retained after the conversion to a passive voice. Onions (*op. cit.* p. 300) mentions this retention as a characteristic of English in its vigour and ungrammaticality. He illustrates with sentences like 'I was not left *a single one*'. In this way, he points out, 'a conciseness is obtained that, however it may defy grammatical analysis, has a pregnancy and directness which cannot be given by any other form of expression'. Such constructions are common in the novels, though they were disapproved of by contemporary grammarians like Lindley Murray (*op. cit.* I 272):

> It was made a great favour of. (*E* 46)
> Every lighter talent had been done full justice to. (*E* 164)
> Every thing . . . would be taken such excellent care of. (*P* 18)
> She was made such a fuss with by everybody. (*E* 166)
> Perhaps get as far as the clover, which was to be begun cutting on the morrow. (*E* 361)
> We are envied our House by many people. (*L* 50, p. 184)
> There is a pretty little Lady Marianne of the party, to be shaken hands with. (*L* 44, p. 158)

I quote these sentences without minuter analysis. In treating such instances, as Joos points out (*op. cit.* p. 93), there are two possible courses for grammarians. We may call them idiomatic to excuse ourselves from understanding how they work, or go more deeply into their function and nature, an experiment which he compares to trying to light a fire in a wooden stove! I prefer the former, more old-fashioned approach.

Why this predilection for the passive voice? There seem to be a number of reasons. Sometimes a change from active to passive made for variety in narrative, or suggested disturbed or conflicting emotions, pointing the difference between what was controlled and what was less controllable in feelings:

> Presently the carriage stopt; she looked up; *it was stopt* by Mr and Mrs Weston. (*E* 188)
> In short, at the time of the play, I received an impression *which will never be got over*. (*MP* 349)
> She walked on; but it would not do; in half a minute the letter *was unfolded again*, and collecting herself as well as she could, she again began the mortifying perusal. (*PP* 205)

Another motive seems to have been to represent tact, constraint and forbearance in her characters. Thus, in the chapel at Sotherton, Edmund Bertram makes rather diffident attempts to induce seriousness and a sense of devotion in the flippant Mary Crawford. He accordingly avoids the too assertive active voice. Countering Mary's suggestion that there would have been little true devotion in a family chapel, Edmund replies:

> The influence of the place and of example may often rouse better feelings than *are begun with*. (*MP* 88)

Similarly, in spite of herself, Emma cannot avoid a certain constraint when disagreeing with Mr Knightley about the prospect of Harriet Smith marrying Robert Martin. Her use of the passive shows this restraint:

> Mr Martin is a very respectable young man, but I cannot admit him to be Harriet's equal . . . By your account, he does seem to have had some scruples. It is a pity that they *were ever got over*. (*E* 61)

Again, the passive is employed to suggest with propriety, but not to dwell on, emotions which she wishes to avoid dealing with; it is a propriety that does not exclude possibilities of irony:

> The great Mrs Churchill was no more. It was felt as such things *must be felt*. (*E* 387)
> Poor blind Mrs Ripley *must be felt for*, if there is any feeling to be had for love or money. (*L* 89, p. 362)

Perhaps the commonest motive for the passive voice, however, is to suggest the passage of time. Not the least of Jane Austen's claims to pre-eminence as a realistic novelist is her ability to describe everyday occurrences without everyday tedium. Her own criticism of *Pride and Prejudice* was:

> The work is rather too light, and bright, and sparkling; it wants shade; it wants to be stretched out here and there with a long chapter of sense, if it could be had. (*L* 77, p. 299)

It was something she was to remedy in later novels; and generally, her witty or deeply felt episodes are anchored in a wider, more placid narration in which no event, or lack of event, is too trivial to mention. It is the passive voice which she often uses to convey both the embarrassments and the longueurs of social intercourse:

> You will not want *to be talked to*. Let us have the luxury of silence. (*MP* 278)
> She . . . sat deliberating over her paper, with the pen in her hand, till *broken in on* by the entrance of Edward himself. (*SS* 287)
> A very awful pause took place. *It was put an end to* by Mrs Dashwood. (*SS* 359)
> It being now too late in the year for such visits to be made on foot, the coach *was beginning to be listened for*. (*P* 50)
> Their conversation . . . *was now put an end to*, by the approach of the whole party. (*PP* 287)
> For a few moments *she was unanswered*. Fanny coloured and looked at Edmund. (*MP* 87)

The preposition at the end of a clause which such a constant use of the passive voice entails was something which much concerned those grammarians who were reluctant to countenance any English usage without parallel in Latin grammar. Hence, even today, what Fowler calls 'the modern superstition against the preposition at the end'. Robert Lowth was more liberal than most grammarians of the eighteenth and nineteenth centuries in this respect. Suiting example to precept, he wrote in 1762 (*op. cit.* p. 127): 'This is an idiom which our language is strongly inclined to; it prevails in common conversation, and suits very well with the familiar style in writing; but the placing of the preposition (earlier) is more graceful, as well as more perspicuous; and agrees very much better with the solemn and elevated style'.[1]

Now, although Jane Austen's style has its roots firmly in the eighteenth century, and owes much, for instance, to Dr Johnson, she knew how to lighten the rather ponderous tendencies of a balanced, Latinate cast of sentence with the leaven of sprightly

[1] It is interesting that Lindley Murray, who copies wholesale from Lowth's grammar, has 'improved' on Lowth's sentence here in his own instructions: 'This is an idiom to which our language is strongly inclined . . .' The rest of the sentence is a verbatim copy of Lowth's!

colloquial English. The type of clause with the preposition at the end, either with a passive or following a relative pronoun, sometimes has this effect:

> What could be meant by such unsteady conduct, what her friend *could be at*, was beyond her comprehension. (*NA* 149)
> Though my uncle . . . exerted himself immediately, there were difficulties from the absence of one friend, and the engagements of another, which at last I could no longer bear *to stay the end of*. (*MP* 299)

Transitive and Intransitive Verbs

In the matter of transitivity and intransitivity, the novelist's usage often differs from our own. The issue is somewhat more complicated than may at first appear. She faithfully reproduced in her characters' conversations, and in her narrative, the elisions and omissions that she heard about her, provided always that they were not inelegant; and one of the commonest of these is the omission of a preposition between verb and object. In this way verbs which are intransitive become nominally transitive. The feeling of the elided preposition is still strong, however. It would, I think, be wrong to call *supper* the object of *stay* here, for example:

> He scarcely needed an invitation *to stay supper*. (*PP* 345)

Still less is *Isabella Thorpe* the object of the verb *to drink* in the remark of that most careful of speakers, Henry Tilney:

> The mess-room will *drink Isabella Thorpe* for a fortnight. (*NA* 153)

Other examples which are also perhaps to be called intransitive verbs with elision of the preposition rather than intransitive verbs turned transitive are the following:

> To submit quietly and *hope the best*. (*MP* 356)
> They can only *wish his happiness*. (*PP* 156)
> Her relations all *wish the connection*. (*PP* 118)
> I am not romantic . . . I *ask* only *a comfortable home*. (*PP* 125)
> Though we *play but half-crowns*. (*MP* 119)

He was hardly able *to sit the box* on account of the rheumatism. (*MP* 189)
She had not *waited her arrival.* (*MP* 42)
As she saw more of her, she *approved her.* (*E* 26)
My own disappointment . . . is very great; but, as for poor James, I suppose he *will hardly ever recover it.* (*NA* 206)

It is a usual idiom to omit the preposition *on* following a verb of motion in phrases indicating the way a journey is to take:

My travelling the Guildford road. (*L* 69, p. 267)
You go the other road. (*L* 139, p. 476)
They were seen to continue the London road. (*PP* 275)
Nor can I discover any right they had . . . to go their late Tour. (*L* 55, p. 211)

If Jane Austen often made intransitive verbs transitive, by eliding prepositions, she as frequently omits objects, thus having the converse effect of making normally transitive verbs intransitive. A verb which attracts attention to itself by being used intransitively is *visit:*[1]

While I *visit* at Hartfield. (*E* 31)
She made the most of the time by *visiting* about with her daughter. (*PP* 318)
Lady Middleton and Mrs Ferrars will *visit* now. (*SS* 240)

Interest is not now used intransitively; *is interesting* being the counterpart of the transitive verb:

I am grown very happy, but that would not *interest.* (*SS* 372)
Any thing *interests* between those who love. (*E* 89)

Take occurs intransitively meaning 'to take the fancy, become successful or fashionable':

We shall be able to call it Waterloo Crescent – & the name joined to the form of the Building, which always *takes,* will give us the command of Lodgers. (*MW* 380)

[1] In part, the difference is semantic: in the novels the noun *visit* often means 'a short formal call'; the compound noun *tea-visit* (*E* 22) occurs. The modern American tendency to make *visit* intransitive by adding *with* ('Are you *visiting with* friends?'), does not occur in the novels. *Visiting with* above has, of course, a quite different meaning of 'paying a visit in the company of' someone else.

Other verbs used intransitively:

> I said nothing about it, because I would not *influence*. (*E* 53)
> It is not a connexion to *gratify*. (*E* 400)
> Let the other young ladies have time to *exhibit* (their talents). (*PP* 101)
> I want to *consult*. I want your opinion. (*MP* 153)
> A note had been . . . left for her, written in the very style to *touch*. (*E* 184)

A further stage of ellipsis occurs when the verb would normally govern a preposition and object, and both are elided:

> She gives a good account of her health; but as she never complains, I dare not *depend*. (*E* 439)
> My uncle has been too good for me to *encroach*. (*E* 440)
> I am sorry to think how little likely my own eldest son . . . is to marry early . . . I wish he were more likely to *fix*. (*MP* 317)
> While the waters (at Cheltenham) *agree*, everything else is trifling. (*L* 133, p. 463)
> Where the waters do *agree*, it is quite wonderful the relief they give (*E* 275)
> Jane Fairfax mistress of the Abbey! . . . every feeling *revolts*. (*E* 225)

On the other hand, if it describes a facial or other gesture, a normally intransitive verb can become transitive, the idea that the gesture conveys being made into the object. This is quite possible in present English, of course; but it is especially common in Jane Austen; one of her favourite turns of phrase, in fact:

> Mr Crawford smiled his acquiescence. (*MP* 88)
> Mr Crawford bowed his thanks. (*MP* 248)
> She curtseyed her acquiescence. (*NA* 176)
> She looked so truly the astonishment she felt. (*MP* 291)

The Subjunctive

It is quite likely that, had it not been for the eighteenth century grammarians, the subjunctive mood would have been practically discontinued in present English, except in very literary language. S. A. Leonard, in his authoritative book on *The Doctrine of Correctness in English Usage, 1700–1800* (p. 201), points out that, before Johnson's Dictionary was published in 1755, the general opinion of most grammarians seems to have been that there were no moods in English. Johnson, however, announced a 'conjunctive mode', at the same time complaining that it was 'wholly neglected' in his day, though 'used among the purer writers of former times after *if, though, ere, before, till* or *until, whether, except, whatsoever, whomever,* and words of wishing'.

To some extent this insistence on the subjunctive was putting the clock back. Earlier eighteenth century letter-writers, innocent of grammar, had often used the indicative *was*, not merely after *if* and *though*, but even with conditional inversion, usage impossible in present English; '*Was he* twenty years older and I as many years younger,' writes Lady Wentworth, in 1707, of a young man of her acquaintance, 'I would lay al the traps I could to gett him' (*Wentworth Papers,* p. 60).

Jane Austen seems to have used the subjunctive in appropriate contexts when she thought about it; a good deal oftener than it would be found in a modern novel. A 'correct' use of the subjunctive was something to which she clearly aspired; we see this from corrections in later editions of her work, done in her lifetime. It seems natural enough that Mr Darcy's housekeeper should maintain that she could not meet with a better master 'if I *was* to go through the world' (*PP* 249); this is the reading of the first (1813) edition. But in the second (1813) and third (1817) editions, the subjunctive form *were* appears. Similarly in this quotation from the second (1816) edition of *Mansfield Park*, where the first (1814) edition has *was:*

Whether his importance to her *were* quite what it had been. (*MP* 417)

The subjunctive in the main clause, *it were* for *it would be* is rare; but comes plausibly enough in a speech of the rather high-falutin Sir Edward Denham in *Sanditon*. The other character who occasionally uses it is Mr Collins. It was clearly a rather pompous archaism in conversation by the early nineteenth century:

It *were* Hyper-criticism, it *were* Pseudo-philosophy to expect from the soul of high toned Genius, the grovellings of a common mind. (*MW* 398)

If . . . she actually persists in rejecting my suit, perhaps it *were* better not to force her. (*PP* 110)

In main clauses, also, *I had* for *I would have* is very occasionally found:

> I *had* not waited these ten days, could I have read your feelings. (*P* 237)

If the subjunctive in main clauses is rare, in various types of subordinate clause it is fairly frequent. The past subjunctive *were* is often found in noun clauses which are the object of verbs of wishing, fearing, doubting, or uncertainty:

> Elinor could not be surprised at their attachment. She only wished that it *were* less openly shown. (*SS* 55)
> Mrs Jenkinson was chiefly employed in watching how little Miss De Bourgh ate . . . and fearing she *were* indisposed. (*PP* 163)
> It was an even chance that Mrs Churchill *were* not in health. (*E* 221)

The present subjunctive *be* is much rarer in such contexts:

> He calculates how soon it *be* possible to get them there. (*P* 235)

The past subjunctive *had*, meaning 'would have' is also found in subordinate clauses, even in conversation, after verbs of thinking:

> I thought the Miss Musgroves *had been* here – Mrs Musgrove told me I should find them here. (*P* 79)
> Who can this be? . . . I thought we *had been* safe. (*SS* 203)
> I did not think you *had been* so obstinate, Catherine. (*NA* 99)

From being essentially a conjunction associated with uncertainty, it follows that *whether* regularly introduces clauses containing the subjunctive:

> It took up ten minutes to determine whether the boy *were* most like his father or mother. (*SS* 31)
> It was an earnest, steadfast gaze, but she often doubted whether there *were* much admiration in it. (*PP* 181)

Temporal clauses sometimes have verbs in the subjunctive mood, especially when there is a suggestion of uncertainty regarding what is to come:

> He could do nothing till he *were* assured of his fate. (*SS* 366)
> When the novelty of amusement there *were* over, it would be time for the wider range of London. (*MP* 203)

Bringing it to a decision within a very short time, as soon as the variety of business before him *were* arranged. (*MP 255*)

Clauses introduced by generalized relatives (often carrying, in fact, concessive import), regularly have a subjunctive verb:

Whatever *were* to be expressed, he could do it. (*MP 337*)
And yet whether Bingley's regard had really died away, or were suppressed . . . whichever *were* the case . . . (*PP 134*)

Conditional clauses, and clauses of manner introduced by *as if*, frequently contain a subjunctive, where this can be distinguished inflectionally:

There will be much less chance of his marrying her, than if she *remain* with him. (*MP 457*)
(General Tilney) proposed it as no unpleasant extension of their walk, if Miss Morland *were* not tired. (*NA 179*)
It seems as if the W. Kent scheme *were* entirely given up. (*L 36*, p. 129)

On the other hand, many speakers do not use the subjunctive in such contexts, and possibly their rather careless usage is deliberately being intended here:

If I *was* her, I would not have put up with it (Mrs Bennet). (*PP 228*)
If it *was* my house, I should never sit any where else (Catherine Morland). (*NA 214*)
The children are all hanging about her already as if she *was* an old acquaintance (Sir John Middleton). (*SS 119*)

In the following instance, however, the indicative is well chosen: Edmund Bertram is the speaker, and he is here facing up to the painful but undoubted fact that Mary Crawford, despite all her charm, is unworthy:

For sometimes, Fanny, I own to you, it does appear more than manner; it appears as if the mind itself *was* tainted. (*MP 269*)

Concord

In matters of grammatical concord we can observe a tendency frequent also with other points of grammar. Obvious and blatant breaking of the rules is deliberate, and generally intended to reflect want of education in the speaker or letter-writer guilty of such usage; but occasionally, Jane Austen perpetrates minor errors herself. It would be pedantic to make too much of these. She is in the tradition of the great English writers from at least the time of Shakespeare onwards, who have always preferred ease and naturalness of expression to a too precise regard for grammaticality.

The Steeles, in *Sense and Sensibility*, and John Thorpe, in *Northanger Abbey*, will furnish us with examples of the vulgar disregard of the rules of concord:

> Edward *have* got some business at Oxford. (*SS* 275)
> He could get nothing but a curacy; and how *was* they to live upon that ?
> (*SS* 273)
> Here *is* Morland and I come to stay a few days. (*NA* 49)

Miss Bates, in *Emma*, is sometimes typically muddled:

> There never was such a keeping apple any where as one of his trees – I
> believe there *is* two of them. (*E* 238)

Servants, also, are ignorant of the rules of concord:

> The horses *was* just coming out (Thomas, the Dashwoods' servant).
> (*SS* 355)

But the more refined characters, and even Jane Austen herself in her narrative, can be a little easy-going in this matter at times. Sometimes the plural aspect of a singular noun, or vice versa, causes inconsistency:

> The pains which they . . . have taken to reason, coax or trick him into
> marrying *is* inconceivable (Mary Crawford). (*MP* 43)
> Of pictures there *were* abundance, and some few good. (*MP* 84)
> The row of Beech *look* very well. (*L* 73, p. 287)

At other times there is the attraction of intervening plurals drawing the singular verb into a plural:

> Nothing but love, flirtation, and officers, *have* been in her head. (*PP*
> 283)

His want of spirits, of openness, and of consistency, *were* . . . attributed
to his want of independence. (*SS* 101)
Your enquiry after my uncle and aunt *were* most happily timed.
(*L* 70, p. 280)

None and *neither* are still bones of contention:

None *were* to be compared with the prospect of Rosings. (*PP* 156)
Neither Jane nor Elizabeth *were* comfortable on this subject. (*PP* 129)

But Jane Austen often side-steps this problem by a neat
repetition of the subject:

The ladies were none of them dressed. (*PP* 344)
You are neither of you large. (*PP* 211)
We none of us expect to be in smooth water all our days. (*P* 70)

There had been a tendency in the eighteenth century to
write *was* after *you* when *you* was singular. *You was* is fairly
frequent, and not necessarily vulgar, in Richardson's novels.
(See Uhrström's *Studies on the Language of Samuel Richardson*,
pp. 18–19). This usage, however, was condemned by the
grammarians, and in the novels only people like the Steeles have
it:

I felt almost as if you *was* an old acquaintance. (*SS* 132)
I felt sure that you *was* angry with me. (*SS* 146)

We do not expect Fanny Price to use such expressions; and this
speech of hers is 'corrected' in later editions:

I thought you *was* against me. (*MP* 346)

Nouns

Certain nouns now inflected with *s* have an uninflected plural in
the novels. The commonest, in view of the frequent topic of
balls and dancing, is *couple:*

To collect young people enough to form twelve or fourteen *couple*.
(*MP* 253)

A train of twenty young *couple* . . . walked after her to church. (*E* 22)
She found in Elinor and her husband . . . one of the happiest *couple* in
the world. (*SS* 374)

So, too, with *pair*:

The Crown Inn . . . where a couple of *pair* of post-horses were kept.
(*E* 197)
We have got apartments up two *pair* of stairs. (*L* 9, p. 20)

Acquaintance never has an *s*, so far as I have observed. The same
form appears as a collective:

They had, therefore, many *acquaintance* in common. (*PP* 142)
The *acquaintance* she had already formed were unworthy of her. (*E* 23)

Taste occurs in contexts where a plural would now be usual:

Upon my word, Miss Anne Elliot, you have the most extraordinary
taste. (*P* 157)
Edward's generous temper, simple *taste*, and diffident feelings. (*SS*
305)

Muffin appears in the singular instead of the plural, a usage also
found in Richardson (*Sir Charles Grandison*, I 310); we may
contrast *toasts* below:

The *muffin* last night – if it had been handed round once, I think it
would have been enough. (*E* 170)

Sort and *kind* regularly have uninflected plurals. Educated
writers tend now to avoid this inconsistency by a phrase like
things of this sort:

How wonderfully *these sort of things* occur. (*PP* 96)
It is . . . an unpleasant thing . . . to have *those kind of yearly drains*.
(*SS* 11)
Neither she nor her daughters were *such kind of women* as Fanny would
like to associate with. (*SS* 228)

The phrase *a series of* is generally followed, rather illogically,
by a singular noun. This was regular eighteenth century usage.
In Johnson's *Life of Savage*, the poet, we are told, was subject

to 'a series of his mother's cruelty' (*Lives of the English Poets*, *II* 357):

> She . . . should have received a partner only through *a series of inquiry*. (*MP* 274)
> Confined within doors by *a series of rain and snow*. (*MP* 286)

An exception is *E* 331 (*a series of* strange *blunders*).

The converse of what we have described in the last paragraph, viz., an inflected plural no longer insisted on, also occurs:

> The window shutters were not painted green, nor were the walls covered with *honeysuckles*. (*SS* 28)
> I hope you will eat some of this Toast . . . I reckon myself a very good Toaster; I never burn my *Toasts*.[1] (*MW* 417)

In earlier periods of English, abstract nouns are more frequently found in the plural, and Jane Austen has many plural abstract nouns which would be hardly acceptable today:

> Better *accommodations* (for dancing) he can promise them. (*E* 250)
> To sooth her distress, lessen her *alarms*. (*SS* 262)
> If you remember any *queernesses*, set them all to the right account. (*E* 439)
> An opportunity of watching the *loves* and *jealousies* of the four. (*P* 80)
> One of the many *praises* of the day. (*P* 84)
> Giving him all the *helps* and directions in her power. (*MP* 166)
> His leaving Eton for Oxford made no change in his kind *dispositions* (The meaning is clearly 'disposition'). (*MP* 21)
> He has no headake, no sickness, no pains, no *Indigestions*. (*L* 117, p. 438)

Frequently the meaning of these abstract nouns in context is 'acts of, instances of (the quality in question)'; a meaning that is borne out when we find abstract nouns preceded by indefinite articles:

---

[1] 'Adams immediately procured himself a good fire, *a toast* and ale,' Fielding, *Joseph Andrews* I, 163. We are reminded by this use with the indefinite article and in the plural of the identity of origin with the other meaning of *a toast*, the name of a lady being figuratively supposed to flavour a bumper of ale etc., in much the same way as a piece of spiced toast did.

F

It was *an encouragement* of vice. (*PP* 364)
Every dinner-invitation he refuses will give her *an indigestion*. (*L* 84,
p. 329)
I shall try for it with *a zeal*! (*E* 259)
Julia's looks were *an evidence* of the fact. (*MP* 175)

Jane Austen has a fondness for the abstract noun as complement to convey a general impression. In this she is a child of the
eighteenth century:

It was unvarying, warm admiration every where. (*P* 73)
The wilderness . . . was darkness and shade, and natural beauty,
compared with the . . . terrace. (*MP* 91)
'Here's harmony!' said she, 'Here's repose! . . . Here's what may
tranquillize every care!' (*MP* 113)
The past suspense . . . had been ease and quiet to the present disappointment. (*NA* 138)

She sometimes uses abstract nouns to refer to people in particular. She means 'an object of my contempt' in the first
quotation here, for example:

The Man who cannot do justice to the attributes of Woman is *my
contempt*. (*MW* 397)
You are determined . . . to make him *the contempt* of the world. (*PP*
358)
Mr Crawford was no longer . . . *her abhorrence*. (*MP* 328)
'It was a hard case . . .' and, 'I do think you were very much to be
pitied'; were the kind responses of *listening sympathy*. (*MP* 122)

Inflected and Phrasal Genitive

There are two ways of expressing possession in English: by the
genitive inflection, and with *of*, as in *the man's hat* and *the leg of
the table*. We retain in full use both *the king's son* (German
des Königs Sohn) and *the son of the king* (French *le fils du roi*);
whereas both French and German speakers have no choice of
construction. These two ways of expressing possession are by
no means always interchangeable, however. The differentiation
may be, as in the two English examples just quoted, between an
animate and an inanimate object. (This is why *the pen of my aunt*
is a literal translation from a French grammar-book rather than

idiomatic English). The two forms also sometimes tend to be a means of differentiating between a subjective and objective genitive, as in *the Queen's actions* and *the betrayers of the Queen;* but in earlier English, where the objective genitive was in any case rather more frequent, it was more often inflectional; as in these examples from the novels, where we should prefer the prepositional genitive: 'the idea of Mr Elliot' etc.:

That *Mr Elliot's idea* always produced irritation in both, was beyond a doubt. (*P* 107)
Though she had not waited for that sentence to be thinking of Edmund, such a memento made her particularly awake to *his idea.* (*MP* 207)
His sight was so inseparably connected with some very disagreeable feelings. (*E* 182)
Admirers of Charles must be attended to. – They seem very reasonable . . . & full of *his praise.* (*L* 44, p. 158)

As we have just said, the names of inanimate things do not normally have the inflected genitive; but an exception to this is nouns denoting time, which sometimes do (*an hour's time, a night's rest,* etc.). This is very much a matter of idiom, however. We should prefer the genitive with *of* in contexts like this today:[1]

By the ten days' end, her nephew's letter . . . (*E* 317)
At about *the week's end.* (*MP* 429)
At *the fortnight's end.* (*L* 133, p. 466)
Mrs Norris thought it an excellent plan, and had it *at her tongue's end.* (*MP* 80)

What is sometimes called the double or pseudo-partitive genitive, seen in such a characteristically English expression as *a friend of his,* is exemplified, as one would expect, in the novels: 'an offer *of Mr. Price's*' (*MP* 402), etc. It is a construction that Fowler (*MEU of* 7) calls 'plainly illogical'. One sometimes has the impression, as with *yesterday morning* above (p. 17), that when Jane Austen stopped to think, her strong logical mind sometimes overcame her sense of idiom; in the following un-

[1] Or should we? That herald extraordinary of modern idiom, *Time* magazine, frequently has expressions like *at week's end.* The succinctness of the inflected genitive is preferred. See S. Potter, *Changing English* pp. 105–6.

idiomatic omissions of the second indication of the genitive here, for instance:

The exchange of a few old-fashioned jewels *of her mother*. (*SS* 220)
The Longbourn party were the last . . . to depart; and by a manœuvre *of Mrs Bennet* had to wait. (*PP* 102)

About that other peculiarly English use of the genitive, the group genitive, however, she has no inhibitions; freely using expressions like 'his son and daughter's carriage' (*E* 108); 'the morning appointed for Admiral and Mrs Croft's seeing Kellynch-hall' (*P* 32); 'her father and sister's solicitudes' (*P* 148).[1]

A now obsolete, or at least very uncommon, use of the genitive found in the novels, is the elliptical partitive genitive. This construction flourished in Middle English. Chaucer tells us, of the Prioress:

Of smale houndes hadde she that she fedde
With roasted flesh. (*General Prologue* 146)

Comparable with this are the following:

I shall like it *of all things* (for *most* of all things). (*PP* 317)
He was not to be *of the party* to Northanger (for *one* of the party). (*NA* 150)
Scarcely any family but *of the residents* left (for *those* of the residents). (*P* 95)

Personal Pronouns

The colloquial omission of a personal pronoun subject where it can be easily supplied from the context is an aspect of English speech that Jane Austen faithfully reproduces. On the whole, it

---

[1] One might well compare with this her very English habit of always adding the plural inflection, when it was needed, to the last element of a proper name. She will have nothing of Gallicisms like *the Misses Bertram*, *the Ladies Fraser*, *Messrs Musgrove*; instead, we regularly find *the Miss Bertrams* (*MP* 90), *the Lady Frasers* (*NA* 209), *the Mr Musgroves* (*P* 42). In a phrase like *idle heir apparents* (*MP* 469), she likewise flouts French precedent. In these respects, as in so many, she is, in Kipling's phrase, 'England's Jane'. Nevertheless, there are French influences occasionally. See p. 177n.

is the more elderly people who omit the subject most; or those
who, like Mrs Jennings and John Thorpe, talk so much that
they have no time to speak precisely:

> They will be all wanting a home. Could not be a better time, Sir
> Walter (Mr Shepherd, a family lawyer). (*P* 17)
> I am monstrous glad to see you – sorry I could not come before – beg
> your pardon (Mrs Jennings). (*SS* 163)
> I saw him . . . turn up the Lansdown Road . . . Did upon my soul; knew
> him again directly (John Thorpe). (*NA* 85)
> Ha! snows a little I see (Mr Elton). (*E* 115)

When the subject is the same in two subordinate clauses, it
has always been quite usual to omit it in the ¯second. But
sometimes the distance between the two verbs in clauses, or
some difference in the subject, may make the omission of a
pronoun awkward or ambiguous. Freedom in the omission of
such pronouns has always been a prerogative of letter-writers,
and also of diarists. (Witness Henry Tilney's parody of what
Catherine Morland will be likely to put in her journal: 'Friday,
went to the Lower Rooms; wore my sprigged muslin . . . etc.'
NA 26.) But in the novels it is only the vulgar letter-writers,
and Jane Fairfax when she is ill and writes in words of 'tremu-
lous inequality', who have such usage:

> Miss Fairfax's compliments and thanks, but is quite unequal to any
> exercise. (*E* 390)
> We . . . are now on our way to Dawlish for a few weeks, which place
> your dear brother has great curiosity to see, but thought I would first
> trouble you with these few lines (Lucy Ferrars, née Steele). (*SS* 365)
> The impossibility . . . of taking a personal leave of Mr Woodhouse,
> . . . and had Mr Woodhouse any commands, should be happy to
> attend to them (Mr Elton). (*E* 140)

Conversely, other vulgar speakers, particularly when they
are excited or expostulating, add extra personal pronouns:
Mrs Jennings, for example, narrating a family quarrel at John
Dashwood's house; or Isabella Thorpe:

> Nancy, *she* fell upon her knees, and cried bitterly; and your brother, *he*
> walked about the room. (*SS* 259)
> And your dear brother, I am sure *he* would have been miserable if I had
> sat down the whole evening. (*NA* 134)

The substitution of the neuter pronoun *it* for *he* or *she* is found a few times in the novels. This is not unprecedented in English. Duncan says of Macbeth '*It* is a peerless kinsman' (*Macbeth* I iv, 58). In each of the following our attention is being drawn to something other than the person: the idea of friendship in the first two examples, for instance:

It had been a friend and companion such as few possessed. (*E* 6)
'How did Miss Campbell appear to like it?' (the flirtation between her fiancé and Jane Fairfax).
'*It* was her very particular friend, you know.' (*E* 202)
Miss Nash thinks her own sister very well married, and *it* is only a linen-draper. (*E* 56)

Another use of the pronoun *it* which occurs more freely than today, is as the object of what would otherwise be an intransitive verb, or where the situation or nature of the object is too vague for more particularity.[1] This idiomatic usage occurs, of course, in Shakespeare ('Lord Angelo *dukes it* well' *Measure for Measure*, III, ii, 91), and one recalls Herbert Morrison's wartime slogan, 'Go to *it*':

Elinor could sit *it* no longer. (*SS* 360)
I saw a mixture of many feelings . . . but habit, habit carried *it*. (*MP* 458)
Well, Miss Morland, I suppose you and I are to stand up and jig *it* together again. (*NA* 59)
They battled *it* together for a long time. (*PP* 324)

A couple of examples occur of the personal pronoun used with the definite article, with the force and function of a noun, equivalent to 'the man, the woman'. The fact that it is really a noun and not a pronoun is proved by the case in the first example here, *the he*, not *the him*:

[1] It is worth recalling, if only because it is one of the funniest exchanges in the novels, that Mr Bennet will not let his wife get away with such a vague use of *it*:
'If it was not for the entail I should not mind *it*.'
'What should you not mind?'
'I should mind not anything at all.'
'Let us be thankful that you are preserved from a state of such insensibility.' (*PP* 130)

She perceived among a group of young men, *the very he,* who had given them a lecture on tooth-pick cases. (*SS* 250)
I have a very good eye at an Adultress, for tho' repeatedly assured that another . . . was *the She,* I fixed upon the right one. (*L* 36, p. 127)

With regard to the case of pronouns, the first person object forms, *me* and *us,* are used as the subject forms *I* and *we* by the less refined:

Neither Mr Suckling nor *me* had ever any patience with them (Mrs Elton). (*E* 321)
You do not know him so well as *me,* Miss Dashwood (Lucy Steele). (*SS* 130)
Nobody could live happier together than *us* (Lady Denham). (*MW* 400)

One feels it would have been quite wrong for Mrs Norris to have used the subject form in the next example; *it is I* is elevated rather than idiomatic. Instead, she pushes forward with:

Depend upon it it is *me* . . . It is *me,* Baddeley, you mean. (*MP* 325)

Likewise this substitution of the object form by Mrs Bennet:

If I was *her,* I would not have put up with it. (*PP* 228)

The descendant of the Old English nominative second person plural pronoun *ye* had been generally supplanted by the accusative *you* long before Jane Austen's day. *Ye* was by then a rare poetic and archaic form. Marianne Dashwood, evincing her sensibility by apostrophizing her birthplace when leaving it, and perhaps consciously echoing Cowper, has it:

And you, *ye* well-known trees! – but you will continue the same. (*SS* 27)

Ye only survives in normal colloquial usage in the novels (as perhaps it still does) in *How d'ye do?* (*E* 188, etc.).

Quite common in her conversation is the use of the possessive adjective second person *your* in a slightly contemptuous, and often argumentative, indefinite usage, which has thriven colloquially from at least the time of Shakespeare.[1] '*Your* water is a sore decayer of *your* horson dead body,' says the grave-digger in *Hamlet (Hamlet*, V, 1, 167):

> Sir Frederick and Lady Wentworth! It would be but a new creation, however, and I never think much of *your* new creations. (*P* 75)
> What nonsense one talks . . . when hard at work . . . *your* real workmen . . . hold their tongues. (*E* 242)
> Oh! I know nothing of *your* furlongs, but I am sure it is a very long wood. (*MP* 95)

Rather as she has a tendency to avoid the personal at times by the use of a passive voice, so Jane Austen also occasionally eschews personal pronouns, preferring such an impersonal phrase as *there is:*

> A little quickness of voice there is which rather hurts the ear. (*E* 279)
> I wish there may not be a little sulkiness of temper. (*MP* 13)
> She saw that there had been bad habits; that Sunday-travelling had been a common thing. (*P* 161)
> There was a tooth amiss. Harriet really wished . . . to consult a dentist. (*E* 451)

Alongside this, we should notice the use of a definite article (perhaps reflecting French influence), where we now have a possessive adjective:

> There was no recovering *the* complexion from the moment that I spoke of 'Fanny'. (*MP* 394)
> Her face is grown longer . . . and so striking is *the* voice and manner of speaking that . . . (*L* 47, p. 168)

Dr Craik (*op. cit.* p. 140) reads into a like use of the article by Mr Elton, the fact which, if Emma had not been so deluded she would have seen, that Elton does not love Harriet. He is discussing Harriet's portrait. A lover, Dr Craik thinks, would have said '*her* eye' and '*her* mouth':

> Exactly so – The shape of *the* eye and the lines about *the* mouth. (*E* 44)

[1] Any fears that this usage might have been growing obsolete should have been dispelled by the egregious Alf Garnett in the BBC TV series '*Till Death us do Part*': 'Edward Heath, he's *your* grammar-school man" etc.

How, then, are we to account for Frank Churchill's similar expression, as he protests his ecstatic devotion to Jane Fairfax near the end of the novel?

> My aunt's jewels. They are to be new set. I am resolved to have some in an ornament for *the* head. Will not it be beautiful in her dark hair? (*E* 479)

Is he protesting a little too much? It goes without saying that the novelist is more than capable of such subtlety. This context, on the other hand, (Elizabeth inspecting Pemberley) does not seem to lack warmth of feeling, despite the impersonal article:

> She beheld a striking resemblance of Mr. Darcy, with such a smile over *the* face, as she remembered to have sometimes seen (*PP* 250)

There is possibly a tendency to use the article more freely when a portrait is being described, rather than a real person.

Demonstratives

Only one point calls for comment. In adverbial phrases indicating duration of time leading up to the present, normally introduced today by the preposition *for*, there is often no preposition, the demonstrative adjective being used instead; *these two months* (*L* 38, p. 98); *this ever so long* (*SS* 182); *this half hour* (*NA* 43).

Relative Pronouns

In early Modern English *that* was by far the commonest relative pronoun. *Who*, originally an interrogative, did not develop fully as a relative till at least the end of the fifteenth century. The modern distinction between *who*, referring to persons, and *which* and *that*, referring to things, though it has been insisted on more and more over the past three centuries, is even now not finally established. True, we no longer use *which* of persons, as authors of the King James Bible did in the Lord's prayer: 'Our Father *which* art in Heaven'; but it is still normal to use *that* with persons. Jane Austen sometimes refers to persons with a *that*-relative:

> Here are many *that* would be interested. (*MP* 62)
> To have somebody about her *that* she is used to see. (*E* 9)

Compared with the more usual:

> You, *who* have been my only comfort. (*SS* 264)

Apart from the fact of *that* being used with persons, *that* and *which* are differentiated in two other respects. *Which* occurs introducing a second subordinate clause, or a clause at some distance from its antecedent:

> Willoughby had given her a horse, one that he had bred himself . . . and *which* was exactly calculated to carry a woman. (*SS* 58)
> An intimacy resulting . . . from Miss Crawford's desire of something new, and *which* had little reality in Fanny's feelings. (*MP* 208)

Which without antecedent can introduce a clause in anticipatory parenthesis to what is to come. *That* could not be used here without ceasing to be a relative and becoming a demonstrative. This is usage which occurs typically in the prolix style of Mr Collins:

> And thirdly – *which* perhaps I ought to have mentioned earlier, that it is the particular advice . . . of the very noble lady whom I have the honour of calling patroness. (*PP* 105)

And elsewhere:

> But if, *which* I rather imagine, your making the match . . . means only your planning it. (*E* 12)
> And I will tell you what, Fanny – *which* is more than I did for Maria – the next time pug has a litter you shall have a puppy. (*MP* 333)

One of the characteristics of the modern adjective clause is its immediate contact with its antecedent. Generally, in present English, when an adjective clause depends on a genitive, the inflected genitive is avoided, since this would mean that the noun indicating the thing possessed would come between the clause and the noun it described. Instead, we prefer the genitive with *of*. In place of Chaucer's 'By my *fader* soule, *that* is deed' (*General Prologue* 782), we should now say 'By the soul of my *father who* is dead'. The older form of the genitive was, nevertheless, slow to die out, and Jane Austen sometimes has it:

> As she wished to get it over before *Henry's* return, *who* was expected on the morrow. (*NA* 193)
> Fanny was ... in her *mother's* arms, *who* met her there with looks of true kindness. (*MP* 377)

Among vulgar usage connected with the relative pronoun, we may mention:
(1) The use of *as* for *that*, still common dialectally:

> And his lady too, Miss Steele *as* was (Thomas, the Dashwoods' manservant). (*SS* 354)

But correlative to demonstrative *that*, *as* is not vulgar:

> Jane's curiosity did not appear of *that* absorbing nature *as* wholly to occupy her. (*E* 174)

(2) The collocation *but what*, introducing an adjective clause including a negative, describing persons:

> There is not one of his tenants ... *but what* will give him a good name (Mr Darcy's housekeeper). (*PP* 249)
> Not that I think Mr. Martin would ever marry any body *but what* had some education (Harriet Smith). (*E* 31)

(3) *Who* for *whom*:

> Whose great kindness I shall always thankfully remember, as will Edward too, *who* I have told of it (Lucy Steele). (*SS* 277)
> The name of the man on *who* all my happiness depends (Lucy Steele). (*SS* 131)

(4) The asyndetic relative clause in the subject relation. In present English we freely omit the relative in the object relation: so did Jane Austen ('the first thing I did', *E* 236); but we rarely nowadays omit a relative pronoun subject, as Chaucer and Shakespeare could ('I have a brother is condemn'd to die' *Measure for Measure*, II, ii, 34). The few modern instances of omitted relatives usually occur before more or less meaningless introductory phrases like 'here is, there is' – 'There is a man

below wants to speak to you', for example. Very occasionally such omissions occur in the novels, but they are not spoken by the most acceptable people. That 'rattle', John Thorpe, however, has some examples:

> Does he want a horse? Here is a friend of mine, Sam Fletcher, has got one to sell. (*NA* 76)
> But here is your sister says she will not go. (*NA* 85)

And also the newly-rich, 'only moderately genteel' Mrs Cole:

> There is poor Jane Fairfax, who is mistress of music, has not any thing of the nature of an instrument. (*E* 215)

Interrogative Pronouns

Both Mrs Norris and Lydia Bennet use *who* for *whom*, in either direct or indirect questions:

> *Who* should I look to . . . but the children? (*MP* 6)
> I am going to Gretna Green, and if you cannot guess with *who*, I shall think you a simpleton. (*PP* 291)

But Mr Knightley says:

> *Whom* are you going to dance with? (*E* 331)

The Articles

Jane Austen's use of the definite, indefinite and zero articles differs from Modern English in one or two points. We do not now much use a favourite device of hers, the indefinite article before indefinite pronouns like *something*, *nothing* or *somebody*:

> There was *a something* in Sir Thomas . . . which made Mr. Yates think it wiser to let him pursue his own way. (*MP* 191)
> There does seem to be *a something* in the air of Hartfield which gives love exactly the right direction. (*E* 75)
> It is *a nothing* of a part, *a mere nothing*. (*MP* 145)
> She was the only girl . . . for you to notice, and you must have *a somebody*. (*MP* 230)

SENTENCE STRUCTURE   173

More rarely, the definite article occurs:

> Exactly *the something* which her home required. (*E* 26)
> After the waste of a few minutes in saying *the proper nothings*. (*P* 226)

We occasionally find the indefinite article with a proper name, meaning 'a person like (the one named)':

> *An Anne Ekins* can hardly be so unfit for the care of a Child as *a Mrs. Holder*. (*L* 87, p. 350)
> *A Harriet Smith* ... would be a valuable addition to her privileges. (*E* 26)

The indefinite article is also used rather differently with proper names to emphasize some special facet or development of a person's nature:

> You must prepare for *a William* when you come, a good looking Lad, civil and quiet. (*L* 130, p. 459)
> Henry at White's! Oh, *what a Henry!* (*L* 97, p. 390)
> Such a heart – *such a Harriet!* (*E* 475)

It was unusual for the proscriptive grammarians of the time to recommend positively any grammatical construction; but Lindley Murray (*op. cit. I* 257) had suggested: 'The article *the* has sometimes a good effect, in distinguishing a person by an epithet: "I own I am often surprised that he should have treated coldly, a man so much *the gentleman*".' Whether fortified or not by such recommendation, Jane Austen has this use of the definite article fairly often:

> A most distinguishing complexion! So peculiarly *the lady* in it. (*E* 478)
> Not handsome, but in person and address most truly *the gentleman*. (*PP* 171)
> His brother-in-law, Mr. Hurst, merely looked *the gentleman*. (*PP* 10)
> With what true sympathy our feelings are shared by Martha, you need not be told; – she is *the friend & sister* under every circumstance. (*L* 57, p. 220)

Perhaps because so many spurious forms of gentility have arisen since the early nineteenth century, a phrase like 'He is quite *the gentleman*' can hardly be taken seriously any longer.

Names of diseases now have a definite article less frequently than formerly. Though people can still catch *the measles* and, perhaps, *the mumps*, we do not now have *the headache* nor, except in substandard speech, *the rheumatism*:

> I am sure you have *the headach*[1]. (*MP* 71)
> She caught *the headach* there. (*MP* 74)
> He was hardly able to sit the box on account of *the rheumatism*. (*MP* 189)

We should now omit the definite article, too, in the following:

> To spend *the Christmas* at Longbourn. (*PP* 139)
> The Master *of the Ceremonies*. (*E* 156)
> Many things to be taken *into the account*. (*P* 198)
> It is *the etiquette*. (*PP* 99)
> The most upright female mind *in the creation*. (*E* 437)
> I have been ... used to have a man lean on me for the length of a street, and you are only a fly *in the comparison*. (*MP* 94)

Beside *in comparison* (*MP* 418).

In the three following contexts it is not merely the presence of the definite article, but the idiom itself that is different:

> He did not know what was come to his master ... he could hardly ever *get the speech* of him[2]. (*E* 458)
> When Edmund ... told her in reply, as he did when she would *give him the hearing*. (*MP* 79)
> It was not very pretty of him not to *give you the meeting* when he was invited. (*SS* 171) (Also *E* 159)

Conversely, we should include the definite article here:

> She was *at window*, looking out for Captain Wentworth. (*P* 78)
> Dinner was *on table*. (*E* 298, *PP* 288)

There is a rather significant omission of the definite article in the following sentences. It is still the custom to refer to members of a family, and family retainers such as *cook, nurse* or *doctor* with no article in familiar speech. Mrs Norris, among whose many

[1] Johnson says of Pope: 'His most frequent assailant was *the headach*'. *Lives of the English Poets*. III, 197.
[2] Cf. Fanny Burney: At length I procured *the speech* of one of the pages. (*Diary* IV, 196)

failings is a tendency to be too familiar with the servants, uses *coachman* with no article in this way:

> Between ourselves, *coachman* is not very fond of the roads between this and Sotherton. (*MP* 77)
> And poor old *coachman* would attend us . . . though he was hardly able to sit the box. (*MP* 189)

It is the indefinite article, to our way of speaking, that is omitted from the following:

> She is *niece to Sir Thomas Bertram.* (*MP* 293)
> He . . . found *matter of commendation and interest.* (*E* 197)
> There is never *convenient time for reading it.* (*L* 89, p. 361)

Here rhythm seems to be a consideration. The article would probably not have been omitted if the noun had not been followed by an attributive phrase. Rhythm probably also accounts for the idiomatic omission in the following, which seems to occur in the letters only:

> Both the boys rowed *great part of the way.* (*L* 59, p. 228)
> We were out *great part of the morning.* (*L* 94, p. 385)
> It rained *great part of the way* there. (*L* 4, p. 9)

With which we can compare Fanny Burney:

> I had afterwards to relate *great part of this* to the Queen. (*Diary* III, p. 445)

On the other hand, the idiomatic omission of the article in *change of air* and in *an hour and half* occurs in the novels as well as in the letters:

> To give her *change of air and scene.* (*E* 390)
> *Change of scene* might be of service. (*PP* 141)
> She ought to try *change of air.* (*L* 130, p. 457)
> The sun was yet *an hour and half* above the horizon. (*MP* 439)
> *An hour and half* ago. (*E* 173) (Also *L* 55, p. 211)
> *The three days & half.* (*L* 28, p. 95)

With *kind of* the indefinite article is sometimes omitted:

> They are very good *kind of* people. (*NA* 68)
> Mrs Allen thought them very pretty *kind of* young people. *NA 236*

And we should certainly have to include an indefinite article here!

> They . . . adjourned to eat *ice* at a pastry-cook's. (*NA* 116)

Adjectives

The modern grammarians' rule that the comparative of the adjective, and not the superlative, is to be used when two things are to be compared, is largely a nineteenth century creation. As S. A. Leonard (*op. cit.* p. 61) puts it: 'No-one in the eighteenth century seems to have taken as a serious anomaly the use of the superlative for comparing two persons or things.' In the novels the superlative degree regularly occurs when only two things are compared:

> Mr. Martin may be the *richest* of the two. (*E* 62)
> Which is the *eldest* of the two Miss Plumbtrees. (*L* 73, p. 286)
> So much the *most* in love of the two. (*E* 315)

Traces of the modern distinction appear, with some lack of consistency, here:

> The *elder* (brother) whose temper was by much *the most communicative*, and who was always the *greater* talker. (*E* 100)
> Henrietta was perhaps the *prettiest*, Louisa had the *higher* spirits. (*P* 74)

We should probably consider the following adjectives too long to be compared with a suffix; but this is normal early Modern English usage. Richardson had compared disyllabic and trisyllabic adjectives similarly without resorting to *more* and *most*; but by the mid-nineteenth century a comparative form like *curiouser* is sufficiently outré to form a facetious chapter heading for *Alice in Wonderland: Curiouser and curiouser*:

> His thoughts took a *cheerfuller* turn. (*SS* 226)
> Learning every word of his part herself, but without his being much the *forwarder*. (*MP* 166)
> The *properest* manner. (*MP* 340)
> He would . . . speak louder & look *Impudenter*. (*L* 103, p. 410)

Adjectives occur after the noun in certain contexts; the reasons for this are emphasis, rhythm and idiom, perhaps dialectal idiom, of the time.[1] A common phrase, for instance, seems to have been *reason good* for *good reason*:

No, my dear Miss Price, and for *reasons good*. (*MP* 109)
'Yes,' said he, smiling – 'and *reason good*'. (*E* 99) (Also *L* 140, p. 480)

The position of *all* after a noun was emphatic:

'So very fond of me!' 'tis *nonsense all*. She loves nobody but herself. (*MP* 424)
Her uncle read well – *her cousins all* – Edmund very well. (*MP* 337)

Jane Austen favours a construction in which a superlative adjective, preceded by a definite article, comes after a noun preceded by an indefinite article. It is a construction that is even more common in Fanny Burney. Does one detect French influence here?[2]

Satisfied that the cause was now on *a footing the most proper*. (*MP* 330)
On *a basis the most assured and satisfactory*. (*MP* 314)
An escape . . . from a connection, for life, with an unprincipled man . . . *a deliverance the most real, a blessing the most important*. (*SS* 184)

The likeliest reason for post-position of adjectives in present English is that the phrase in which the adjective occurs goes back, ultimately, to Law French. Hence Jane Austen, too, has

[1] We may compare the East Midland dialectal *times many*, for *many times*, still frequently heard.

[2] In addition to the statement of the *Memoir* that Jane Austen read French easily, there is the probability that her spoken French was improved by acquaintance with her first cousin, Eliza, Countess de Feuillide, née Eliza Hancock, who stayed at Steventon occasionally from the time that Jane was eleven, and who remained in England after her husband had been executed by the Revolution in 1794. Apart from collocations like those above, other Gallicisms seem to be the use of *at all events* and *at present* with French overtones of meaning (p. 189); *to penetrate* in the sense of 'to move the emotions' (p. 67); perhaps the definite article in place of a possessive with parts of the body (p. 168); and possibly the odd use of a genitive like this:

A letter . . . which she eagerly caught from the servant, and, turning *of a death-like paleness*, instantly ran out of the room. (*SS* 181)

heir apparent (*MP* 469), *heir expectant* (*E* 449), a *pair royal* of Braggers (*L* 63, p. 247), and, on the basis of such collocations as *ambassador extraordinary*, phrases like 'to sit up *one hour extraordinary*' (*MP* 387) and 'a *dish extraordinary*' (of tea) (*MW* 326).

Adjectives as Adverbs

'Adjectives,' wrote Robert Lowth (*op. cit.* p. 125), 'are sometimes employed as adverbs; improperly, and not agreeably to the genius of the English language.' This statement is very debatable; the issue, in any case, is certainly not as clear-cut as Lowth seems to imply. There *are* clear instances where a form without the characteristically adverbial suffix *-ly* is wrong, and sounds vulgar; but there are other contexts, even today, where the form without *-ly* sounds, if anything, more idiomatic. There are at least two reasons for this. One is the sense that an adjective complement suits the verb in question as well as, or better than, an adverb. The other is a historical reason. In Old English the chief adverbial suffix was *-e*, an ending that could be added to stem adjectives, or to derivative adjectives ending in *-lic*; so *strang* and *stranglic* were adjectives meaning 'strong', and *strange* and *stranglice* were adverbs meaning 'strongly'. The modern distinction that the root without *-ly* is an adjective, and the root with the suffix *-ly* added is an adverb, grew up only gradually (the eighteenth century grammarians were influential in insisting on the differentiation); and it is even now not universal. *Kingly* and *godly*, for example, are still adjectives, not adverbs; while certain words like *daily*, *hourly* and *leisurely* can be either part of speech. Very occasionally, the ambiguity arises in Jane Austen's English, as in her famous statement: 'An artist cannot do anything *slovenly*'. (*L* 11, p. 30) Again, when one of her characters, Mrs John Dashwood (or a twentieth century speaker, for that matter), says: 'They will live so *cheap*' (*SS* 12), there are reasons in the history and idiom of English why this is not vulgar, but at least as acceptable as 'They will live so *cheaply*'. *Cheap* is elliptical for *good cheap*, an adverb phrase meaning 'at good market' (French *à bon marché*).

Jane Austen's instinct for distinguishing between what is unacceptable (and therefore to be kept for vulgar characters), and what, though not perhaps having grammar-book sanctions, is idiomatic and tolerable English; her instinct and judgement, in other words, as to what can and cannot be said without jeopardizing one's position in the best society, never fail her. Here, in this matter of using adjectives as adverbs, are her vulgarians, with their obvious solecisms:

> I think they are vastly agreeable, provided they dress *smart* and behave *civil* (Anne Steele). (*SS* 123)
> If ever you tell your sister what I think of her, you cannot speak too *high* (Lucy Steele). (*SS* 240)
> Jane speaks so *distinct* (Miss Bates). (*E* 158)
> Mr. Morland has behaved vastly *handsome* indeed (Mrs Thorpe). (*NA* 135)

Here are some less reprehensible instances, where the possibility of an adjective complement is not excluded:

> Let her be an active, useful sort of person, not brought up *high* (Mr Collins, quoting Lady Catherine). (*PP* 106)
> Jane Fairfax did look and move *superior*. (*E* 219)
> So *anxious* for her health and comfort, so very *feeling* as he now expressed himself. (*MP* 414)

Right and *wrong*, *quick* and *slow*, and associations like *speaking plain* and *writing even* are instances where the grammarians' insistence on the adverbial suffix *-ly* was slow to operate. Most of the following sound, if anything, archaic rather than vulgar usage, even today:

> An innate propriety and simplicity of taste, which in general direct him perfectly *right* (Elinor Dashwood). (*SS* 19)
> She must feel that she has been acting *wrong* (Jane Bennet). (*PP* 148)
> 'Do not imagine, madam,' she continued, 'that I was taught *wrong*!' (Jane Fairfax). (*E* 419)
> Anne . . . was . . . beginning to breathe very *quick*. (*P* 183)
> James was . . . given a charge to go very *slow*. (*E* 128)
> Speaking *plain* enough to be very intelligible. (*E* 170)
> How can you contrive to write so *even?* (Miss Bingley). (*PP* 48)
> You write so *even*. (*L* 85, p. 336)

Here, too, we might include the idiomatic and now obsolete
expression *to fresh arrange*:

> Lady Russell had *fresh arranged* all her evening engagements. (*P* 158)
> In *fresh arranging* . . . the noble fire which the butler had prepared.
> (*MP* 273)

So much for the modification of verbs. The use of an adjective form as an adverb of degree is more acceptable at this date,
and the older characters, especially, tend to use expressions like
monstrous pretty, *prodigious good*, etc. Generally, heroes and
heroines do not have such turns of phrase, and Jane Austen is
not often given to them in her letters; but the elderly and vulgar
characters are:

> You shall see a *monstrous pretty* girl (Sir John Middleton). (*SS* 108)
> An *exceeding good* income (John Dashwood). (*SS* 226)
> My uncle and aunt were *horrid unpleasant* (Lydia Bennet).   (*PP* 319)
> I hear he is quite a beau, and *prodigious handsome* (Anne Steele).
> (*SS* 125)
> I hope you will . . . find it all *mighty delightful* (Mrs Norris). (*MP* 220)
> She told me that it was *certain true* (Mrs Phillips). (*PP* 331)

The last quotation here runs thus in the first edition; the later
editions produced in the author's lifetime have *certainly true;* 'a
very clumsy correction', as Dr Chapman says. Mrs Phillips,
wife of a middle-aged attorney in Meryton, would be likely to
use the former expression. In the narrative itself, I have found
only two examples where the adjective form does duty for an
adverb of degree:

> In Darcy's breast there was a *tolerable powerful* feeling towards her.
> (*PP* 94)
> A *remarkable stout*, forward child. (*P* 79)

There is a third context in which adjectives occur as adverbs:
this is as a sentence adverb, the only instance being *sure* instead
of *surely*. This again seems usually to indicate either a vulgar or
an elderly speaker. It was a common usage of eighteenth
century dramatists like Goldsmith and Sheridan, and is still, of
course, a characteristic of English spoken in Ireland:

Should not the Colonel write himself? – *sure*, he is the proper person
(Mrs Jennings). (*SS* 286)
This is very strange! – *sure* he need not wait to be older (Mrs Jennings). (*SS* 281)
Sure Sir Thomas could not seriously expect such a thing (Mrs Norris).
(*MP* 28)

The only heroine to use such an expression is Catherine
Morland, who perhaps indicates thereby her unsophisticated
upbringing:

Does not he want Captain Tilney to go away? – *Sure*, if your father
were to speak to him, he would go. (*NA* 152)

Adverbs

The intensifying adverb which is probably most associated with
Jane Austen is *vastly*;[1] but in fact, she obviously considered the
words *vast* and *vastly* in their frequent colloquial use, as substandard. The semi-genteel characters use them fairly frequently; the elderly ones, occasionally; but the exemplary
young characters, not at all:

She was *vastly pleased* at your all going (Mrs Allen). (*NA* 68)
Mr. Morland has behaved *vastly handsome* indeed (Mrs Thorpe).
(*NA* 135)
Though I have broke it to her, and she bears it *vastly well* (John
Dashwood). (*SS* 295)
I'm sure there's *a vast many* smart beaux in Exeter (Anne Steele).
(*SS* 123)

Characteristically, Henry Tilney disapproves of extravagant
intensifiers. Catherine Morland's loose use of the adverb
amazingly is taken with a quizzical literalness:

'I really thought before, young men despised novels *amazingly*.'
'It is *amazingly*; it may well suggest amazement if they do – for they
read nearly as many as women'. (*NA* 107)

[1] Though frequent in the eighteenth century, the word was always
objected to by purists, except when it literally meant 'enormously'. Lord
Chesterfield, writing in *The World* No. 101 (Dec. 5th, 1754), instances
a lady who described a snuff-box as '*vastly* pretty, because it was so *vastly*
little'.

A similar playfulness prompts her description of a small room, in the letters, as 'quite *monstrously* little' (*L* 37, p. 132).

With adjectives which derive from past participles there existed until recently a hesitation about modifying with the adverb of degree *very*. A true past participle, it was thought, could not be modified by *very* alone; *much* or *very much* were advocated instead. *Very pleased* and *very delighted*, for instance, were denounced in Victorian times as 'Americanisms'. The whole history of opposition to this construction has been catalogued by Visser (*op. cit. II*, 1224). At least one headmistress was fighting rearguard actions against the use of *very pleased* instead of *very much pleased* on schoolgirls' reports down to the middle of this century. Jane Austen seems to have been aware of the feeling against *very* with a participial adjective. Instances with *very much* greatly outnumber those with *very*:

> Mr. Woodhouse's spirits . . . are sometimes *much depressed*. (*E* 275)
> Mr. Darcy seemed *much pleased*. (*PP* 98)
> Mrs. Dixon must be *very much disappointed*. (*E* 161)
> Finding himself & his horse to be *very much tired*. (*L* 24, p. 81)
> The girls were *very much delighted*. (*L* 82, p. 323)
> Uncle Henry was *very much amused*. (*L* 111, p. 427)
> She cannot be *too much guarded* in her behaviour. (*PP* 289)

Alongside:

> With a *very saddened* heart. (*MP* 282)
> Emma was *very decided* in thinking such an attachment no bad thing. (*E* 342)

Jane Austen's occasional use of *something* as an adverb for *somewhat* is now substandard:

> He has a wide . . . mouth & very good teeth, & *something* the same complexion. (*L* 87, p. 353)
> Has not Miss Crawford a gown *something* the same ? (Edmund Bertram) (*MP* 222)

Contrariwise, *somewhat* now tends to be restricted to adverbial uses, whereas here it appears as the equivalent of *something*:

> As if he had *somewhat* in particular to tell her. (*SS* 172)
> Time would undoubtedly abate *somewhat* of his sufferings. (*MP* 460)

The use of the near adverb *here* where *there* is now preferred is fairly common; it is found, also, in Richardson (*Sir Charles Grandison*, I, 11):

Do let us have the pleasure of taking you home. *Here is* excellent room for three. (*P* 91)
Mr. Woodhouse considered eight persons at dinner together as the utmost that his nerves could bear – and *here* would be a ninth. (*E* 292)
Here are officers enough at Meryton to disappoint all the young ladies in the country. (*PP* 138)

There and *where* commonly occur in abstract contexts to describe personal relationships. *There* is generally italicized:

Had she endeavoured to find a friend *there* (in Jane Fairfax) instead of in Harriet Smith. (*E* 421)
If she suspected any prepossession elsewhere, it could not be in that quarter. '*There*, to be sure,' said she, 'I might have thought myself safe'. (*SS* 266)
Mr. Darcy can please *where* he chuses. (*PP* 82)
That sweetness which makes so essential a part of every woman's worth in the judgment of man, that though he sometimes loves *where* it is not, he can never believe it absent. (*MP* 294)

With the verb *look* in the sense of 'to appear', it is now normal to have an adjective complement, found in Jane Austen's usage also ('She looks very *neat* & *tidy*', *L* 74.1, p. 500); but alongside this construction, adverbs are also found with this verb:

Though looking most *wretchedly*, she ate more. (*SS* 193)
You look very *nicely* indeed. (*MP* 222)
The table ... holds a great deal ... without looking *awkwardly*. (*L* 25, p. 82)

We can compare Fanny Burney:

We went to the play, and saw Mrs Siddons in Rosalind. She looked *beautifully*. (*Diary* IV, 303)

This construction is a testimony to the influence of the grammarians. It arises from a misconceived notion of the right use of predicative adjectives. Adjectives were felt to be incorrect even when they were warranted.[1] This represents the converse of

---

[1] Such sentences seem still to be characteristic of American English. See Brian Foster *The Changing English Language* p. 213.

the use of adjectives as adverbs, discussed above (p. 178). Once, an adverb occurs with *feel*:

> I stood for a minute, feeling *dreadfully*. (*E* 179)

Beside the modern *good-looking* (*NA* 15), *well-looking* occurs with the same meaning, and also its converse, *ill-looking*, meaning 'ugly':

> A remarkably fine family, the sons very *well-looking*. (*MP* 13)
> Handsome is as handsome does, he is therefore a very *ill-looking* man. (*L* 75, p. 292)

The *ill/well* distinction is clearly implied here:

> What sort of looking man is Mr. Martin? (*E* 29)

Well as an adjective complement now generally refers to health. We now prefer *good*, for instance, in contexts like these:

> It is really very *well* for a novel. (*NA* 38)
> Gentlemen of the navy are *well* to deal with. (*P* 17)

There has also been a tendency since the early nineteenth century to substitute more precise adverb phrases for single adverbs of location: *in the front*, *towards the back* etc., for adverbs like these:

> Some (cloaks) are long *before*, & some long all round. (*L* 37, p. 133)
> The room . . . was the one he chiefly occupied, and looking *forwards*. (*E* 89)
> The room in which the ladies sat was *backwards*. (*PP* 168)
> They are gone down to Newcastle, a place quite *northward*, it seems (Mrs Bennet). (*PP* 336)

Such usage may mislead. When we are told that Mr Musgrove always sits *forward*, the meaning is not, as it would be today, 'bolt upright', but 'in the front seat':

> Mr. Musgrove always sits *forward*. So, there was I, crowded into the back seat with Henrietta and Louisa. (*P* 39)

Negative Adverbs

Jane Austen is not fond of the reduced form of the negative adverb. It is generally the vulgar speakers in the novels who use abbreviations like *can't, don't*, etc. In this respect she is of the eighteenth century. In one of the *Spectator* essays (No. 135), Addison had written that '*mayn't, can't, sha'n't, won't* and the like' had 'very much untuned our language and clogged it with consonants'. Though, as we learn from the fifth chapter of *Northanger Abbey*, the novelist was no admirer of *The Spectator*, she seems to have been of Addison's opinion in this matter. Exceptionally *do'nt* (sic) occurs in the letters (*L* 134, p. 469); but the following uncontracted collocations are everywhere more normal when the speakers are not vulgar:

John has charming spirits, *has not he?* (*NA* 58)
Will not it be a good plan? (*E* 277)
I am sure I have spoke at least a dozen times: *have not I*, Betsey? (*MP* 440)
It must be our cousins . . . Anne, *must not it?* (*P* 105)
Do you not think they are something in Miss Morton's style? (*SS* 235)
Is not it a fine old place? (*NA* 157)
It would quite shock you to see me do such a thing; now *would not it?* (*NA* 58)

Probably one objection to these abbreviations was that they led to grammatical errors. *Don't* was a reasonable abbreviation of *do not*, and *an't*, which seems to have been pronounced [*a*:nt], for *are not*;[1] but they were both used as abbreviations of the singular form as well; *don't* meaning 'does not' and *an't* meaning 'am not' and 'is not'. This was, and still is, substandard:

They are very pretty ma'am – *an't* they? (Mrs John Dashwood). (*SS* 235)
I shan't go if Lucy *an't* there (Mrs Jennings). (*SS* 292)
I have . . . secured a box for tomorrow night. *A'n't* I a good boy? (Charles Musgrove). (*P* 223)
Well and whose fault is that? Why *don't* he repair it? (Mrs Jennings). (*SS* 286)
Well, it *don't* signify talking (Mrs Jennings). (*SS* 194)

[1] See Jespersen, *MEG* V, 23, 1_8. As an abbreviation of *are not, an't* appears till late in the nineteenth century without suggesting vulgarity. It is used, for example, by the clergymen in Trollope's Barchester novels.

Double and multiple negatives are always a sign of vulgarity:

No, ma'am, he did *not* mention *no* particular family. (A waiter at Lyme). (*P* 106)
Now he had no fortune, and *no nothing* at all (Anne Steele). (*SS* 273)

The negative adverb *nay*, much commoner in earlier English, but now only dialectal, survives occasionally in the novels. It is used, not in reply to a question, but to introduce some kind of a contradiction to a previous statement or idea:

'I did not know that he ever had any such plan . . .'
'*Nay*, I had it from you. You wrote me word of it.' (*E* 344)
'He would certainly have done more justice to . . . prose . . . You would give him Cowper.'
'*Nay*, mama, if he is not to be animated by Cowper!' (*SS* 18)

Adverb Phrases

The inclusion or omission of a preposition with an adverb phrase is also something of a shibboleth of gentility in the novels; but, as with the use of adjectives as adverbs, it is not a simple matter of every instance not conforming to strict grammar being 'the mark of the beast', as Lord Chesterfield put it.[1] Nor is it a question, with such phrases, of the gradual loss of prepositions, as the language developed, by the eroding processes of time and usage. It may sometimes, indeed, be the contrary process: when a person says 'I work *nights*' this may be not so much an ellipsis for *at nights* as a descendant of the Old English adverbial genitive *nihtes*, much earlier than *at night* or *by night*.

As always, Jane Austen's ear is sharp. When Lucy Steele writes: 'I have burnt all your letters, and will return your picture *the first opportunity*' (*SS* 365), her style confirms her vulgarity. And also when her sister says: 'He had been sent for *Wednesday* to Harley-street' (*SS* 273). The semi-gentility of Mrs Norris, Harriet Smith and Mrs Jennings's daughter, Mrs Palmer, are in evidence here:

[1] In a letter of September 27th 1749, to his son: 'Even his pronunciation carries *the mark of the beast* along with it. He calls earth, *yearth* . . . etc.'

Would you have her stay within *such a fine day as this?* (*MP* 72)
He was four-and-twenty *the 8th of last June.* (*E* 30)
I met Colonel Brandon *Monday morning* in Bond-street. (*SS* 115)

It is surprising to find the punctilious Mr John Knightley of their company; but he is not, of course, the model that his brother is, and moreover he is cross when he says: 'If we were obliged to go out *such an evening as this* . . . what a hardship we should deem it'. (*E* 113)

In examples such as this, marking a point, not an extent, of time, the best people would hardly omit a preposition; but with words like *all* or *the whole* the preposition can be omitted. It is not far-fetched to see a tradition of no preposition here going back to King Alfred. In Old English such sentences would have been in the accusative, also with no preposition, to indicate extent of space or time:

Let him *ealne weg* þæt weste land on ðæt bæcbord. Alfred *Orosius* (*EETS, OS* 79, p. 17, 1.10)

i.e. 'He had the waste land on the port side *the whole way*'. So in Jane Austen:

Elizabeth . . . was . . . resolved not to be out of sight of the inn *the whole of that morning.* (*PP* 260)
The report . . . of his coming no more to Netherfield *the whole winter.* (*PP* 129)

With extent of space or time generally the omitted preposition is more acceptable than with a single point of time:

I have been acquainted with you by character *many years* (Mr Elliot). (*P* 187)
Unless you will give me the pleasure of your company *the little way* our road lies together (Anne Elliot). (*P* 169)
She distinguished him . . . at such a distance as to have him in view *the greater part of the street.* (*P* 179)
Her happening to be not in perfectly good spirits *the only winter which she had afterwards spent there.* (*P* 14)

Every way for *in every way* is a usual idiom, though the latter phrase also occurs (*E* 450):

In paying that attention to Miss Fairfax, which was *every way* her due. (*E 421*)
There was perplexity and agitation *every way*. (*MP304*)

Of course, now always an adverb phrase, often of little meaning, occurs as both an adjective phrase and an adverb phrase in the novels. As an adjective phrase it signifies 'to be expected in the natural course of events':

I consider it as a thing *of course* at her time of Life. (*L* 84, p. 330)
Your refusal of my addresses is merely words *of course*. (*PP* 108)
The persons to be invited required little thought. Besides the Eltons it must be the Westons and Mr. Knightley; so far it was all *of course*. (*E 291*)

When *of course* occurs as an adverb phrase, it tends to be less interjectional than modern usage, to relate more closely to the verb than to the sentence as a whole, and to have fuller meaning than is usual today. We should now expand the following phrases to *as a matter of course* or *in due course*:

The invitation was accepted *of course* and at a proper hour they joined the party in Lady Catherine's drawing room. (*PP* 172)
Must it not follow *of course* that when he was understood, he should succeed? (*MP 327*)

With the adverb phrase *for ever* in the following, it is not the phrase itself, but its position in the sentence that we should now alter. *For ever* counts as an adverbial of frequency rather than of time, and as such would now come before the verb it modifies. When we put *for ever* after the verb, we mean not, as here, 'constantly', but 'for always':

And while Meryton was within a walk of Longbourn, they would be going there *for ever*. (*PP* 213)
There are few people much about town that I do not know. I have met him *for ever* at the Bedford. (*NA 96*)

In the last instance we should also now expand the tense: 'I have been for ever meeting him'. This position of *for ever* may sometimes be misleading. Thus when Mary Crawford says 'I shall be at Mansfield *for ever*' (*MP 361*) at a time when she is about to leave for London, she merely means, 'I shall, in imagination, be constantly thinking about Mansfield'.

The adverb phrase 'in the way' now generally means 'in such a position as to obstruct or impede'. This meaning is found also in the novels ('He meets with a young woman . . . His aunt is *in the way*. – His aunt dies', *E* 428); but more usually the phrase means 'available, at hand,' or (*US*) 'around':[1]

> I came here . . . intending to rehearse it with Edmund . . . but he is not *in the way*. (*MP* 168)
> If he is not *in the way* his Partner will do just as well. (*MW* 365)

Likewise the converse:

> I would not have been *out of the way* for a thousand pounds. (*MP* 380)

In Modern English the adverb phrase *at present* is used in contrast with what is to happen in the future. In the novels it often has a backward reference, contrasting, not with what is to be, but with what has gone before:

> His person can hardly be called handsome, till the expression of his eyes . . . is perceived. *At present* I know him so well, that I think him really handsome. (*SS* 20)
> As for regret . . . I have done with that . . . *At present*, if I could be satisfied on one point . . . (*SS* 344)

The modern usage, however, does occur (*P* 141). The French *à présent* can also have this backward reference, as Dr Chapman points out. French precedents are also recalled in the use of the adverb phrase *at all events* meaning not, as now, 'at any rate', but 'at all costs' (French *à tout événement*).

> Elinor had not spirits to say more, and eager *at all events* to know what Willoughby had written, hurried away. (*SS* 182)
> Should the result of her observations be unfavourable, she was determined *at all events* to open the eyes of her sister. (*SS* 159)
> Her wretchedness I could have borne, but her passion – her malice – *At all events* it must be appeased. (*SS* 328)

[1] The two meanings are well illustrated in the compliment paid by Charles II to his Lord Treasurer, the Cornishman Godolphin: 'Never in the way, and never out of the way'.

For the sense of 'at any rate' in conversation, the word *however* appears. Its adversative force is often weakened, since it occurs when there is not much preceding to contradict. This is, I think, slightly substandard.

> 'A devilish long fortnight it will appear to me.'
> 'Then why do you stay away so long?' replied Catherine.
> 'That is kind of you, *however* – kind and good-natured'. (*NA* 123)
> 'A famous good thing this marrying scheme . . . What do you think of it, Miss Morland?'
> 'I am sure I think it a very good one.'
> 'Do you? . . . I am glad you are no enemy to matrimony *however*'. (*NA* 122)
> I am astonished . . . that you should be so ready to think your own children silly. If I wished to think slightingly of any body's children, it should not be of my own *however* (Mrs Bennet). (*PP* 29)

Prepositions

Prepositions are small words, but in the aggregate they do much to contribute to the period quality of a writer. We have seen (p. 152) that Jane Austen was particularly fond of deferring prepositions to the end of sentences or clauses. Apart from this, a good many special uses of prepositions call for comment. The following are noteworthy:

After is used in its older abstract meaning of 'according to':

> Every thing depended, exactly *after* her expectation, on his getting that preferment. (*SS* 276)

Against also occurs in an abstract sense, that of 'in preparation for' some (usually hostile or formidable) eventuality:

> It is a comfort to be prepared *against* the worst. (*SS* 275)
> I shall prepare my most plaintive airs *against* his return. (*MP* 59)

At is used more widely with place-names than is usual today:

> We shall be *at* Newcastle all the winter. (*PP* 317)
> There she comes . . . looking as unconcerned as may be, and caring no more for us than if we were *at* York. (*PP* 113)
> She preferred it to any place she had ever been *at*. (*NA* 212)

There is also the idiomatic *what* (a person) *is at* meaning 'what he is aiming at, working for', sometimes with the idea of subterfuge. Since the early nineteenth century the phrase seems to have become more colloquial:

Who but Henry could have been aware of what his father was *at?* (*NA* 211)
Fanny . . . was . . . earnestly trying to understand what Mr. and Miss Crawford were *at*. (*MP* 305)

By paper occurs meaning 'on paper, in writing':

I have something of consequence to inform you of, which I was on the point of communicating *by paper*. (*SS* 288)

An especially common use of *by*, now much restricted, is in the sense 'in respect to, on behalf of' (another person); it is particularly connected with the quality of one person's behaviour in regard to another. Since the quality of actions in society is such a major concern of the six novels, this kind of context often occurs. I append a few of the many examples:

Captain Wentworth is not very gallant *by* you, Anne, though he was so attentive to me. (*P* 60)
What was due – or rather what would be kind *by* me. (*E* 268)
Her influence . . . originated in an act of kindness *by* Susan, which . . . she (Fanny) at last worked herself up to. (*MP* 396)
The duty of woman *by* woman. (*E* 231)
That she should have the very same . . . office to perform *by* Harriet, which Mrs. Weston had just gone through *by* herself. (*E* 403)

We should now have to introduce many such adverb phrases with an often rather lifeless formula such as *in regard to, in respect to*, etc. The further back into our language we go, the more full of meaning, and even emotion, the simpler preposi- tions tend to be.[1] When Malory makes Sir Ector say of Sir Lancelot that he is the truest lover that ever loved woman *of a synful man* (*Morte Darthur*, Caxton's ed., p. 860), we can only elaborate this with some such abstract expression as *considering that he was a sinful man*, doing no justice to either the compres-

[1] See R. D. Emma *Milton's Grammar* p. 123, on a similar economy in Milton's use of prepositions.

sion or the warmth of the original phrase. We can compare, in
similar terms, Jane Austen's use of *for*, meaning 'in favour of',
and *from*, meaning 'away from'.

> Lady Russell, whose first views on the projected change had been *for*
> Bath. (*P* 14)
> He is decidedly *for* Clapham and Battersea. (*L* 9, p. 22)

> He was neither so unjust, nor so ungrateful, as to leave his estate *from*
> his nephew. (*SS* 4)
> I shall then have been some time *from* home. (*L* 90, p. 365)

In frequently occurs where *on* appears today; for instance *in
his way* for *on his way* (though the latter phrase occurs:
MW 355):

> It was possible that he might stop *in his way* home. (*P* 142)
> *In* our return to Barton. (*SS* 243)
> Something that he told me *in* our journey hither. (*PP* 185)

As also, for something written on a page:

> Yes, papa, it is written out *in* our second page. (*E* 79)

We also find *in behalf of* for *on behalf of* (*NA* 109) and the
Shakespearean *in such a night* (*Merchant of Venice*, V, i, 1) for
on such a night:

> I do not know that, *in* such a night as this, I could have answered for my
> courage. (*NA* 167)

For the following six instances with *in*, we should perhaps
substitute *at* for the three first, *into* for the fourth, *during* for the
fifth, and *about* for the sixth:

> *In* the very beginning of our relationship. (*PP* 304)
> The park was very large ... They entered it *in* one of its lowest
> points. (*PP* 245)
> She ... put it (*sc.* a letter) hastily away, protesting that she ... would
> never look *in* it again. (*PP* 205)
> You ought ... never to admit them *in* your sight. (*PP* 364)
> *In* harvest, it must be quite out of their power to spare a horse. (*MP* 58)
> Her upper house-maid and laundry-maid, instead of being *in* their
> business, are gadding about the village. (*P* 45)

Very characteristic are predicative phrases introduced by *in*: *in exercise, in beauty, in anger*, etc., and the frequent *in spirits*, meaning 'in good spirits':

> That any one who knew so well how to teach, should not have their powers *in exercise* again. (*E* 461)
> Then she will be *in beauty*. (*MP* 394)
> She is not *in anger* against us. (*SS* 275)
> How can Mr. Bingley . . . be *in friendship* with such a man? (*PP* 82)
> She began to think that he must be *in liquor*. (*SS* 318)
> Jane had not written *in spirits*. (*PP* 182)
> Mrs. Poore & her mother, whom I was glad to see *in good looks & spirits*. (*L* 28, p. 96)
> We are engaged tomorrow Evening. What *request* we are *in!* (*L* 43, p. 151)

Another common predicative phrase is *in hopes*. *To be in hopes* is equivalent to the verb *to hope* and is often followed by a clause:

> Emma was more than half *in hopes* of Mr. Elton's having dropt a hint. (*E* 59)
> I . . . was *in hopes* the question would be followed up by others. (*MP* 198)

Typical of her concern with moral issues are sentences like 'It was considerate *in* you'[1] where *of you* is the modern idiom, the meaning being 'on the part of' a person:

> Mr. Perry . . . told him how shabby it was *in* him, their best player, to absent himself. (*E* 68)
> I should have expected better judgment *in* Colonel Campbell. (*E* 228)
> I am going to send *Marmion* out with it – very generous *in* me, I think. (*L* 63, p. 248)

Apart from its use as a preposition to indicate possession, which we have discussed already, the preposition *of* appears in various idioms: 'tall *of* her age' occurs regularly, though the modern 'tall *for* their age' (*SS* 234) is also found:

> She was small *of her age*. (*MP* 12)
> Well-grown and forward *of their age*. (*MP* 13)

[1] A characteristic which Angus Wilson parodies in his short story *Such Darling Dodos*: 'I think it vastly disobliging *in* you, cousin'. *Such Darling Dodos* Penguin Books, p. 70.

G

In comparison of is a regular idiom:

> It is nothing *in comparison of Rosings*. (*PP* 352)
> *In comparison of Norland*, it was poor and small. (*SS* 28)

Of an evening and *of a Sunday* are examples of an idiom that has become vulgar since the early nineteenth century:

> Mrs. Price scarcely ever stirred out of doors, except *of a Sunday*. (*MP* 401)
> My Mother did not go out *of an evening*. (*L* 44, p. 156)
> I have made myself two or three caps to wear *of evenings*. (*L* 13, p. 35)

Of and *on* have always overlapped each other's sphere of usage; we should now paraphrase with *on* in the following:

> His face the colour of mahogany . . . nine grey hairs *of a side*. (*P* 20)
> Mother had chanced to send him *of a message* to father. (*MP* 142)
> In the sweet dependence *of his having* a most comfortless visit. (*E* 109)

'To be put, forced, or driven *on* an expedient or course' is no longer English idiom. *To* is usual in such contexts today. *On* or *upon* regularly occur in such contexts in the novels:

> You are forced *on* exertion. (*P* 232)
> 'I blush for you, Tom,' said he . . . 'I blush for the expedient which I am driven *on*'. (*MP* 23)
> He has not been forced *upon* any exertion. (*P* 233)
> It is always good for young people to be put *upon* exerting themselves. (*NA* 234)

Upon occurs more often than in Modern English; often where *on* now suffices:

> She is always *upon* the gad. (*P* 45)
> He had desired Perry to be *upon* the watch. (*E* 70)

So also in the moving account, by her sister Cassandra, of Jane's own funeral:

> I was determined I would see the last, and therefore was *upon* the listen. (Letters Appendix, p. 517)

'To have a complaint or illness *on* one' is another idiom that seems to have slid down the social scale since the novelist's day:

> She has had a nervous complaint *on* her for several weeks. (*SS* 227)
> This Discharge was *on* me for above a week. (*L* 145, p. 493)
> Dr. P. should see Lady B. with the Gout *on* her. (*L* 90, p. 366)

The origin of the phrase 'It is *on* the cards' is suggested by this obsolete use of *on* :[1]

> Everybody's assuring her . . . that it (Speculation) was the easiest game *on the cards*. (*MP* 239)

To in the pregnant sense of 'in comparison to' occurs:

> A whole evening of back-gammon with her father was felicity *to* it. (*E* 377)
> What do they do for her happiness, comfort, honour, and dignity . . . *to* what I shall do. (*MP* 297)

A similar use of this preposition is the following; slightly substandard, and originating, presumably, from 'gaming':

> It will be all *to* one a better match for your sister (Mrs Jennings). (*SS* 196)
> Tom Musgrave looks all *to* nothing, the smartest . . . Man of the two. (*MW* 347)

Phrases in which *to* occurs with the meaning 'to the extent of' are fairly common today: *punctual to the minute, done to a turn*, etc. But they tend to appear in greater variety, and to be less stereotyped, in the eighteenth and early nineteenth centuries:

> We see him tomorrow by dinner time *to a certainty*. (*E* 188)
> Her husband . . . being *to a precision* the most charming young man. (*NA* 251)
> She performed her promise of being discreet, *to admiration*. (*SS* 265)
> I was very tired, but slept *to a miracle*. (*L* 92 p. 376)

---

[1] Another phrase that has its origin in card-playing would seem to be the following: 'What's your Game?' cried he . . . 'Vingt-un is the game at Osborne'. (*MW* 358)

One can compare Richardson:

> The grandmother and aunt, to whom the Girl is dutiful *to a proverb*. (*Sir Charles Grandison* I 6)

To is fairly common in the pregnant sense of 'to go to' or 'in order to have':

> And was asked by him to join their party the same evening *to Astley's*. (*E* 471)
> He had been sent for Wednesday *to Harley-street*. (*SS* 273)
> They have Edward's carriage *to Ospringe*. (*L* 58, p. 357)
> She joined Mrs. Jennings in the drawing-room *to tea*. (*SS* 315)

'To make a fuss *with* a person' was clearly a regular idiom:

> I looked upon him as the sort of person to be made a fuss *with*. (*MP* 433)
> She was made such a fuss *with* by everybody. (*E* 166)

But the following use of *with*, by Lucy Steele, is presumably substandard:

> We . . . did not know what was become *with* him. (*SS* 273)

Within doors and *without doors* occur as prepositional phrases meaning 'indoors' and 'outdoors':

> To wear over her Shoulders *within doors*. (*L* 74·1, p. 501)
> It might be all talked over as well *without doors* as *within*. (*MP* 257)
> As soon as she was *within the door*. (*E* 322)

Similarly *within side* together forms the preposition *inside*:

> Harriet . . . had never in her life been *within side* the vicarage. (*E* 83)

Conjunctions

There was a time in the history of English, in the late Middle English period, when almost any preposition could be made into a conjunction by the addition of *that*. This is a freedom that has been much restricted, now that it has left us an adequate number of conjunctions to introduce the various types of adverb clause. Usually, the additional *that* has been lost, except with a few conjunctive groups like *in that* and *save that*. We no longer use *that* with *for*, for example; but in the six novels *for that* occurs once:

> In a few minutes the servant returned, and . . . said that he had been mistaken, *for that* Miss Tilney was walked out. (*NA* 91)[1]

Besides that also occurs once:

> For *besides that* the circumstances did not in her opinion justify such . . . amazement . . . her wonder was otherwise disposed of. (*SS* 71)

Nor do we now use *against* or *except* as conjunctions:

> A voluntary partner secured *against* the dancing began. (*MP* 274)
> Her coming on tuesday evening which nothing is now to prevent *except* William should send her word. (*L* 50, p. 185)

So that, and also *so as*, introduce clauses of proviso in the novels, as well as clauses of purpose. The former usage, of very long standing in the language, has since Jane Austen's day grown archaic:

> Where shall we sit? Any where *so that* Jane is not in a draught. (*E* 330)
> I take any part you choose to give me, *so as* it be comic. (*MP* 131)

The conjunctive group *but however*, with *however* in the Austenian sense of 'at any rate' (p. 190), is frequent in conversation and letters; but, as Dr Chapman reminds us, it is used mainly by the more illiterate, like the Steeles, Miss Bates, and Mrs Allen:

> To be in different kingdoms, I was going to say, *but however* different countries (Miss Bates). (*E* 159)
> Any place would do . . . *but, however*, do not speak to Mr. Darcy about it, if you had rather not (Lydia Wickham, née Bennet). (*PP* 386)
> I have some idea he is (an only son); *but, however*, he is a very fine young man (Mrs Allen). (*NA* 69)

[1]This is perhaps vulgar, in any case (*erlebte Rede*); we recall Mrs John Gilpin in the poem of Jane Austen's beloved Cowper:
> *For that* wine is dear
> We will be furnished with our own
> Which is both bright and clear.

And also Lucy Steele (*SS* 277). Nevertheless, Edmund Bertram uses the expression once (*MP* 155). At a further level of illiteracy, there is Thomas, the Dashwoods' servant, who says *but howsever*:

> They was going further down for a little while, *but howsever*, when they come back ... (*SS* 354)

Only also occurs redundantly with *but* occasionally:

> I am most happy to hear it – *but only* Jane Fairfax one knows to be so very accomplished (Mrs John Knightley). (*E* 104)
> *Only* to be sure it was paying him too great a compliment, *but* she did think there were some looks a little like Mr. Elton (Harriet Smith). (*E* 220)

Occasionally such redundancy is put to deliberate literary effect in the narrative. At a crucial point in *Emma* the heroine's mingled confusion and gratification at Mr Knightley's 'unfinished gallantry' in taking and pressing her hand but not kissing it, is cleverly suggested by the confusion of construction here:

> And *whether* it was that his manners had in general so little gallantry, or *however* else it happened, *but* she thought nothing became him more. (*E* 386)

Jane Austen freely omits the conjunction *that* introducing noun clauses. This, of course, is regular modern usage; but we should perhaps hesitate to omit it in instances like the following, where the clause is introduced by a circumlocution instead of a simple verb:

> It is a sign I was not there to take care of you. (*E* 295)
> It was a clear thing he was less in love than he had been. (*E* 316)
> I was in hopes you might have got some good news from town. (*PP* 301)

While we speak of an omitted conjunction here, because the term is difficult to avoid, historically there has been no omission. As Jespersen points out (*MEG* III, 2.31): 'Both *I think he is dead* and *I think that he is dead* are evolved out of original parataxis of two independent sentences: *I think: he is dead* and *I think that: he is dead'*.

It is equally wrong to think of 'omission' in any historical sense in the following type of sentence, where a noun clause is dependent on a noun or an adjective, and where, in consequence, for the last few centuries, and especially in the last hundred years, the tendency has been increasingly to include prepositions or particles like *as to* or *of* between the noun and a following clause. So far from being an omission of a preposition formerly included, the reverse is true: the further back we go in the language, the more common are sentences like the following, with no preposition:

All . . . ended . . . in praise of the Thrush, *conjectures how* she would be employed. (*MP* 375)
You know, Mrs. Weston, you and I must be *cautious how* we express ourselves. (*E* 296)
I came determined to know the truth; though *irresolute what* to do when it was known. (*SS* 210)
How they were all to be conveyed, he would have made a *difficulty* if he could. (*E* 108)

The last sentence, with its inversion of the clause and its governing noun, is a typically bold extension of normal grammatical usage.

Besides *that*, the conjunctions *how* and *if* very occasionally appear to introduce clauses as objects of verbs of saying; but certainly in the first instance below (Thomas, the manservant), and probably in the second (Mrs Jennings), substandard usage is indicated:

She said *how* she was very well. (*SS* 355)
I declare *if* she is not gone away without finishing the wine! (*SS* 194)

The occurrence of a noun clause object after the verb *like* is now rare in standard English, according to the *NED*. We prefer some kind of noun and infinitive construction. In the novels this earlier usage is sometimes found:

William did not like she should come away. (*MP* 16)
I do not like, William, that you should leave . . . without this indulgence. (*MP* 252)
I can only imagine that Mr D. prizes any Picture of her too much to like it should be exposed to the public eye. (*L* 80, p. 312)

When the verb *consider* takes a double object, the conjunction *as* is usually included before the second, where it would not now be thought necessary. Sometimes *as* is included before a noun clause in such constructions. This is hardly possible today:

> She could not but *consider* it *as* absolutely *unnecessary*. (*MP* 36)

Alongside the rarer, but more modern:

> As to its being *considered necessary*. (*MP* 36)
> They *consider* it (the American War) *as* certain, and *as* what is to ruin us. (*L* 99.1, p. 508)
> His situation is an evil – but you must *consider* it *as* what satisfies your friend. (*E* 472)

Grammatical Conversion

Jane Austen shows great freedom, and even daring, in her conversion and use of almost any part of speech as any other part of speech. Shakespeare was the precursor to whom she might look in this; Shakespeare whose writings, in the words of Henry Crawford (*MP* 338), are 'part of an Englishman's constitution'. At least two of her conversions emanate from *Hamlet:*

> Ever since her being turned into a Churchill she has *out-Churchill'd* them all in high and mighty claims. (*E* 310)

Hamlet's *out-Herods Herod* is of course echoed; and an even more famous passage here:

> How many times have we mourned over the dead body of Julius Caesar, and *to be'd and not to be'd*, in this very room. (*MP* 126)

Various other bold transformations occur: conversions into verbs from common and abstract nouns, from adjectives and adverbs, even from proper names:

> Her being handsomely *legacied* hereafter. (*NA* 245)
> He is *calomeling* & therefore in a way to be better. (*L* 111, p. 425)
> She would hesitate, she would teaze, she would *condition*. (*MP* 417)
> To be going so soon . . . seemed to *distance* every pain. (*MP* 443)

Anne haggard, Mary coarse, every face in the neighbourhood *worsting*. (*P* 6)
I was in the greatest fright . . . lest she should *out* with it all (Lucy Steele). (*SS* 133)
Let me not suppose that she dares go about, *Emma Woodhouse-ing* me. (*E* 284)

Nouns, also, are manufactured at will from other parts of speech. Even a clause or a phrase can be preceded by an article and function as a noun:

After a civil reception, a short sentence about being waited for, and a '*Let Sir Thomas know*,' to the servant. (*MP* 298)
With . . . no confidence in her own taste – the '*how she should be dressed*' was a point of painful solicitude. (*MP* 254)
She was so busy . . . in talking and listening, and forming all these schemes in the *in-betweens*. (*E* 24)

This is the first *NED* quotation for *in-betweens*. Her coinage apparently caught on; even more so, apparently, *grown-ups*, an indispensable word nowadays, and one first illustrated in the *NED* from her writing:

They bring Isabella & one of the *Grown ups*. (*L* 90, p. 369)

With which we can compare this quotation from *Persuasion*:

There was a numerous family; but the only two *grown up* . . . were Henrietta and Louisa. (*P* 40)

Exclamations and interjections, also, are made into nouns, as are adverbs like *always* and *tomorrow*, relative pronouns and relative adverbs like *which, how* and *where*, and prepositions like *for, against* and *under*:

I could not pay Mr. Herington! That was the only *alas !* of the business. (*L* 92, p. 376)
Unconscious of the . . . change of countenance, the fidget, the *hem !* of unquietness. (*MP* 185)
'You are always kind.'
There was no bearing such an '*always*'. (*E* 380)
A very few *tomorrows* stood between the young people . . . and happiness. (*E* 318)

H

Henry is indifferent as to *the which*. (*L* 80, p. 312)
Wanting to hear . . . all *the wheres* and *hows* of a circumstance which highly entertained her. (*E* 351)
I was privy to all *the fors* and *againsts*. (*P* 200)
Frank and Mary are to have Mary Goodchild to help as *Under*[1] till they can get a cook. (*L* 97, p. 392)

Adjectives are also converted freely into nouns. That they are fully nouns is shown when they can take a plural suffix. We can see an intermediate stage if we compare the use of *agreeable* in the first quotation following with *disagreeables* in the second:

All the *agreeable* of her speculation. (*MP* 248)
The preparing and the going abroad in such weather . . . were *disagreeables* . . . which Mr. John Knightley did not like. (*E* 113)

A very common expression is *the chief*, meaning 'the main part':

The chief of the party were now collected. (*MP* 249)
Never satisfied with the day unless she spent *the chief* of it by the side of Mrs. Thorpe. (*NA* 36)

Other interesting conversions of adjectives to nouns are the following:

We saw nobody but our *Precious*. (*L* 118, p. 441)
(Music) is *a necessary* of life to me (Mrs Elton). (*E* 276)
His own two thousand pounds . . . should be his *all*. (*SS* 267)
One accompaniment to her song took her agreeably by surprize – a *second* (i.e. an underpart in harmony), slightly but correctly taken by Frank Churchill. (*E* 227)
I do not think we have had an Heiress here, or even a *Co* – since Sanditon has been a public place. (*MW* 401)

With this last can be compared Mary Crawford's indelicate pun, apropos of her upbringing among high-ranking naval officers:

Of *Rears*, and *Vices* I saw enough. (*MP* 60)

[1]i.e. as an under-servant, presumably in the kitchen, without the full rank of cook. Cf. Barrie's *The Admirable Crichton* (Act I):
A *tweeny*, that is to say my lady, she is not at present, strictly anything; a *between* maid; it is she . . . who conveys the dishes from one end of the kitchen table . . . to the other end.

Nouns are freely used attributively as adjuncts; sometimes where we should prefer a noun in the genitive or an adjectival suffix. Thus in the novels we find *bridemaids* (*MP* 203) and *bride-people* (*E* 6) – i.e. wedding guests on the bride's side; *a navy officer* (*MP* 400), beside *naval fervour* (*P* 167); *the pic-nic parade of the Eltons* (*E* 352); *a tête-à-tête drive* (*E* 129); and the rather frequent phrase *in an under voice* (*MP* 192), for which we might now substitute the Italian equivalent *sotto voce*.

Nouns are quite commonly formed from verbs. Particularly characteristic are compound nouns formed from the conversion of phrasal verbs. Of course, not all Jane Austen's examples are original to her; but it is typical of her to use such colloquially inspired constructions freely, and to add to their number occasionally:

> There would be a general *cry-out* upon her extreme good luck (first *NED* example). (*E* 61)
> 'There shall be cold meat in the house'.
> 'Well – as you please; only don't have a great *set out*' (second *NED* example). (*E* 355)
> I wish you had been there, my dear, to have given him one of your *set downs*. (*PP* 13)
> The whole of his *Break-off* with Lady H. is very well done. (*L* 98, p. 395)
> I know so many . . . who have found themselves entirely deceived . . . What is this, but a *take in?* (*MP* 46)
> She would be (happy) but that she thinks there will be another *put-off*. (*E* 120)
> That was the *wind-up* of the history; that was the glory of Miss Hawkins. (*E* 183)
> The pleasure of coming in upon one's friends before the *look-out* begins. (*E* 190)

No-one will need reminding that such conversions are also characteristic of recent, and particularly trans-Atlantic, usage: the *brush-off*, the *try-out*, the *run-around*, etc.

Allied to grammatical conversion is the formation of agent-nouns from verbs by the addition of an *-er* suffix. While this process is in theory possible with every verb, wherever the idea of agency occurs, in practice not every writer feels as free as she evidently did to form these nouns at will. She has: 'a very liberal *thanker*' (*E* 447); 'He is no *complimenter*' (*E* 464); 'the principal *arranger* of the plan' (*P* 86); 'a *gainer* (*E* 11);

'She looks like a rejected *addresser*' (i.e. suitor, L 75, p. 294); and so on. Moreover, the reference is not invariably to a person:

> To die . . . is equally to be recommended as a *clearer* of ill-fame. (*E* 387)
> The recollection of what had been done for William was always the most powerful *disturber* of every decision against Mr Crawford. (*MP* 364)

Direct and Indirect Speech

It is usual to say that conversation is represented in writing in two ways: by citing the exact words, with the concomitant quotes, question marks and so on; that is, by direct speech; or by as it were straining what is to be said through the mind of the narrator, so that the tenses and pronouns are transformed, and the idioms and characteristics of the original, so far as they are colloquial, are lost. Then the special marks of punctuation to represent conversation are dispensed with, and the speech is said to be reported or indirect.

This two-fold division is an arbitrary one, and in fact an oversimplification. It is possible, and with Jane Austen it was almost usual, to vary and hybridize these two methods. Consider this passage from *Emma*:

> Mr Woodhouse was almost as much interested in the business as the girls, and tried very often to recollect something worth their putting in. 'So many clever riddles as there used to be when he was young – he wondered he could not remember them! but he hoped he should in time.' (*E* 70)

Is this direct or indirect speech? There are inverted commas, yet the tenses are converted from present to past (*can* becomes *could*, for example). The first person has become the third person, yet the accents are so unmistakably those of Mr Woodhouse that Jane Austen can be said to represent speech more than she is reporting it.

We have no word for this subtle blend of direct and indirect speech in English. For both the term used to describe it and for much discussion of the subject itself, we must refer to German.

Erlebte Rede 'experienced speech' is something we can constantly exemplify from the six novels, and a whole book on Jane Austen's varied techniques in representing speech has been published.[1]

A good example of this variety occurs in the second chapter of *Mansfield Park*. The ten-year-old Fanny Price is very miserable on first arriving at Mansfield, and her cousin Edmund Bertram tries to find out why:

'My dear little cousin,' said he with all the gentleness of an excellent nature, 'what can be the matter?' And sitting down by her, was at great pains to overcome her shame ... and persuade her to speak openly. 'Was she ill? or was any body angry with her? or had she quarrelled with Maria and Julia? or was she puzzled about any thing in her lesson that he could explain? Did she, in short, want any thing he could possibly get her, or do for her?' For a long while no answer could be obtained beyond a 'no, no – not at all – no, thank you;' but he still persevered, and no sooner had he begun to revert to her home, than her increased sobs explained to him where the grievance lay. He tried to console her.

'You are sorry to leave Mamma, my dear little Fanny,' said he. (*MP* 15)

Of the four passages in inverted commas here, only the first and the last are straightforward direct speech. The second passage is Edmund's own words, except that the tenses and pronouns are transmuted. The third passage ('no answer beyond a "no, no – not at all – no thank you"') illustrates another favourite device: the embedding of a small bit of direct speech into the structure of a narrative sentence, treating it, by a typical grammatical conversion, as if it were a unit, a single part of speech. Here are some more examples:

A pleasant 'thank you' seemed meant to laugh it off. (*E* 294)
'Miss Price all alone!' and 'My dear Fanny, how comes this?' were the first salutations. (*MP* 97)
In looking back after Edmund ... they were united, and a 'there he is' broke at the same moment from them both. (*MP* 81)

[1]W. Buhler *Die 'Erlebte Rede' im englischen Roman. Ihre Vorstufen und ihre Ausbildung im Werke Jane Austens.*

Such varied techniques demand a certain adroitness in the reader. Jane Austen recognized this. On reading through *Pride and Prejudice* just after it had been published, she wrote to Cassandra:

> There are a few typical errors; and a 'said he' or a 'said she' would sometimes make the dialogue more immediately clear; but
>   I do not write for such dull elves
>   As have not a good deal of ingenuity themselves. (*L* 76, p. 298)

Certain specific effects could be obtained by *erlebte Rede*. One of the most notable is that of distance and formality. General Tilney, for example, in *Northanger Abbey*, is a rather sinister, formidable man, whose presence imposes restraint not only on his young visitor, Catherine Morland, but also on his own family and household. In this next passage Catherine is being shown over the Abbey by him, and she is more interested in its ancient remains than in its modern conveniences. We may note how gradually in the narrative the General's accents are heard, though nothing is explicitly stated as to his speaking, and there are no inverted commas; as he proceeds, we feel how his dignified politeness, which only half masks an autocratic temperament, constrains Catherine and prevents her investigating as she would wish to. The effect could not be gained by direct speech. The words 'but if he had a vanity', mark the beginning of *erlebte Rede*:

> The new building was not only new, but declared itself to be so; intended only for offices, and enclosed behind by stableyards, no uniformity of architecture had been thought necessary. Catherine could have raved at the hand which had swept away what must have been beyond the value of all the rest, for the purposes of mere domestic economy; and would willingly have been spared the mortification of a walk through scenes so fallen, had the General allowed it; but if he had a vanity, it was in the arrangement of his offices; and as he was convinced, that, to a mind like Miss Morland's, a view of the accommodations and comforts, by which the labours of her inferiors were softened, must always be gratifying, he should make no apology for leading her on. (*NA* 184)

One more example, one of the cleverest, must suffice. Unlike the last, this passage uses inverted commas; but it is still *erlebte Rede* rather than direct speech, for the tenses are converted. Here Jane Fairfax is at her most 'disgustingly' reserved. Emma is asking the questions, fruitlessly. Finally the questions are dispensed with, and the sum total of information that Jane will give is placed together, in all its non-committal meagreness:

> She and Mr. Frank Churchill had been at Weymouth at the same time. It was known that they were a little acquainted; but not a syllable of information could Emma procure as to what he truly was. 'Was he handsome?' 'She believed he was reckoned a very fine young man.' 'Was he agreeable?' 'He was generally thought so.' 'Did he appear a sensible young man; a young man of information?' – 'At a watering-place, or in a common London acquaintance, it was difficult to decide on such points. Manners were all that could be safely judged of, under a much longer knowledge than they had yet had of Mr. Churchill. She believed everybody found his manners pleasing.' Emma could not forgive her. (*E* 169)

MODES OF ADDRESS

Modes of address are a good deal more formal in the novels than they are today; and the dispensing with formality by characters in the novels is generally considered reprehensible. For instance, the only person in *Emma* regularly to call Mr Knightley by his Christian name is his brother John (*E* 99). Indeed, when Emma is betrothed at the end of the book she is still uncertain what to call him:

> ' "Mr. Knightley." – You always called me, "Mr. Knightley;" and, from habit, it has not so formal a sound. – And yet it is formal. I want you to call me something else, but I do not know what.'
> 'I remember once calling you "George", in one of my amiable fits, about ten years ago. I did it because I thought it would offend you; but, as you made no objection, I never did it again.'
> 'And cannot you call me "George" now?'
> 'Impossible!' (*E* 462)

The chief person to give offence by a cavalier dismissal of titles is Mrs Elton. Her use of the surname alone, *Knightley*, is a final proof, for Emma, of her vulgarity:

> Insufferable woman! . . . Knightley! never seen him in her life before, and call him Knightley! (*E* 279)

Informality and disrespect in these matters is not countenanced. Even Catherine Morland, young and inexperienced though she may be, can snub John Thorpe for this:

> 'Old Allen is as rich as a Jew – is not he?'
> 'Oh! Mr. Allen, you mean'. (*NA* 63)

Over-formality does occur, however, occasionally, as when the punctilious Sir Walter Elliot refers to his daughters, and even addresses them, as *Miss Elliot* and *Miss Anne Elliot* (*P* 18,

157). This is the usage of the elderly: 'She could see nothing worse in Lady Denham, than the sort of oldfashioned formality of always calling her (her ward) *Miss Clara*' (*MW 392*).

It is Mrs Elton's free use of Christian names that incenses Frank Churchill. Though engaged to Jane Fairfax, he himself does not presume so far as to use her Christian name:

> That officious Mrs. Elton . . . 'Jane,' indeed! – You will observe that I have not yet indulged myself in calling her by that name. (*E* 441) (See also *E* 324)

Even worse, Mrs Elton uses both Christian name and surname with no prefix:

> 'Jane Fairfax and Jane Fairfax.' Heavens! Let me not suppose that she dares go about Emma Woodhouse-ing me! (*E* 284)

Contrast this with Mrs Weston, who is not on Christian name terms even with her step-son's fiancée:

> 'It is Frank and Miss Fairfax,' said Mrs. Weston. (*E* 476)

Emma herself is a stickler in such matters. Miss Taylor has been her governess, and on marrying is still referred to by her with formality, as *My dear Mrs Weston* (E 225). The reply is *My dear Emma*. In Emma's own tutelary relationship with Harriet Smith, Harriet addresses Emma as *Miss Woodhouse* (*E* 406) and the reply is *My dear Harriet*.

A convenient half-way stage towards informality, for ladies, as Dr Chapman points out in the appendix on modes of address in his edition of *Pride and Prejudice* (pp. 409–412), was the use of *Miss* with the Christian name. This was not old-fashioned or over-formal when the person in question was outside the immediate family circle. Thus Mrs Musgrove addresses Anne Elliot, her daughter-in-law's sister, as *Miss Anne* (*P* 44). This was a form of address that was evidently acceptable to Jane Austen herself, as we see from this passage in one of her letters, where she is praising the speaker's affability, not, I think, laughing at him for being 'easy':

> Bickerton . . . a very sweet boy . . . I have never seen Bickerton without his immediately enquiring whether I had heard from you – from '*Miss Cassandra*', was his expression at first. (*L* 44, p. 156)

The eldest sister in the family had the right to be known as *Miss* followed by the surname alone. Thus *Miss Steele* is Anne Steele, the elder sister, as distinct from *Miss Lucy Steele* or *Miss Lucy*. Similarly *Miss Bennet* always refers to the eldest daughter, Jane, if she is in the scene (*PP* 224), *Miss Dashwood* to Elinor (*SS* 72), and so on. On these grounds, objections have been raised to the donnish and dying habit of referring to Jane Austen herself as *Miss Austen*,[1] the objectors pointing out that she would never have been called by this title, since it would have been reserved for her older unmarried sister, Cassandra. The point is hardly worth contesting, but in fact those people – Otto Jespersen, for example – who refer to *Miss Austen* can be justified from the novels. When the elder sister was not present, the custom was not observed. Elizabeth Bennet, at Rosings, for example, where there is no possibility of confusing her with Jane, is addressed and referred to as *Miss Bennet* (*PP* 176). Moreover, Jane Austen jocularly refers to herself as ' *'tother Miss Austen'*, in a letter (*L* 15, p. 45).

The distinction in this matter is nicely illustrated in an anecdote of Tom Bertram's:

> I afterwards found that I had been giving all my attention to the youngest, who was not out, and had most excessively offended the eldest. Miss Augusta ought not to have been noticed for the next six months, and Miss Sneyd, I believe, has never forgiven me. (*MP* 51)

The custom might also mean that few people knew the Christian name of the eldest daughter:

> Miss Wapshire – I wish I could be certain that her name were Emma; but her being the Eldest daughter leaves that circumstance doubtful. (*L* 28, p. 97)

With men the position was rather different, since there is no differentiation in mode of address between a married and an unmarried man. The senior member of the family had the right

---

[1] Most recently by Brigid Brophy in her notes to the Pan edition of *Pride and Prejudice*. She calls 'Miss Austen' a 'sad solecism'. Against this, however, we have the fact that Fanny Burney, not the eldest of Dr Burney's daughters, is addressed as *Miss Burney* by everybody from George III downwards.

to be styled *Mr* with no Christian name. Thus *Mr Frank Churchill* is necessarily distinguished from his uncle and guardian, *Mr Churchill*. In *Mansfield Park* the situation is different again, in that the head of the family is a baronet, Sir Thomas Bertram. The designation *Mr Bertram* therefore devolves upon the eldest son, Tom. Mary Crawford is glad when Tom is away and Edmund can be unambiguously referred to without the addition of his Christian name:

> My sister and Mr. Bertram – I am so glad your eldest cousin is gone that he may be Mr. Bertram again. There is something in the sound of Mr. Edmund Bertram so formal, so pitiful, so younger-brother-like. (*MP* 211)

Generally, the use of the Christian name by men to women seems to have marked at least an understanding of the kind leading to betrothal:

> In the whole of the sentence, in his manner of pronouncing it, and in his addressing her sister by her christian name alone, she instantly saw an intimacy so decided . . . as marked a perfect agreement between them. (*SS* 59)

This is Elinor Dashwood's observation of the relationship between Willoughby and her sister Marianne. Later, after his desertion of Marianne, Willoughby has the grace to hesitate over her Christian name:

> To obtain something like forgiveness from *Ma* – from your sister. (*SS* 319)

The next two instances are Henry Crawford paying his addresses, and his sister Mary supporting his suit with a like familiarity:

> Yes, dearest, sweetest *Fanny* – Nay – (seeing her draw back displeased) forgive me . . . but by what other name can I call you? . . . No it is 'Fanny' that I think of all day. (*MP* 344)
> My dear *Fanny*, for so I may call you, to the infinite relief of a tongue that has been stumbling at *Miss Price* for at least the last six weeks. (*MP* 303)

Members of the same sex were not on Christian name terms as quickly as they are today. It is a mark of her excessive approval of the Steeles that Mrs Dashwood was calling Lucy

by her Christian name so soon after their acquaintance (*SS* 254).
In her disapproval of informality, Jane Austen contrasts with her
great predecessor, Richardson. Sir Charles Grandison and his
sister Charlotte stand in a similar relationship to Harriet
Byron, heroine of *Sir Charles Grandison*, as Henry and Eleanor
Tilney do to their friend Catherine Morland, heroine of
Northanger Abbey. But this sort of conversation is unthinkable
in the latter book:

> 'And will you one day let me see what you write?'
> 'Most willingly, madam'.
> 'Madam!' interrupted she, 'So formal? Charlotte say!'
> 'With all my heart, my ever-amiable, my ever-kind Charlotte.'
> (*Sir Charles Grandison*, I, 291)

Men, too, used Christian names to one another far less than
they do now. Brothers called each other by Christian names,
but Mr Knightley and Mr Weston, though friends of long
acquaintance, address and refer to each other as *Knightley* and
Weston (*E* 36). Mr Woodhouse, with old-fashioned formality,
refers to his son-in-law as *Mr John Knightley* (*E* 103), to
distinguish him from his brother; he does not address or refer
to him as *John*. Similarly, Captain Wentworth refers, in her
presence, to *Mrs Charles Musgrove* (*P* 114) to avoid confusion
with the lady's mother-in-law.

Some abbreviations of Christian names were acceptable:
Lizzy (*PP* 113) and *Eliza* (*PP* 37) for Elizabeth Bennet;
Nancy for Anne Steele (*SS* 258). The name *Fanny* is itself an
affectionate form of *Frances*; but only the vulgar Mr Price
abbreviates his daughter's name to *Fan* (*MP* 439). What was
not acceptable in speech, though it was in writing, was the use
of *Mr* with an initial as an abbreviation of the surname. Even
today, this sounds vulgar. Here is Mrs Elton offending trebly
by using surnames for men she has not long known, reserving
Mr for her husband only, and abbreviating *Elton* to *E*:

> Weston and Cole will be there too; but one is apt to speak only of those
> who lead. – I fancy Mr. E. and Knightley have every thing their own
> way. (*E* 456)

However, surnames are abbreviated to initials in Jane Austen's
letters, and also occasionally in the letters of socially acceptable

characters in the novels. Frank Churchill writes of *Miss W.* (*E* 441), and seems to give no offence.

There is a tendency for some of the young ladies to refer to young men, often young men of their choice, by their surnames alone. Isabella Thorpe speaks of *Morland* (*NA* 119); Lydia Bennet of *Wickham* (*PP* 318); Mrs Dashwood (SS 77) and Marianne (SS 177) both refer to and address *Willoughby* with no formality. With Marianne, however, it is perhaps sensibility rather than good sense that is thus manifested. We recall Lydia Languish, of Sheridan's *The Rivals*, her head full of novel-reading, addressing her *beloved Beverley*. Lydia Bennet, Isabella Thorpe, and, in her unregenerate days, Marianne Dashwood, are all three in this over-romantic tradition. Certainly Marianne's older and wiser sister, Elinor, does not speak of *Ferrars*; nor does Elizabeth Bennet speak of *Darcy*, Fanny Price of *Bertram*, nor Anne Elliot of *Wentworth*.

Servants, male and female, in large households, were addressed by surname alone; a usage which survived well into this century. 'How has *Wright* done my hair?' asks Mrs Elton, fishing for compliments (*E* 324); and Lady Bertram attributes much of Fanny's good looks on the night of her ball to the fact that 'I sent *Chapman* to her' (*MP* 272). This was the usage of larger establishments, however; the Bates's maid-of-all-work is known by her Christian name of *Patty* (*E* 173). Similarly, while the butler at Mansfield is *Baddeley* (*MP* 180), the Dashwoods' only manservant is *Thomas* (*SS* 354).

The title *Esquire* was not the more or less meaningless (and sometimes ironic) alternative to *Mr* that it tends to be today. Sir Walter Elliot took pleasure in writing in his copy of the baronetage:

Heir presumptive, William Walter Elliot *Esq.* (*P* 4)

Esquire was the rightful designation of the landed gentleman who had no other title. Congratulating her nephew, James Edward Austen, on the occasion of his leaving school, Jane Austen writes:

One reason for my writing to you now, is that I may have the pleasure of directing to you *Esq.* – I give you Joy of having left Winchester. (*L* 134, p. 467)

It was not uncommon for husbands and wives to use *Mr* and *Mrs* when referring to each other, and in *Pride and Prejudice*, Mr and Mrs Bennet, and in *Sense and Sensibility*, Mr and Mrs Palmer address each other in this way: 'Impossible, Mr. Bennet' (*PP* 7); 'There, Mrs. Bennet' (*PP* 62); 'Don't you, Mr. Palmer?' (*SS* 113). This last is in an earlier tradition, not found, so far as I have observed, in the later novels. We can compare the usage of Mr and Mrs Hardcastle in *She Stoops to Conquer*.

Sons and daughters, even when grown up and married, addressed their parents frequently as *sir* and *ma'am* or *madam*. Fanny Price calls her not particularly venerable father, as well as her uncle Sir Thomas Bertram, *sir* (*MP* 439, 275). Frank Churchill is liberal with *sir* in conversation with his father, Mr Weston. Emma often addresses her father as *papa*, but occasionally as *sir* (*E* 280). Elizabeth Bennet also has *sir* when addressing her father, and with her mother, occasionally *mamma*, but more often *madam* (*PP* 99) or *ma'am* (*PP* 20). The middle-aged Miss Bates addresses her mother as *madam* (*E* 157); likewise Mrs John Dashwood, addressing her mother, Mrs Ferrars (*SS* 235). *Sir* and *ma'am* are indeed common forms of address among acquaintances, even when (perhaps particularly when) they are quarrelling:

'*Sir*, it is a moor park, we bought it as a moor park.'
'You were imposed on, *ma'am*.' (*MP* 54)

When remonstrating, there was, and still is, a tendency for people to be more formal, in a half ironic way:

Upon my word, *Miss Anne Elliot*, you have the most extraordinary taste! (*P* 157)
I tell you what, *Miss Lizzy*,... you will never get a husband. (*PP* 113)

Father and *mother* do not seem to occur as appellatives. Mr Darcy refers to *my father*, but also, more formally, to *Mr Darcy* (*PP* 200); and Julia Bertram announces Sir Thomas's sudden return from the West Indies with the words: '*My father* is come! He is in the hall at this moment' (*MP* 172). However, other relationships are underlined, in conversation, rather more than they are today. One remembers a remark in one of the letters: 'I like first Cousins to be first Cousins, & interested about each other. They are but one remove from (brother and sister)' (*L* 105, p. 415). Mrs Norris calls Lady Bertram *sister* (*MP* 167), and the Bertrams address her as *aunt* (*MP* 18). Edmund calls Fanny 'my dear little *cousin*' (*MP* 15), and she sometimes replies with *cousin* (*MP* 26). Quite frequently, an aunt or uncle may be distinguished by a surname completing the appellation – never a Christian name, so far as I have observed: *my aunt Norris* (*MP* 25); *my uncle Phillips* (*PP* 68). Mrs Bennet says '*my sister Phillips*' (*PP* 307).

One minor difference is that the -*in-law* suffix does not always refer, as nowadays, to the relations one acquires by marriage. This meaning does occur (*SS* 171, *NA* 206); but the words *mother-in-law* (*SS* 5, *E* 444) and *sister-in-law* (*SS* 222) also occur to indicate a step relationship, as with the Dashwoods, and Frank Churchill and Mrs Weston. More often than not the suffix -*in-law*, meaning the normal modern relationship by marriage, is omitted. 'Can it really be as my *brother* imagined,' Emma asks herself when warned by her brother-in-law that Mr Elton is aspiring to her hand (*E* 118).

The custom of one person referring to another in the third person and by name, as if that person were not present to be spoken or written to directly, occurs occasionally; 'always suspect' is Dr Craik's comment (*op. cit.* p. 175) on this practice. And certainly, in the first two examples below, an attempt at imposing one's will by slightly devious means is suggested. The other quotations seem harmless. 'The loss of a Fanny Knight' in the last sentence, refers to the prospect of her favourite niece changing her name by marriage:

Perhaps I may sometimes have felt that Harriet would not forget what was due – or rather what would be kind by me (Emma Woodhouse to Harriet Smith). (*E* 268)

It requires a gentlewoman – a Julia Bertram. You will undertake it I hope (Henry Crawford to Julia Bertram). (*MP* 135)
I was sometimes quite provoked, but then I recollected my dear Elizabeth and Jane, and for their sakes had patience with her (Mrs Gardiner in a letter to Elizabeth Bennet). (*PP* 325)
I do wish you to marry very much . . . but the loss of a Fanny Knight will be never made up to me. (*L* 140, p. 479)

It is curious, therefore, in view of instances of this kind, that she disapproves of this usage when her niece Anna Austen has it in one of her attempts at a novel:

> I do not like a Lover's speaking in the 3rd person; it is too much like the formal part of Lord Orville. (*L* 95, p. 387)

Lord Orville is a character in Fanny Burney's *Evelina* who has this trick of speech. There are not many examples of this usage in the novels, however. With Fanny Burney, as with Richardson and her other predecessors, Jane Austen takes what she needs without following to extremes. It is the peculiar triumph of the six novels that this moderation and propriety never preclude spontaneity or depth of feeling.

BIBLIOGRAPHY

I. Texts

Boswell, J. *The Life of Samuel Johnson, LL.D.*, ed. G. Birkbeck Hill. Oxford, 1934.

Burney, Fanny. *Evelina*, ed. E. A. Bloom. Oxford, 1968.
Diary and Letters of Madame d'Arblay (née Fanny Burney), ed. Charlotte Barrett. London, Macmillan, 1904–5.

Fielding, H. *Joseph Andrews* (Shakespeare Head edition). Oxford, 1926.
Tom Jones. The History of a Foundling (Shakespeare Head edition). Oxford, 1926.

Johnson, S. *The Lives of the English Poets*, ed. G. Birkbeck Hill. Oxford, 1905.

Richardson, S. *Pamela, or, Virtue Rewarded* (Shakespeare Head edition). Oxford, 1929.
The History of Sir Charles Grandison (Shakespeare Head edition). Oxford, 1931.

Verney Letters and Papers of the Eighteenth Century, ed. Lady Verney. London: Benn, 1930.

Wentworth Papers, The, 1705–1739, ed. J. J. Cartwright. London: Wyman, 1883.

II. General

Austen-Leigh, J. E. *A Memoir of Jane Austen, by her Nephew*, ed R. W. Chapman. Oxford, 1926.

Babb, H. B. *Jane Austen's Novels; the Fabric of Dialogue*. Ohio, 1962.

Bradbrook, F. W. *Jane Austen and her Predecessors*. Cambridge, 1966.

'Style and Judgment in Jane Austen's Novels' in *The Cambridge Journal* IV (1951), pp. 515–537.

Brophy, B. Notes to the Pan edition of *Pride and Prejudice*. London: Pan Books, 1967, pp. 290–311.

Buhler, W. *Die erlebte Rede im englischen Roman. Ihre Vorstufen und ihre Ausbildung im Werke Jane Austens.* Zürich and Leipzig, 1936.

Cecil, Lord David. *Poets and Story-tellers.* London: Constable, 1965.

Chapman, R. W. 'Names, Designations and Appellations', *SPE Tract* XLVII (1936).

Copley, J. *Shift of Meaning.* Oxford, 1961.

Craik, W. *Jane Austen: The Six Novels.* London: Methuen, 1965.

Jane Austen in her Time. London: Nelson, 1969.

D'Arcy, M. D. *Jane Austen's English,* unpublished BA dissertation. Liverpool, 1949.

Emma, R. D. *Milton's Grammar.* The Hague, 1964.

Empson, W. *The Structure of Complex Words.* London: Chatto and Windus, 1951.

Foster, B. *The Changing English Language.* London: Macmillan, 1968.

Fowler, H. W. *A Dictionary of Modern English Usage* (second edition revised by Sir Ernest Gowers). Oxford, 1965.

Garrod, H. W. 'Jane Austen: a Depreciation' in *Transactions of the Royal Society of Literature* VIII (1928), pp. 21–40.

Jespersen, O. *A Modern English Grammar,* vols. I–VII, Heidelberg, London and Copenhagen, 1922–1949.

Johnson, S. *A Dictionary of the English Language.* London, 1755.

Joos, M. *The English Verb.* Wisconsin, 1964.

Kaye-Smith, S. and Stern, G. B. *Talking of Jane Austen.* London: Cassell, 1943.

More Talk of Jane Austen. London: Cassell, 1950.

Laski, M. *Jane Austen and her World.* London: Thames and Hudson, 1969.

Lascelles, M. *Jane Austen and her Art.* Oxford, 1939.

Leonard, S. A. *The Doctrine of Correctness in English Usage 1700–1800.* New York, 1962.

Lewis, C. S. *Studies in Words.* Cambridge, 1960.

'A Note on Jane Austen' in *Essays in Criticism* IV (1954), pp. 359–371.

Lodge, D. *The Language of Fiction.* London: Routledge and Kegan Paul, 1966.

Lowth, R. *A Short Introduction to English Grammar*. London, 1762 (Facsimile reprint by the Scolar Press, 1967).

Murray, L. *English Grammar* (first London edition). London, 1805.

Mustanoja, T. F. *A Middle English Syntax*, part I. Helsinki, 1960.

New English Dictionary on Historical Principles, The ed. J. A. H. Murray, Henry Bradley, W. A. Craigie and C. T. Onions. Oxford, 1884–1928.

Onions, C. T. 'The English Language' in a symposium, ed. Sir Ernest Barker, on *The Character of England*, pp. 280–302. Oxford, 1947.

Page, N. 'Standards of Excellence: Jane Austen's Language' in *Review of English Literature*, VII, iii (1966), pp. 91–98.

Palmer, F. R. *A Linguistic Study of the English Verb*. London: Longmans, 1965.

Phillipps, K. C. 'Lucy Steele's English' in *English Studies* Anglo-American Supplement (1969), pp. lv–lxi.
'Jane Austen's English' in *Neuphilologische Mitteilungen* LXX (1969), pp. 319–338.

Piozzi, H. L. (Mrs Piozzi, formerly Mrs Thrale). *British Synonymy, or an Attempt at Regulating the Choice of Words in Familiar Conversation*. London, 1794 (Facsimile reprint by the Scolar Press, 1969).

Platt, J. 'The Development of English Colloquial Idiom during the Eighteenth Century' in *Review of English Studies* II (1926), pp. 70–81, 189–196.

Potter, S. *Changing English*. London: Deutsch, 1969.

Quiller-Couch, A. *On the Art of Writing*. Cambridge, 1916.

Raybould, E. 'Of Jane Austen's Use of Expanded Verbal Forms' in *Studies in English Language and Literature presented to Professor Karl Brunner*, pp. 175–190. Vienna, 1957.

Ryle, G. 'Jane Austen and the Moralists' in *Critical Essays on Jane Austen*, pp. 106–122, ed. R. B. Southam. London: Routledge and Kegan Paul, 1968.

Schorer, M. 'Fiction and the Matrix of Analogy' in *Kenyon Review* XL (1949), pp. 539–560.

Stoffel, C. *Intensives and Down-toners*. Heidelberg, 1901.

Strang, B. *Modern English Structure* (second edition). London: Arnold, 1968.

Sweet, H. *A New English Grammar, Logical and Historical*, parts I and II. Oxford, 1892–8.

Tucker, A. E. H. 'Religion in Jane Austen's Novels' in *Theology* LV (1952), pp. 260–265.

Tucker, S. *Protean Shape*. London: Athlone Press, 1967.

Uhrström, W. *Studies on the Language of Samuel Richardson*. Uppsala, 1907.

Vallins, G. H. *The Pattern of English*. London: Deutsch, 1956.

Visser, F. Th. *An Historical Syntax of the English Language*, parts I–III. Leiden, 1963–9.

Williamson, M. 'Colloquial Language of the Commonwealth and Restoration'. *Pamphlets of the English Association* LXXIII (1929).

Wright, A. H. *Jane Austen's Novels: a Study in Structure*. London: Chatto and Windus, 1953.

Wright, J. *The English Dialect Dictionary*. Oxford, 1898–1905.

Wyld, H. C. K. *A History of Modern Colloquial English*. Oxford, 1936.

SUBJECT INDEX

Abstract noun: words used less concretely than today, 62–5; and *vice versa*, 66–7; in plural, 161; with indefinite article, 161–2; used where concrete nouns now normal, 162

Address: use of *sir, madam*, etc., 214; mention of kinship in, 214–15; use of third person in direct, 215–16. See also Proper names.

Adjective: comparison of, 176; postposition of, 177–8; as adverbs, 178–81; as adverbs of degree, 180; conversion into verbs and nouns, 200–2

Adverb: inversion after, 120, 130; adjective form as, 178–81; intensifying, 181–2; negative, 185–6; now replaced by phrase, 184; conversion into verbs and nouns, 200–2

Adverb phrase: and omitted prepositions, 186–8; position of, 188–9; reference to past and future, 189

Agent nouns in *-er*, 203–4

Americanisms, foreshadowings of, 106–7

Aspect, verbal: and expanded tenses, 111–17

Auxiliary verb: and past tenses, 109–10; and emphasis, 119–20; expression of possibility by, 120–2; expression of compulsion by, 122–4, 137–40; future, 125–6; conditional, 127–30; and inversion, 120–1, 130

Boswell, James, 36, 54, 106, 138, 143
Burney, Fanny, 13, 63, 85, 89, 95, 110, 112, 118, 132, 142, 174, 175, 177, 183, 210, 216
Byron, Lord, 106

Chesterfield, Lord, 61, 181, 186
Christian names: used too familiarly, 211–12; abbreviation of, 212–13
Colloquialisms, 20–1
Complement, replaced by adverb, 183–4
Compulsion, expressions of, 123, 138
Concord, faulty, 157–9
Condition, inversion to express, 130
Conjunction: omission of, 198–9; vulgar usage with, 197, 199; additional, 198–200
Conversion, grammatical, 107, 200–4
Cowper, William, 91, 167, 197

Definite article: in place of possessive, 168–9; idealizing, 173; and names of diseases, 174; where now omitted, 174
Demonstrative pronoun, 169
Derivatives, unusual, 107
Direct and indirect speech: and auxiliaries, 127; varied techniques in, 204–7. See also Erlebte Rede
Domestic vocabulary, 98–100
Double entendre in vocabulary, 70–1

Erlebte Rede: and auxiliaries, 127, 138; to suggest constraint, 206–7
Etymology, meanings nearer the, 33–7
Euphemism, 82–3
Expanded tenses: frequency of, 111–12; and expression of emotion, 112–13; confused with predicative participles, 113–14; no passive form of, 114–15; expanded present participle, 115; absence where now usual, 116

Fielding, Henry, 13, 40, 81, 98, 161
Financial metaphors, 65–6
Forcefulness, words with less and more, 23–5
French: influence on vocabulary, 21–2; on syntax, 177, 189; resistance to French influence, 164

Game laws, vocabulary of, 97–8
Genitive: inflected and phrasal, 162–3; objective, 163; and expressions of time, 163; double, 163–4; group, 164; elliptical partitive, 164
Gerund: alternative forms of, 131; prefixed with *a–*, 132; frequency of, 132, 134–5; in plural, 132–3; passive form, 134; with possessive, 146; where infinitive now usual, 134
Gilpin, William, and the vocabulary of the 'picturesque', 90–3
Goldsmith, Oliver, 180, 214
Grammarians, 13–14, 125, 146, 154–5, 176

Impersonal constructions, preference for, 168
Indefinite article: and abstract nouns, 161–2; and indefinite pronouns, 172; and proper names, 173; familiar omission of, 174–5; idiomatic omission of, 175–6

Indefinite pronoun: and article, 172; as adverb, 182
Indicative mood, for subjunctive, 157
Infinitive: exclamatory, 135; accusative and, 135–6; where gerund now usual, 136–7; attributive, 140; wider implications of, 140–1; consecutive, 141; perfect, 142; omission of, 142–3; latent, 143. See also *to be to* construction
Interrogative, with and without *do*, 118
Interrogative pronoun, 172
Inversion: after adverb, 120–1, 130; conditional, 130; absence of where now usual, 130
Italian, 20–1, 203

Johnson, Dr Samuel, 17, 26, 33, 36, 38, 39, 54, 56, 62, 100, 106, 127, 138, 155, 160, 174

Key words, 55–9

Latinate words, 86–8
Letter-writing, 101–2
Lowth, Robert, grammarian, 125, 131, 141, 146, 151

Matchmaking, vocabulary of, 74–83
Medicine, 100–1
Misleading words, 40–44, 184, 188–9
Murray, Lindley, grammarian, 142, 144, 149, 151, 173

Narrow horizons, reflected in vocabulary, 88–90
Navy, the, 53, 97
Negative: with and without *do*, 117–18; negative adverb, contracted and uncontracted forms, 185; double and multiple negative, 186; *nay*, 186
Neologisms, 103–4
Noun: with no plural inflection. 159–60; plural inflection where none now usual, 161; conversion into verbs, 200–1; freely used as adjuncts, 203. See also Abstract noun

Passive voice: and expanded tenses, 114–15; and gerund, 134; frequency of, 147–52; and retained object, 149; and preposition at end, 151–2
Past participle: confusion of forms with past tense, 146–7; used loosely, 147
Pejorative meanings, 25–30
Perfect tense: resultative, 109; of experience, 109
Personal pronoun: omission of, 164–5; redundant, 165; replaced by *it*, 166; used virtually as noun, 166–7; subject

and object forms, 166–7; avoidance by impersonal phrase, 168
Personal qualities, vocabulary of, 78–81
Phrasal verb: frequency of, 71–4; conversion into nouns, 203
Piozzi, Mrs, formerly Mrs Thrale, 52, 132
Possessive adjective: avoidance by use of definite article, 168–9; argumentative-indefinite *your*, 167–8
Preposition: at end, 151–2; elision of, between verb and object, 152–3; omission with adverb phrases, 186–8; with compressed meaning, 191–2; introducing predicative phrase, 193; conversion into nouns, 202
Present participle: parenthetic use of, 144; and punctuation, 144; used loosely, 144–5; no passive form of, 145; frequent use attributively, 146; with redundant personal pronoun, 146
Present tense: dispositional present, 108–9; for past, vulgar use of, 109
Proper names: and indefinite article, 173; conversion into verbs, 201; and omission of *Mr.* etc., 212; abbreviated to initial, 212–13; usage with servants, 213
Punctuation, 144

Rank, preoccupation with, reflected in vocabulary, 93–7
Relative adverb: use in abstract contexts, 183; conversion into nouns, 202
Relative pronoun: *which* and *that* compared, 169–70; referring to preceding genitive, 170–1; vulgar usage with, 171–2; conversion into nouns, 201–2
Richardson, Samuel, 39, 45, 60, 69, 71, 72, 74, 82, 87–8, 95, 143, 159, 160, 183, 196, 212

Scott, Sir Walter, 64, 104
Shakespeare, William, 29, 67, 94, 119, 140, 166, 171, 192, 200
Sheridan, Richard Brinsley, 180, 213
Social intercourse, vocabulary of, 83–6
Step relationship, expression of, 215
Subjunctive mood: in main clauses, 154–6; in subordinate clauses, 156–7; indicative in place of, 157

To be to construction: with fewer compulsive overtones, 138; and present participle, 139; future tense of, 139; negative form of, 139–40

Trade names, 102–3
Transitive and intransitive verbs: different from modern usage, 49–50; and elision of preposition, 152–3; and omission of object, 153–4; *it* added to normally intransitive verb, 166

Verney Memoirs, The, 14, 116, 145

Vulgar usage, 17–19, 20–1, 23, 32, 67, 81, 89, 104–6, 109, 145, 146–7, 157, 158–9, 165, 167, 171–2, 178–81, 187, 190, 195, 196, 197, 199, 208–13

Weather, vocabulary of the, 100
Wentworth Papers, The, 14, 155
Wider meaning of abstract nouns, 44–8, 75
Wordsworth, William, 120, 123

WORD INDEX

a, 175–6
a–, *as in* a–shooting, 133
abroad, 88
accent, 85
accommodation, 70
account, 65
accustomary, 107
acquaintance, 160
acquit, 49
act, *v*, 35
addition, 69
address, 77–8
addresses, 78
admire, 32
admit, 68
advancement, 66
after, 190
against, 190, 197
aggravate, 51
agree, 154
agreeable, 202
air, 78
al–fresco, 21
alliance, 77
allow, 68–9
ally, *v*, 77
altogether, 44
amiable, 25
amount, 65
a'nt, 185
apothecary, 101
apparent, 43
appearance, 95
apply, 49
appointment, 58
arrear, 65
article, 69
as, 141, 171, 200
ascertain, 33–4
assiduous, 31
at, 190–1
at all events, 177, 189
at present, 177, 189
attach, 74–5
attorney, 107

backwards, 184
beau, 19
beauty, 162, 193
before, 184
blameable, 107
bloom, 80
bones, make any, 20

bore, *n*, 21
branch, 67–8
break–off, 203
break through, 72
breed, *v*, 20
bring in, 72
Broadwood, 103
broke, 147
burst, *n*, 63
business, 50
but however, 12, 197
but only, 198
but what, 171
buzz, *n*, 83
by, 191
by no means, 119

candid, 26–7
candour, 26–7
canvass, 34
cap, setting one's – at, 21
capable, 93
capital, *a*, 89–90
cards, on the, 195
caro sposo, 21
catch, on the, 20
character, 42, 48
chat, 25–6
cheek–glowing, 133
chief, the, 202
closet, 30
collect, 69
come across, 72
come-at-able, 103
come into, 72
come to, 72
comfort, *n*, 47
comfortable, 47
common sense, 50
complacency, 13, 27, 38
complaisance, 13, 87
complicate, *a*, 107
compliment, 31–2
comprehend, 44
con amore, 22
condition, *v*, 200
connect, 77
connection, 77
conscious, 82
consciousness, 70, 82
consequence, 94
consider, 200
Constantia wine, 102

consult, 154
continue, 49
conversation, 83
conversible, 83
cottage ornèe, 21
countenance, 79
country, 88
couple, 159–60
course, 66
coze, 103
crop, 102
cross, v, 64
cross a letter, to, 102
cry-out, 203
cut up, 73

deedily, 104
degree, to a, in a, 23
delicacy, 53
depend, 154
deputation, 97–8
detach, 76
determine, 48
develop, 41
development, 41–2
direction, 78
dirty, 100
disagreeables, 202
discontent, 27
discourse, 83
discover, 35–6
disengagement, 76
disgusting, 22
disinterested, 51
dismission, 107
distance, second, 92
distinction, 81
distinguish, 81
do, 117–21
dog-tired, 21
don't, 185–6
draw in, 74
dress, v, 98–9
druggist, 106–7

ease, 52, 79
easy, 79, 209
eclat, 32
elegance, 51–3, 79
elocution, 48
embodied, 97
emergence, 13, 48
Emma Woodhouse-ing, 201
encroach, 154
enough, the outside of, 21
engage, 74–6
enthusiasm, 56–7
envelope, n, 101
esquire, 213
essay, n, 35

establish, 42
establishment, 77
even, to write, 179
event, 34–5
every way, 187–8
evil, 22
except, conj., 197
expensive, 31
experimental, 36
explore, 24
expose, 23–4

fact, 35
fag, 21
fail, 134
famous, 89
felicity, 87
female, 29–30
fine, 80
fish, 99
fix, 76, 154
floated, 100
for, 192
for ever, 188–9
forgot, 147
for that, 197
fortune, man, woman of, 94
forwards, 184
frank, 101
fresh arrange, 180
from, 192
fuss with, make a, 196

genius, 24–5
genteel, 26, 52, 59
glow, n, 80
governess-trade, 76
Gowland, 103
grateful, 13, 48
great, 29
grown-ups, 103, 201
guess, I, 106

half-gentlemen, 93
half, not above, 21
hand, 75
handsome, 80
have, 107, 139
he, 166–7
hem!, 201
here, 183
high, 67
hobby horse, 99
honeysuckles, 161
hop, n, 21
hopeless, 50
hopes, be in, 193
horrid, 18–19
how, 199
how do you do? 121, 167

however, 12, 190

ice, 176
idea, 12, 36–7
if, 199
illaudible, 107
illegitimacy, 82
illiberal, 54
imaginist, 103
immethodical, 107
improvements, 93
improver, 93
in, 192–3
in-betweens, 103, 201
in comparison of, 194
induce, 49
indulge, 28
infer, 51
influence, 154
in for, to be, 19
in liquor, to be, 193
inmate, 29
insensible, 40
in spirits, to be, 193
intelligence, 86
interest, 96, 153
interested, 97
in the way, 189
invalides, 21
irritable, 27–8
irritation, 27–8
it, 166

jib, v, 104

kind, 160

lady, 105
lay out, 71
lay out for, 71
liberal, 53–4
light, 66
like, v, 199
line, 106
liveable, 83
look, 183–4
look off, 74
lounge, 43
love-child, 83

mad for, to be, 21
made, to be, 97
manners, 61, 96
may, v, 121–2
me, it is, 167
measures, 48
menus plaisirs, 22
mighty delightful, 180
mind, 13, 52, 59–62

Miss Austen, 210
mizzle, 103
monstrous pretty, 180
moor park, a, 102
mother-in-law, 215
muffin, 160
must, 122–4
must have, 123–4

narrow-minded, 54
natural daughter, 82
nay, 186
neither, 159
nice, 18
nidgetty, 104
none, 159
noonshine, 100
notice, 84–5
novel-slang, 19
nuncheon, 100

object, n, 30
of, 193–4
of an evening, 105, 194
of course, 188
of her age, 193
on her, have a complaint, 105, 195
one, 128
open, a, 79
open on, 73
open weather, 100
oppress, 23

pair, 160
partial, 50, 105
participate, 50
particular, 31
parts, 86
party, 106
peculiar, 30
penetrate, 67
person, 60, 79
personal, 79–80
pewter, 19
piano, 21
picturesque, 90–3
pitiful, 32
place, n, 95–6
place, v, 64, 95
planning, 71
pop off, 20
position, 46
powers, 86
precise, 54
pretty, 80–1
prevent, 34
private man, 94
prodigious handsome, 180
propriety, 55
prospect, 91

public, *n*, 94–5
puppy, 86
purport, 48
push, 63
put forward, 73
put-off, 203
putrid, 100–1
put to, 72

qualification, 48, 97–8
quality, 93
quit, 106
quite, 42–3
quiz, 85–6
race, 89
rate, 32–3

rational, 13, 55–6
rattle, 85
receipt, 48
receive, 68
recover, 49, 153
regard, *n*, 25, 70
regard, *v*, 66
remark, *n*, 84
representative, *n*, 94
repulsive, 23
respectable, 26, 59
rest, *n*, 20
revolt, 154
revolve, 67
ridicule, 99–100
ring up, 73
rout-cakes, 99
Rumford, 102

scheme, 28
second, *n*, 202
secure, 33
self-complacency, 27
se'nnight, 100
sensation, 87–8
sense, 37–40
sensibility, 37–40
sensible, 39–40
series, 160–61
serious, 57–8
set out, 203
seven shillings, 98
shall, 125–6
she, 167
should, 127–30
side-screens, 91–2
sink, 63
sit down, 73
situation, 45
sly, 28
so as, 197
solicitude, 87

solid, 26, 58
something the same, 105, 182
somewhat, 182
sort, 160
so that, 197
spars, 99
speak, 64
speak for, 73
speculation, 70
spencer, 103
spunge, 20
stab, 64
stand up, 73
start, 84
stout, 67
stretch, *n*, 64
strong, 47
succeed, 66–7
successless, 103
suffer, 24
superior, 59
support, 59
sure, *adv*, 180–1
surgeon, 101
sweep, *n*, 103–4

take, 153
take-in, 203
taste, *n*, 160
tax, *n*, 65
tea, dish of, 98
tea, drink, take one's, 98
tea-board, 98
tea-visit, 153
tease, 25
tenacious, 95
that, *rel*, 169–70
the, 172–4, 177
there, 135, 168, 183
this, 169
tittuppy, 104
toast, 161
to a certainty, precision *etc*, 195
to be to, 123, 137–40
tolerable, 58
touch, 154
touch up, 73
tough, *n*, 107
tout ensemble, 22
town, 88–9
transpire, 51
treasure, 105
treat about, 73
trials, 50
turn away, 71
turn off, 71
turn up, 71
twelvemonth, 100
Twining, 103
typical, 206

unagreeable, 107
unconscious, 82
under, *n*, 202
under voice, 203
understanding, 60
undescribable, 107
undoubtedly, 44
unexpensive, 107
unfrequently, 107
upon, 194
use, did not, 125
used to, 124–5, 136

valuable, 46
value, 46
variety, 46
vastly, 181
very much pleased, 182
view, *n*, 45
visit, 153

wafer, 101
Wedgwood, 103
What's your game? 195
where, 183
which, 170
who, 170–1
wild, 21
will, 125–6
wind-up, 203
wish I may, I, 122
within doors, 196
within side, 196
work out, 49
worst, *v*, 201
would, 127–30
wring, 50

ye, 167
yesterday, 17
your, 167–8